RANGER

CONFIDENTIAL

Living, Working, and Dying in the National Parks

ANDREA LANKFORD

FALCONGUIDES

GUILFORD, CONNECTICUT
HELENA, MONTANA
AN IMPRINT OF GLOBE PEQUOT PRESS

To buy books in quantity for corporate use
or incentives, call **(800) 962-0973**
or e-mail **premiums@GlobePequot.com.**

FALCON GUIDES®

FalconGuides is an imprint of Globe Pequot Press.
Falcon, FalconGuides, and Outfit Your Mind are registered trademarks of Morris Book Publishing, LLC.

Text designer: Libby Kingsbury
Layout artist: Mary Ballachino
Project manager: John Burbidge

Library of Congress Cataloging-in-Publication data is on file.

ISBN 978-0-7627-5263-8

Printed in the United States of America

10 9 8 7 6 5 4 3

For the one who pulled me back from the edge.

The season's over and they come down

From the ranger station to the nearest town

Wild and wooly and tired and lame

From playing "the next to nature" game

These are the men the nation must pay

For "doing nothing," the town folks say

But facts are different. I'm here to tell

That some of their trails run right through—well

Woods and mountains and deserts and brush

They are always going and they always rush.

—From *Oh, Ranger! A Story about the National Parks* by
Horace Albright and Frank J. Taylor, 1928

CONTENTS

INTRODUCTION

For twelve years I lived and worked in some of the most sublime places in the world. Zion, Yosemite, and the Grand Canyon were all landscapes I was proud to protect. I participated in search and rescues, wildland firefighting, and law enforcement. I directed traffic around tarantula jams. I pursued bad guys while galloping on horseback. I jumped into rescue helicopters bound for the dark heart of the Grand Canyon and plucked the damned from the jaws of the abyss. I raced the sunset. I won arguments with bears. I dodged lightning bolts. I pissed on forest fires. I slept with a few too many rattlesnakes.

Hell, yeah, it was the best job in the world. And fortunately I survived it.

One of my dearest friends was not so lucky.

Park rangers bring to mind images fit for a postcard. A square-jawed outdoorsman wearing a stiff-brimmed Stetson rides horseback through lonely canyons. A freckle-faced young woman hikes to an altar of wildflowers under a shadowy cathedral of redwoods. A friendly guy stands on the porch of a hewn-log ranger station and waves to the happy campers passing by. These sylvan scenes make for pretty portraits of a ranger's life, but as every park ranger eventually learns, sunny postcards tell only half a story.

Even paradise has its problems. Criminals go on vacation too. In the United States, a park ranger is more likely to be assaulted in the line of duty than is any other federal officer, including those who work for the U.S. Bureau of Alcohol, Tobacco and Firearms (ATF); the Secret Service; and the Drug Enforcement Administration (DEA). A park ranger is twelve times more likely to die on the job than is a special agent for the Federal Bureau of Investigation (FBI). In light of such numbers, some describe park rangers—like grizzly bears, wild orchids, and sea turtles— as "endangered."

Within these pages you will meet a few of the park rangers behind these statistics and read some of the stories behind the scenery of America's national parks. If my imaginary postcards were actual portraits of real park rangers I came to know and love during my intense and extraordinary career, the square-jawed out-doorsman would be Chris Fors, a hardy New Englander who used his sturdy expression to hide the fear and disillusionment he faced while working at the Grand Canyon. The freckle-faced young woman hiking through the trees would resemble Mary Litell, a rock climber determined to break the glass ceiling at Yosemite Valley. And the friendly ranger with a kind wave and goofy smile? That would be Cale Shaffer, a short guy with a big dream: to become a mountaineering ranger on Denali, North America's tallest mountain.

I cherish the memories I have of working alongside park rangers like Chris, Mary, and Cale. For better and worse, our time with the National Park Service (NPS) changed us in ways we could never have anticipated. In the beginning we were four passionately dedicated rangers willing to risk our lives to protect the national park ideal. But age wreaked havoc on our idealism, a little courage bled from each tragic experience, and hope seemed elusive when so many lives were lost. In the end I watched someone toss a beloved ranger's ashes into the Grand Canyon.

Rangers rarely share their experiences with those outside the clannish NPS. Chief rangers and park superintendents have politically fragile careers. NPS public information officers are reticent about the darker sides of the park experience. Concessionaires— multi-million-dollar companies that run the hotels, restaurants, and gift shops inside national parks—think bad news equals bad business. Park rangers, including those at the highest ranks, have been disciplined, frivolously indicted, and even fired because they told the truth about living, working, and dying in a national park.

This is a work of nonfiction. The park rangers are real people. The stories are true. Quoted dialogue and statements are taken directly from government documents, dispatch recordings, other media sources, journals, letters, and the recollections of myself or the people I interviewed. In one chapter only ("Pine Pigs") I portray minor events as if they occurred in one day. In a few instances I combine several conversations into one for the sake of narrative efficiency. I occasionally use my imagination when dramatizing the actions, thoughts, and motivations of the park ranger who dies by this story's end. With the exception of a few high-profile incidences, I omit the names of the deceased to allow them and their families some privacy.

Reader beware. Ranger reality is rated R. Nature doesn't always play nice. Public servants curse from time to time. Search and rescue can involve wet work. Cliffhangers don't always have happy endings.

The service thus established shall promote and regulate the use of the Federal areas known as national parks . . . which purpose is to conserve the scenery and the natural and historic objects and the wild life therein and to provide for the enjoyment of the same in such manner and by such means as will leave them unimpaired for the enjoyment of future generations.

—The National Park Service Organic Act, 1916

Well . . . the only thing I can say is . . . Yosemite is one Goddamn beautiful place to get locked up.

—Man arrested for driving while intoxicated in a national park, 1993

1

THIS IS YOUR BRAIN ON THE GRAND CANYON

Nude from the waist down, the woman arched her back off the gurney and kicked a padded ankle restraint across the room. Obviously the Valium wasn't working. The doctor yelled for something stronger. A male park ranger fought with the woman's kicking legs while I leaned all my weight on her upper torso so a nurse could inject the drug into the catheter I had put in her arm. With all her panting and senseless blabbering, you would have thought we were trying to sedate a lunatic. But this young woman was not insane. She was just a girl who went hiking in the Grand Canyon.

It was April 1997. We were in the emergency room inside a medical clinic on the Grand Canyon's South Rim. The park ranger struggling to maintain his hold on the hiker's tan legs was Cale Shaffer, my newest and youngest employee. Sweat stains blossomed all over Cale's uniform shirt, and his dark brown bangs were falling in his face. An Outdoor Recreation grad from Pennsylvania, my newbie ranger stood five-foot-five in his hiking boots. Cale was twenty-two but could pass for fifteen, and the Eagle Scout hadn't rubbed off him yet. He looked much too young to be wrestling with the legs of a half-naked woman while a nurse had both hands in the woman's crotch, trying to slide a rubber tube up the patient's urethra in order to empty her bladder.

The sick hiker responded to this medical intervention in a bizarre, almost sexual manner, moaning and wiggling her hips out of the nurse's range. "Whoa there Nelly," the nurse said with an awkward giggle. A decade of rangering had desensitized me to a variety of disturbing sights, sounds, and smells. But in front of my Boy Scout of an employee, the carnality of this poor woman's delirium burned my cheeks with embarrassment. I made a little wish for the woman: Please, when this latest victim of the Arizona desert wakes up in intensive care a week from now, don't let her remember a thing about her trip to the Grand Canyon.

Earlier that afternoon, Cale found the hiker during a routine patrol of the Bright Angel Trail. He used his radio to call for a ranger-medic to respond, and within a half hour a skilled pilot landed the park helicopter on a patch of flat red rock. I stepped out, grabbed my medical packs, and climbed the slope to the trail where Cale introduced me to a young woman sitting next to a puddle of vomit. The hiker's vacant stare helped me make my diagnosis. To be certain, I held up her empty 1.5-liter canteen and asked her how many of these she had drunk that day.

"Six," she said, "maybe seven."

Nearly two gallons of water consumed in five hours. This explains why, by the time we landed on the canyon's South Rim, Cale and I were sitting on the hiker to keep her from jumping out of the rescue helicopter. "Let me out of here," she had screamed at us. "I need to pee!"

Hydrate or die. This is never more true than when trekking in the Grand Canyon. But an overzealous effort to stay hydrated on a desert hike can also kill you. Too much water consumed too quickly can dilute your blood to the point that your sodium level drops to a critical level. Excess water in your diluted blood moves across membranes to places more salty. The brain is as good a place as any for this fluid to go—but there is only so much water the brain will accept without complaining. Not everyone with hyponatremia (also known as low blood sodium or water intoxication) goes nympho or tries to jump out of flying helicopters. Some become comatose and die. Some go into seizures. Some turn into fountains of vomit. Some see a kaleidoscope of angels. Some try to drink their flashlights. One bit a rescue volunteer so hard he drew blood. That's your brain on a water overdose—swollen and soggy and making you do things normally reserved for bad acid trips.

Once our sick hiker was medically stabilized and on her way to the Flagstaff ICU, Cale and I drove the ambulance back to the rescue cache for supplies. On the way, my new employee hounded me with newbie questions. If he encounters another psychotic man hurling rocks at hikers, should he arrest him, write him a ticket, or ask him to stop? Can he put in for overtime pay if he misses his unpaid lunch hour for five days straight? Were the deadly scorpions he shook out of his boots each morning really deadly? How could he prevent the bighorn ram lurking behind Sheep's Corner from butting him off the trail? And would I please explain, one more time, how you tell the difference between heat cramps, heat exhaustion, heat syncope, heat stroke, dehydration, and hyponatremia?

The last question troubled Cale most of all. Even physicians have difficulty diagnosing a heat illness without the benefit of blood lab results. A few days earlier Cale had concluded that another delirious hiker was hyponatremic and refused to give the man a drink of water when he asked for it. Later, a field blood test showed that Cale's patient wasn't water intoxicated—he was dehydrated! What the guy needed most was water, and Cale had withheld it. Everything turned out okay (a more experienced ranger was flown in and gave the man fluids by IV), but Cale continued to beat himself up over it. He felt bad. He felt stupid. He was making so many mistakes.

"We all feel that way when we first start out." I told him. "It gets better with time. I promise."

* * *

Ten years earlier, in the spring of 1987, I strapped on a gun belt and placed a "Smokey Bear Stetson" on my head for the first time. (Although NPS uniform hats are now made by Stratton, rangers still call their hats "Stetsons" for the first company that made them.) After obtaining my Forestry degree in my home state of Tennessee, I worked at Cape Hatteras National Seashore. At the time, I had felt like a young ranger with too much responsibility, prematurely kicked out of the nest by a harried supervisor. Ten years later I was the distracted district ranger at the Grand Canyon who, as my superior had done a decade earlier, had to apologize for my failure to orient my employee properly to the complexities of his new job. I claimed the latest chain of events as my excuse. My district was the busiest (in numbers of search and rescue missions) backcountry area in the nation. Last summer had been the deadliest hiking season in the park's history. The staff had yet to recover from the aftermath of so many fatalities, and the emergencies kept coming, leaving us little time for educating the park visitor and protecting the natural resource. As I recently explained to a reporter, "People come to the Grand Canyon and die; we clean up the mess."

My superiors were less than thrilled with the picture my public comment painted, but they knew we could not afford a repeat of last year's carnage. They developed a creative financing strategy that afforded me some additional funding to do my part in implementing a new program to prevent heat-related deaths in the Grand Canyon. I used a portion of this budget to hire Cale Shaffer. To stretch those funds even further, I asked Cale to assist me in coordinating the activities of a volunteer rescue team. This so-called volunteer rescue team was composed of a raggedy bunch of juvenile delinquents, otherwise known as "hoods in the woods."

Despite the high hopes we had for our new hiker-safety program, the year was off to a grim start. In March a private plane crashed while flying in a blizzard over the canyon's North Rim. After two weeks of searching the snowy forests by air and land, a cadaver dog found the female victim. When I reviewed the report, I noted that Cale Shaffer had photographed the accident site and assisted with the recovery of the remains. The senior ranger at the scene told me that the force of the crash had "augered" the victim's torso into the snow.

God Almighty! Cale seemed much too young to be unscrewing human body parts out of snowbanks. He had been a ranger less than a week. What was I thinking when I allowed him to go on that assignment? Shouldn't a district ranger protect her youngest employee from such atrocities?

By the end of my impromptu employee counseling session, the post-sunset rush hour out of the park had come and gone. I dropped Cale off at the shack he shared with another ranger and a wildland firefighter. Then I went home, ate dinner, and prayed that the phone didn't ring. When I finally made it to bed, I couldn't sleep. Awake, I considered the consequences of exhausted rangers responding to increasingly hazardous missions. I conducted a risk-versus-benefit analysis of my using disadvantaged youth to patrol a dangerous trail. I mentally reshuffled the paperwork piling up on my desk. I outlined strategies for keeping the strained relationship I had with my supervisor from deteriorating any further. I picked apart all the rescue operations that went poorly: the children who died on the trail; the people who drowned; the people who fell to their death before we could get a rope to them; the missing hikers we never found. I beat myself up over it. I felt bad. I felt stupid. I was making so many mistakes.

The following night, my neighbor, ranger Chris Fors, walked across the street with a six-pack under his arm. Sitting at my kitchen table, we proceeded to test how many beers it would take to drown our discontent. Chris and I were both in our early thirties. We both started at seashore parks back east before traveling thousands of miles from our friends and families to work out west. At first we had loved being park rangers, but now something felt horribly out of whack. Death haunted us, the Grand Canyon scared us, park managers disappointed us, and our careers were not following the script.

Today Chris Fors would agree: My promise to Cale Shaffer was a lie. Life for a park ranger in a big park did not get better with time. It just got different. But for me to acknowledge this truth required less beer and more years of sober reflection. And at the Grand Canyon, meditative retreats on mountaintops were a luxury our jobs did not allow.

2

PLOVER PATROL

On his first day working for Cape Cod National Seashore, the district ranger issued Chris Fors his gear—a black plastic briefcase, a metal clipboard, a ticket book, a box of bullets, and a revolver. The gun, a hand-me-down from the FBI, was an old .38 Smith and Wesson six-shooter. It was a cool pistol, though. It looked like an antique.

After showing his new employee around the office, it was time for a lunch break. The boss suggested that Chris try a local diner in the nearby community of Provincetown, Massachusetts. Chris Fors had a deeply masculine voice and his Yankee accent was quite strong, but to an original Cape Codder, even a born-and-bred New Englander like Chris would always be an outsider.

When the young ranger entered the diner and ordered his food, the locals in the place didn't pay much attention to him. He wasn't wearing a uniform, and with his Scandinavian skin, short blond hair, wire-rim glasses, and young face, he looked like a tourist. Just another college kid sitting alone at a table, eating his fried clam strips. A pair of salty Cape Codders slid into the booth in front of him. The men appeared to be on their lunch break from the dock or the cannery. Chris could overhear their conversation. They were bitching about the ranger's new employer, the National Park Service.

A sixty-mile peninsula of gravel and sand that reaches out into the Atlantic like a beckoning finger, Cape Cod is one of the longest expanses of uninterrupted sandy shoreline on the East Coast. It is also one of the few remaining nesting habitats for the piping plover, a bird named for its whistling song—a plaintive *peep-lo, peep-lo*—that, like the Hank Williams whippoorwill, sounds as though the bird is calling for a long lost lover. Weighing less than a cup of coffee and covered with feathers the same smoky beige as dry sand, the piping plover has a black ring around its neck. A black band across its forehead connects two disproportionately large eyes. Thumb through the *Peterson Field Guide to Birds of North America* and you will see that the piping plover (*Charadrius melodus*) is not the most beautiful bird in the book, but it is certainly one of the cutest. It is a teddy bear among North American shorebirds, and we almost lost it forever, twice.

The first time was in the years before 1918, when fashion called for real bird feathers in women's hats. After the Migratory Bird Treaty Act passed in 1918, plover populations rebounded until the boom years following World War II. The Migratory Bird Treaty protected birds from plumage hunters; it did not, however, protect them from cars and condominiums. Threatened once again, the piping plover became an endangered species in 1986. By 1988 the Cape Cod population had dwindled to thirteen breeding pairs.

Plovers build their nests out of nothing more than dimples in the sand. Sometimes the birds decorate their nests with sea-polished rocks and shiny fragments of seashells before the female lays four mottled eggs. The sandy color camouflages these eggs from predators, such as foxes and seagulls, but it also contributes to the eggs being crushed by shoes and off-road vehicle (ORV) tires. Chris Fors arrived at Cape Cod in May 1989. The summer nesting season for piping plovers had begun, and the park superintendent had ordered the closure of several beaches to ORVs.

These closures turned the piping plover into the spotted owl of the East Coast.

As he ate his lunch in that Provincetown diner, Chris eavesdropped on the angry locals. The men were working themselves into a fury, complaining about park policies and verbally burning the little piping plover in effigy. "Let's go on an egg-stomping hunt," one man said. "No," said the other, "let's take a shotgun and blow a bunch of the little bastards to bits."

Then one of them suggested something so radical the young ranger nearly choked on a french fry.

"Why don't we torch the ranger station?"

"Yeah," the other one agreed, "like those guys did in Tennessee!" Recently, in response to another unpopular park policy in another national park, some locals in Tennessee had burned down an entrance station in the Great Smoky Mountains. The men had seen it in the paper. It sounded like something they should do too.

This conversation put Chris Fors on high alert. The men left the restaurant and climbed into a couple of rusty pickup trucks. When Chris rushed to write down the license plate numbers, he didn't have a pen on him!

Chris returned to the ranger station and showed his new boss a napkin with license plate numbers written by a finger dipped in ketchup ink. The district ranger was astonished. The new kid had turned up quite a doozy. On his first day! Before he even had a uniform! What a shit magnet!

The incensed locals ended up being more talk than action, or perhaps they noticed that the federal government had them under surveillance. In any case, they didn't torch any government buildings. They didn't blow any "little bastards" to bits. However, these men were far from the last confrontational locals threatening violence that Chris would encounter.

* * *

9

As a boy, Chris Fors did not want to be a park ranger; he wanted to be a fireman. Whenever the sirens came through his neighborhood, he ran out of the house, jumped on his bike, and pedaled like mad to the end of the street. Watching the fire trucks go by, Chris felt a little jolt of adrenaline. It felt good. It was a comforting distraction from the arguing and drinking going on at home. One summer, when Chris was ten, his dad loaded him and his two sisters into the car and they headed west for the Great American National Park Vacation. When he recalled the trip many years later, what remained foremost in his mind, other than the fact that Mom had stayed home, was the tragic event at Yellowstone. He had left his Matchbox cars, his entire collection, under a lodgepole pine at their last campsite. But by the time Chris remembered his forgotten toys, Dad was well on his way to the next park on the list. It was too late to turn back.

The vacation felt odd and sad. Dad kept an open can of beer between his legs as he drove, and whenever a cop came up in the rearview mirror, he asked Chris to hide the beer for him. On their way to see the Grand Canyon, they stopped in Las Vegas for the night and got a hotel room. Chris and his sisters watched television while Dad went out. The next morning their father announced that the vacation would be cut short. They had spent all their vacation money. On their way back to Massachusetts, they took a short side trip to see the Grand Canyon.

Chris's first view of the seventh natural wonder of the world made little impact on his young mind. He was ten years old. Old enough to know that something was wrong with a dad who drinks all the time. Old enough to be depressed about his parents' impending divorce. Young enough to be even more depressed about the toys he'd left behind in Yellowstone National Park. In light of all this, the Grand Canyon was just another big empty hole in the ground.

When Chris was sixteen he volunteered as an "on-call" probationary firefighter. At nineteen he became an emergency medical technician (EMT). He paid his way through college by working as an emergency dispatcher and an ambulance driver. An exceptional artistic talent earned him a spot in a landscape architecture program at a prestigious school in Rhode Island. While his classmates designed entryways to shopping malls and lawyers' offices, Chris drew up plans for fire stations and fire engines. It took less than a year to see that a career in landscape architecture would be long on salary but short on adrenaline. He dropped out of the design school and enrolled in the Natural Resources program at the University of Massachusetts.

It wasn't easy to decide what to be. A fireman? An EMT? A cop? How about a game warden? The times his father had taken him hunting and fishing were islands of good family memories in a stormy sea. Chris was already leaning toward the profession of game warden when a friend told him about a park ranger course they were offering at UMass. If you took the ranger class, you could apply for a summer job at Cape Cod National Seashore. Park rangers were cops, firemen, EMTs, *and* game wardens! You could be a park ranger and do it all! All of the fun stuff in one job. For one paycheck. Neat!

* * *

Public nudity at Cape Cod was a cocklebur in the briefs of the superintendent. And he passed this minor, yet ever-present, irritation onto his rangers. "This particular freedom—there's nothing like it," one nudist told a reporter for the *Provincetown Banner.* "It's not a sexual thing; it's a spiritual nature-loving thing." The Park Service, however, remained unsympathetic to the close-to-nature attributes of nude sunbathing. Unofficial clothing-optional beaches resulted in public spectacles. Looky-loos bottlenecked traffic on the highways. Some people were trampling fragile plants by running up to the tops of sand dunes for a better view. Rangers were told to use "the lowest level action necessary to ensure compliance." This was code for enforce the law, but don't write any tickets—and for God's sake, be sure to "remove your sunglasses and smile when you talk to these people."

Sure, okay, Chris thought; getting out of his patrol car to talk to topless women was fine by him. But there were times he wondered if things had gotten out of hand. Especially when he had to approach families carrying lawn chairs, beach towels, and seahorse float rings, pull the male adult aside, and say something like, "I'm sorry sir, but I don't recommend this beach."

"What do you mean?" The tourist wanted to know. "This beach looks fine to me."

"There are all kinds of beaches here at Cape Cod National Seashore. There's the topless beach and there's the full frontal beach, the straight beach, the lesbian beach, and the gay beach. Did you see all the cars parked on the side of the highway? Well, those are the people who came to see the scenery. No, not the natural scenery—the au naturel scenery, if you know what I mean. And I'm afraid some of those people aren't the type you want within two miles of your wife and kids. I suggest you drive over to . . ."

"But we've walked all this way, with all this stuff."

"Uh, but this beach is where, uh, the homosexuals, they, uh."

"Look, ranger, I don't have anything against homosexuals."

"But sir, these guys call themselves 'The Dune Bunnies.' See those sand dunes there? They climb to the top of the highest dune, strip down, and get it on right there in the open, in broad daylight. It's quite the free sex show, let me tell ya."

"Here? In the park?" The tourist couldn't fathom what the twenty-two-year-old park ranger was telling him.

Lewdness was not a rare thing at Cape Cod. Chris participated in a few undercover sting operations where young male rangers posed as homosexuals in an attempt to put a stop to the exhibitionist sexual trysts taking place along a park nature trail through a charming grove of trees rangers called the "Enchanted Forest."

The rangers took a lot of heat for their "overzealous law enforcement." Even sexual adventurers don't like being busted. Nor do nudists, topless women, or losers who drive all the way from Canada to hide in the bushes and spy on sunbathers.

Some days Cape Cod rangers used all-terrain vehicles (ATVs) to patrol the sand roads that remained open even when the beaches were closed to motorized traffic. During such ATV patrols, Chris Fors stayed busy with keeping Jeeps out of the plover nesting areas, dogs on leashes, and bathing suits on bodies.

One hot July day, Chris stopped his ATV at a point where he could see between two dunes to the beach. On the sand was a woman he had warned earlier for topless sunbathing. The woman had put her top on as he had asked, but as most people did, she had removed it again as soon as the ranger left. Now she was topless again, lying on her stomach, and a man was standing above her. It looked strange. Something was wrong about it, but Chris couldn't tell what. Until he saw the jerking motions.

He must have appreciated the poetic justice and the craziness of it all. Because on that day in July, when Chris saw the pervert masturbating above the oblivious topless sunbather, the ranger knew he was going to make his first arrest. A righteous arrest. An arrest the superintendent had to agree with, and one the chief ranger couldn't second-guess. A man was committing a flagrant act of open and gross lewdness in front of a defenseless woman. Here? In the park? Not on his watch! Chris cranked down on the accelerator of his ATV. He couldn't wait to bust that perverted freak.

As soon as the perverted freak saw the ranger, he zipped it up and sprinted for the bushes. Chris caught and cuffed the guy, and when the sunbather figured out what had nearly happened, she ran up to her hero and said, "Thank you, trooper!"

Standing next to the bikini-clad lady, Chris felt great, like a good guy. Still, did she have to call him a trooper? Couldn't she see the patches on his ball cap and on his sleeve, the brown arrowhead-shaped fabric with the bison and the sequoia tree and the snowcapped mountains under the words "National Park Service"? Was it really that difficult to figure out? Wasn't it obvious? He didn't work for the state. He wasn't a trooper. He wasn't a police officer, and he wasn't a forest ranger, either. There are national forests, and there are national parks. Cape Cod National Seashore was a national park. He was a park ranger. If she was going to call him a hero, was it too much to ask that she give credit where credit was due?

"I'm a park ranger, ma'am."

"Oh, yeah, right. Ranger, trooper, whatever," she said. "Thank God you showed up when you did!"

After a week of saving topless damsels from drooling perverts and protecting cuddly critters from ignorant brutes, the time came when Chris and a few other Cape Cod rangers felt as though they deserved a night on the town. They got off work and went home and showered for the second time that day. Then they put on their best shirts and their cleanest jeans and headed out to a local bar. Hey, maybe some girls would be there. Pretty girls who would like to meet some park rangers. But once the rangers entered the club, it was obvious they were not welcome by some of the locals.

"Here come the pine pigs," murmured someone at the end of the bar. Then the lead singer of the Provincetown Jug Band, a town favorite, grabbed the microphone and announced the arrival of the "Tits and Ass Plover Patrol." Laughter filled the dark room. Chris smiled and tipped his beer bottle to the band. It was funny. Still, he wished they would hurry up and start singing the next song. But the crowd loved the joke, so the band milked it until it was dry.

Four months on the Tits and Ass Plover Patrol and Chris began to feel a peculiar pull. Yellowstone. Yosemite. The Grand Canyon. The big parks. The "Crown Jewel" parks. The parks symbolized by the arrowhead patch he wore on his sleeve. The parks with bigger animals to protect, bigger scenery to guard, and bigger bad guys to bust. Sure, Cape Cod was cool. But a ranger born in the east longed to be out west where the national park idea began—in the wildest, rockiest, most majestic landscapes of western North America.

Back then if you told Chris Fors that, after living and working in a big park in western North America, a park ranger would suffer from paranoia, anxiety attacks, and nightmares—gruesome dreams that would wake him up screaming and grasping at his sheets—the twenty-two-year-old New Englander would have called you a loon.

3

FAINT AT HEART

I became a park ranger because I had nothing better to do. Just as my parents had predicted, a Forestry degree from the University of Tennessee did not make my résumé a valuable commodity. And my career goals were vague. I knew only that I wanted to work outdoors. I applied for a job as a forester for a logging company but later learned that a woman had less than a spotted owl's chance of working for that outfit. I worked a summer as a naturalist for the Tennessee State Parks. I volunteered for the USDA Forest Service. I had experience as a zookeeper and contemplated becoming a veterinarian.

The one profession I never considered was that of a federal cop. Yet when a boyfriend invited me to join him on a six-week course for people wanting to be law enforcement rangers for the National Park Service, I said, why not? At the time I was an honors graduate who bagged groceries for a living. Learning how to drive fast, shoot guns, and handcuff people sounded like fun. I was flattered when a district ranger from Cape Hatteras National Seashore called and offered me a summer job before I had even finished the academy.

In April 1987, at the age of twenty-three, I packed everything I owned into a sputtering car and drove across the state of North Carolina. I lived on Bodie Island in a mobile home I shared with my boyfriend, who was also a ranger. Our singlewide trailer sat on

16

an exposed cinder-block foundation. The view outside our dining room window was the lee side of a sand dune growing lush with beach grass and sea oats. Most days, the dune provided a measure of protection from the elements. But when the nor'easters blew in, our weather-beaten trailer shrieked and moaned like a scorned banshee.

* * *

In the coastal waters off Cape Hatteras, near the shoals we call the Graveyard of the Atlantic, swims a mighty and fearsome fish. The largest ever reeled in weighed thirty-one pounds. Twelve-pounders are not uncommon. They have strong jaws, sharp teeth, and fighting spirits. Landing one is a rush. The locals call them "blues," and when a pack of Atlantic bluefish attacks a school of smaller fish, they call it a "bluefish blitz."

During my patrols along the coasts of North Carolina's Outer Banks, I saw days when the fishing was good and days when the fishing was damn good. I saw days when all a man had to do was toss a hook into a splashing mass of violence and he was sure to pull something out. I saw days when a bluefish blitz instilled a terror so profound that smaller fish jumped out of the water and onto the shore by the hundreds because a gill-flapping death in the sand was preferable to the teeth of the blues. I saw days when women and children walked the beach to scoop up scores of live sea trout, dropping fish into buckets as if they were berries from a bush.

When word of a blitz got out over the C bands, men ran down the beach like kids let loose on an Easter egg hunt. Jeep Chero-kees braked so hard they threw sand. Beers toppled and spilled on floorboards. Red-faced fishermen tripped in their waders as they raced one another to the tide line, their fishing poles swinging wildly. When the blues were blitzing, things got a little crazy. If you knew what was good for you, you stayed out of the way.

An inebriated and overly enthusiastic cast was surely responsible the day I encountered a twelve-year-old girl with two inches of tri-barbed metal hook in her foot. The hook had penetrated all the way through the meat of her heel, bringing the squid bait with it. It was Memorial Day weekend. I had been a ranger less than six weeks. My understanding of emergency medicine was embarrassing. But I did know one thing: No matter how loud the girl's mother screamed at me to do something for her daughter "right now!" I was not qualified to pull barbed hooks out of human flesh.

For this I called the paramedics. After the ambulance arrived, I stood behind the medics and watched over their shoulders. One medic gently wiggled the hook with his gloved hand. The movement jiggled the squishy squid that dangled from the rusty barb and forced a yellow glob of fat tissue out of the exit wound.

This was when I hit the ground like a sack of rocks.

The paramedics had to abandon their patient to care for the park ranger lying unconscious on the beach. When I woke up, they were checking my blood pressure and taking my pulse. They shouldn't have bothered. There is no cure for humiliation. I stood up, pulled my Smokey Bear hat out of the sand, and brushed it off. They'll think I'm not tough enough, I thought. They'll say it's because I'm a woman. Maybe I'll be fired.

But I wasn't fired. "Don't worry," my supervisor said. "I've felt that way many times. Next time you get that dizzy feeling, just sit down before it takes you with it."

* * *

Coming from Mike Anderson, those words meant a heap-full. Anderson, the Bodie Island district ranger, had survived a gunfight the year before. In spring 1986 a man landed a stolen airplane on a remote airstrip in the national seashore and Ranger Anderson was there to greet him. "I felt in control of this man until he started shooting at me," Anderson later said. Fortunately, neither man was hit. Anderson started shooting back, and the suspect took off running for the wetlands. A huge manhunt followed. Five days later, the local police pulled an emaciated man out of the reeds. I imagine the fugitive's first day in jail was downright comfy after the four mosquito-bitten nights he spent in the marsh.

After hearing this story at the academy, I had expected my new boss to be an intimidating former-Marine type. Instead, when I shook the hand of the Bodie Island district ranger, I saw an attractive man in his thirties with a boyish face and two plump cheeks that blushed easily. Also, he looked a little humbled. The other rangers told me that dodging bullets had unsettled the district ranger, changed him somehow.

Anderson assigned me to the early shift. It sucked waking up at "oh-five-hundred," but I was the newbie, and someone had to patrol the beaches each morning to look for sea turtle tracks. When weeks passed without my seeing any of the tracks I was tasked with finding, I began to worry. "How will I know for sure if I see one?" I asked a more experienced ranger.

"You'll know," he said.

The day I found my first track, I realize how right he was. A blind man wouldn't have missed these tracks: He'd trip over them. Now I understood why a park visitor had recently reported seeing a sea monster emerge from the ocean. The creature that made these tracks was gargantuan. At sizes approaching three hundred pounds, loggerhead sea turtles are designed for the buoyancy of water, not the tedium of land. It takes hours for a mother turtle to drag her body up the beach, dig a hole, lay up to one hundred eggs, cover them with sand, and then crawl back down to the water. A mother's yearly journey to lay her eggs brings another meaning to the word "labor." It shouldn't surprise us when a turtle lays her nest below the high-tide line.

One of my duties as a Cape Hatteras ranger was to drive the beaches early each morning and search for signs of freshly laid turtle nests. If I found a nest below the tide line or close to civilization, I dug up the eggs—which resemble Ping-Pong balls—carefully loaded them into a bucket of sand, and buried them right side up in a safer place. Then I documented the location of the nest and kept track of the incubation schedule.

Eighty-five days after I moved my first turtle nest, I found scores of tiny tracks leading from the nest to the ocean. It felt like Christmas morning when I discovered several baby turtles still fighting their way up the sandy banks of the hole. I expected the turtles to be brown or greenish-yellow like their mother, but the baby loggerheads were dark violet, like bruises. I picked one up and held it in my palm. The turtle flapped its flippers on my skin. It tickled, like a child's butterfly kiss.

It hurt to think about the chances against this one turtle surviving to adulthood. To a baby sea turtle, the world is a war zone. Even if the nest eludes the noses of raccoons and dodges the destruction of a hurricane, some eggs fail to hatch. Of the ones that do hatch, not all the turtles make it to the water. Ghost crabs snatch the hatchlings in their claws and drag them down into their holes. Gulls swoop in and pluck them off the beach. Once I found the carcass of a turtle baked to death by the hot sun. Of the lucky ones that reach the ocean, not all will escape the hunger of sharks. There are gill nets to avoid . . . red tides and pollution . . . poachers looking for shells for jewelry and meat for soup . . . plastic bags and party balloons that float in the water like jellyfish but once eaten by a deceived turtle lead to an agonizing death.

Less than 1 percent of sea turtle eggs end up becoming an adult. The turtle I held in my hand came from a nest of eighty-one eggs. The odds were depressing. Yet this turtle continued to flap its flippers against my skin. Undaunted by the giant holding it, stubborn in its desire to reach the water, compelled by a pull as irresistible as gravity, this turtle wasn't giving up. This turtle wanted to make it. This turtle was so precious.

How could I not join the fight to keep this endangered species from becoming extinct? How could I not risk my life so that "my" baby turtles could someday return and lay their own eggs? How could I not give up retirement benefits, health insurance, and decent housing for a job this important? How could my parents talk any sense into me? Now that I had been down on my knees in the sand with a baby turtle struggling for its life in the palm of my hand.

This was my induction. My call to duty. My pledge of allegiance to the park ranger credo: "Protect the park from the people, the people from the park, and the people from themselves." Up to this point I had been killing time—spending a summer living with my ranger boyfriend on the beach until a better opportunity came my way. Now the stakes were clear. There were things in this park that needed protecting, and it was my job to protect them. Fainting was no longer an option.

Fueled by the righteousness of endangered sea turtles, I began to attack my ranger duties with a zealot's vigor. I kicked sand on illegal beach fires. I spoiled the tans of nude sunbathers, confined Labradors to leashes, and confiscated fireworks from twelve-year-olds. I ruined parties by flipping open cooler lids and dumping out the contents, exposing the undersized flounder hidden beneath beer and ice. One day the dispatcher passed on a report so heinous it had me pounding my hands on my steering wheel. North of the park, some moron had tied a rope to a loggerhead turtle and dragged it down the beach behind his truck. The turtle died. Witnesses said the suspect had been driving a white pickup. For weeks after, I stopped and interrogated the hapless driver of every white truck that crossed my path.

* * *

You can drive a motor vehicle on many Cape Hatteras beaches, but some sections remain open to foot traffic only. One afternoon a campground ranger and I were lounging on the beach behind our trailers when a ruddy-faced fisherman on an ATV drove right past three CLOSED TO MOTOR VEHICLES signs and headed toward us. The audacity of this violation had me livid. How dare he? This beach is for piping plovers, tern eggs, and sea turtles. This beach is for fragile plants that keep sand dunes from blowing away. This beach is for children who want to build sand castles without being run over by drunks on ATVs.

Over my bikini-clad body was this guy getting away.

I ordered my friend to run home and call for an on-duty law enforcement ranger. Then, barefoot and wearing nothing but a white crochet bikini, I ran toward the man on the ATV, stood in his path, threw my hand up like a traffic cop and yelled, "Park ranger! Stop right now." I was alone and out of uniform, but the man didn't challenge my authority. With a stunned expression, he waited politely for the on-duty ranger coming to write him a ticket. Ten minutes later, when my male coworker arrived on the scene, I displayed my catch with pride. After my fainting fiasco, I needed this demonstration of my ability to gain compliance from those who break laws in a national park.

Many years passed before I grasped what my male coworker surely noticed right away. The ATVer's cooperative attitude had less to do with my "command presence" than with the unaware yet ingenious way I had blocked his escape—with my long legs spread wide in front of his ATV, my hands pushing back against his handlebars, and my posture giving him an incredible view of what little cleavage I have.

4

AS YOSEMITE FALLS

Near the door to the Yosemite Valley Ranger Station sat a huge cross section of an ancient tree. According to the sign, the sequoia had been a thousand years old when it fell in 1919. Plastic labels tacked into the wood pointed out rings of tree growth that corresponded to the years of major human events, such as the Battle of Hastings in 1066, the signing of the Declaration of Independence in 1776, the start of the Civil War in 1861, and the year Yosemite became a national park—1890. During the summer of 1993, park ranger Mary Litell passed this exhibit so often during the course of her workday that, before too long, she forgot it was there.

One deceptively calm evening, after passing the tree exhibit on her way home from work, Mary crossed the street and walked along the backside of the Pioneer Cemetery. There, underneath the shade of five evergreens, a large but otherwise unpretentious hunk of granite marked the grave of Yosemite's first park ranger— Galen Clark, who became the park's first civilian guardian in 1867. From Clark's grave, with three good kicks you could have sent a pinecone into the yard of the cabin Mary shared with two male coworkers. But tonight the ranger would not make it home before dark. Just as she turned the corner near Clark's headstone, she heard the screaming.

Behind the Park Service corral, a colossal wall of granite formed a natural amphitheater that intensified the panicked cries for help coming from a ledge three hundred feet above the ground. The anguish in those screams quickened the ranger's pulse and sent a jolt of empathic fear into the hearts of the patrol horses resting in their stables. Sprinting toward the sound, Mary ran into a group of neighborhood kids, children of park employees. The kids had been playing in the woods behind their houses. Now they carried haunted expressions on their faces. "He fell," they said, pointing to the cliffs.

Later it became clear what happened. Hours earlier, two young men, brothers, had leaned as far as they dared over the handrails to watch the water plunge over Yosemite Falls. From the trail they spotted what looked like a shortcut down to the valley. They stepped off the trail. The farther they went, the more difficult the route became until the brothers were scaling the rocky benches under the Lost Arrow Spire. Here there were no handrails, and the mellow feeling from the marijuana the men smoked at the overlook had long since faded. The decomposed granite was flaking off in their hands. Their feet were sending rocks crashing down the nearly vertical slab. When one of them fell, his brother started screaming.

Mary ran up the bouldered slope. Where the granite became scree, she met rescuers Rick Folks and Mike Ray. At the base of the cliff they found something caught in the lower branches of an oak. The large mass tangled up in the tree branches was a man—a very messed-up man. No way was he alive.

Mary yelled up at the man's brother, who was still screaming, and told him to stay put; the rangers would come and get him. Using her park radio, she described the situation to the dispatcher as Mike Ray climbed up to where the tree branches met the scree. Mary watched Ray reach his fingers toward the crumpled man's throat to confirm that this was indeed a fatality.

The rescuers were startled when the man inhaled a wheezy breath.

Mike Ray had aspirations of becoming an emergency-room doctor and knew exactly what to do. He opened the man's airway. Then, using his own body as a backboard to protect the patient's spine, he curled the man out of the tree. Two paramedic rangers arrived, and within minutes an airway tube was down the patient's throat, an IV line was in his vein, his body was on a stretcher, and he was being carried down through the difficult terrain. The ranger-medics worked their injured patient with an urgent calm. Their steady voices told Mary and the other less-experienced rangers what to do.

Mary and five rescuers carried the basket stretcher down the rugged slope. The critically injured man had been unconscious until now. He began to squirm. A medic shouted, "Grab his hands!" Before anyone could stop him, the patient grabbed the plastic airway tube the medics had slid down his throat and pulled it out of his own mouth. He said, "Jesus." Then his heart stopped beating. The rangers initiated CPR, but it was obvious to all but the newbies that this one wasn't going to have a happy ending.

That night the doctor at the park clinic told Mary that even if the guy had fallen onto a table in front of a team of trauma specialists prepped for surgery, he still wouldn't have made it.

It was disappointing. Mary was a cross-wearing Catholic. She had hoped for one of those times when God slaps his palm on his forehead and says, "Oh, shit, John Smith? I meant John Schmidt!" so he sends in a couple of rangers to correct his mistake. She had seen a miracle like this only a week earlier when the dispatcher had reported a severely injured man "under the Green Dragon." No one had been optimistic about that guy making it either. "Green Dragons" were those diesel-fueled, tour guide–equipped, open-air trams that caterpillar the valley roads all day, slowing traffic and pulling a long chain of green-and-yellow cars filled with tourists. If a man was under one of those, his number had been called.

Emergency sirens echoed off the valley walls as the rangers raced to find the green dragon with the man under it. There were several to check, and they were scattered all over Yosemite

Village. But every tour guide the rangers contacted swore up and down they hadn't run over any stray tourists that day. Precious lifesaving minutes ticked by. Rangers radioed in their frustrations to dispatchers who were very confused. Then Mary got an idea.

Minutes later she found him lying unconscious under blood-stained granite along a rock-climbing route called "the Green Dragon."

The guy should have died. In a race against the setting sun, the rangers medically stabilized the climber and got him flown out of the valley before the stroke of darkness turned the park helicopter into a pumpkin. As she watched the rescue helicopter fly into the sunset, Mary decided this ranger gig was a keeper.

* * *

Mary was a ranger who had to learn things the hard way. Like Rule Number One: Measure your head before you order your ranger hat—or you'll have to stuff paper towels inside the headband to keep the hat from falling down over your eyes. Rule Number Two: If you must wear mascara to work, make it waterproof—the guys will laugh at you when you turn into a raccoon during a water-sprayed rescue mission under Yosemite Falls. Rule Number Three: Say "I don't know" if a park visitor asks a question and you don't know the answer. There will always be a crowd standing around you when a camper asks, "Oh, ranger, what kind of squirrel is that?" If you draw a blank and say, "Uh. A bushy-tailed squirrel?" a guy with a video camera will be there to say, "It's called a California gray squirrel," the disgust dripping from his voice.

Mary Litell was no Jane Goodall. That's for certain. But then rangers would have more time for studying the natural history of Yosemite squirrels if people would just stop falling off cliffs. But people will continue to fall off cliffs as long as leaves continue to fall off trees. And over the years, layers upon layers of stories about people falling off cliffs have accumulated into fat files of multicolored papers stuffed into brown cardboard boxes stacked head-high in a walk-in closet inside the special agent's office. And these stories, which the rangers once typed onto quadruplicate-copy government forms and now type into government computers, are as surreal and melodramatic as any of the so-called legends the Ahwahneechee and their descendants passed down orally from generation to generation over the past two hundred years.

* * *

A young Swiss woman traveled to America with her bold and athletic boyfriend, a Czechoslovakian climber. During their days at Yosemite, the Czech climber grabbed his ropes and climbing equipment and set out to climb the Lost Arrow Spire over the course of several days. Before he left, the climber asked his girlfriend to occasionally monitor his progress through a pair of binoculars.

On days one and two, the climber's girlfriend eyed the cliff face, watching her lover ascend the route. On day three she lost sight of him. On day four she spotted a rock climber's haul bag hanging from the rock. On day five she saw no sign of her boyfriend, and the haul bag was in the same spot as it had been before. On day six, when she saw that the haul bag had not moved, the girlfriend was beyond concerned; she was frantic.

Back at camp, a visibly anxious woman convinced two Hungarian climbers to hike with her to the cliff above the spire. At the top, one Hungarian rappelled down the rock alongside the Czechoslovakian's route. The Hungarian found the Czech's gear, a shirt, a hammer, and an anchor set in the granite. Attached to the anchor was a daisy chain (a length of multilooped webbing climbers use to attach themselves and their gear to anchors). The daisy chain appeared to have been cut or smashed in two. The Hungarian ascended back up the rope and ran down the trail to notify the park rangers.

Within minutes of receiving this report, Mary Litell was in the park rescue helicopter, her eyes scanning the Lost Arrow Spire for clues. She spotted a pile of red and black rags lying on the rocks below and asked the pilot to move in closer. The winds were "squirrelly" that day, making the maneuver difficult for the pilot. He hovered as close as he dared to the granite, tilting the helicopter to give Mary a better look. The rotor wash shooed away a flock of crows that had been sitting on the pile of rags, revealing to Mary that the rags weren't rags. They were a human body. Leaning out of the helicopter door, the webbing of her seat belt the only thing keeping her from falling, she snapped an instant photo of the scene.

Back at the rescue cache, Mary showed this photograph to me, the incident commander. (After two summers at Cape Hatteras and four years in Zion National Park, I had transferred to Yosemite. Now a permanent full-time ranger, I was given the leadership role for this particular mission.) As I studied the photograph, Mary informed me that this climber must have fallen eight hundred feet several days ago while climbing the Lost Arrow Spire. Then she pointed to the snapshot of a tattered lump of clothing and decomposing flesh and said, "I don't think he's going to make it."

A rescue helicopter dropped a recovery team near the body before flying Mary to the top of the cliff to find the victim's girlfriend. Mary was looking for a woman with long blond hair and wearing blue shorts, a yellow shirt, and skinny sandals. But instead of the girlfriend, Mary spotted thirty people dressed from head to toe in black, a pack of ninjas standing in a circle and tossing around nunchakus at the edge of the cliff. What the hell? The pilot landed the helicopter, and Mary walked out to investigate. When she returned, the ranger had a driver's license in her back pocket and a dozen nunchakus cradled in her arms. "You're not going to believe this," she told the pilot. "A guy was teaching a martial arts class in the Yosemite backcountry."

At the park morgue, a concrete room adjacent to the search and rescue (SAR) cache, two park rangers waited for the body to arrive. In Yosemite the federal government has exclusive jurisdiction, giving the NPS full responsibility over legal issues such as enforcing laws and investigating deaths inside the park. A handful of rangers are therefore trained to perform as coroners.

If you are thinking people do not become park rangers to do coroner duty, you would be right. Nevertheless, the job must be done. Rangers trained for coroner duty receive no additional pay. However, the experience might help a ranger compete for a better paying job as an NPS special agent.

After the body recovery team rolled the gurney with the Czech climber's remains into the morgue, the ranger-coroners delicately searched for wallets, jewelry, and other objects of evidence or identification.

When the helicopter landed in Ahwahnee Meadow, Mary got out, walked to her patrol car, and dumped all the nunchakus into the trunk. The incident commander sent her to Sunnyside Campground, where the girlfriend was waiting for someone from the NPS to contact her. Like most rangers, Mary would have rather juggled knives while attached to a flaming rope dangling over a mile-high cliff than do a death notification. This was going to be her first.

At Sunnyside Campground, Mary walked up to the dead climber's girlfriend. Surely the girlfriend suspected the worst, but until someone in uniform said it out loud, she was holding onto a glimmer of hope. Mary saw her words put out that glimmer in the girlfriend's eyes. But it was the ranger, not the grieving girlfriend, who first broke down into tears. The two women hugged. The girlfriend said this had happened to her before, years ago in Europe. He, too, was a rock climber. He, too, fell to his death while scaling a cliff.

Later that night, after the recovery mission had wound down, the wayward martial arts instructor met Mary in front of the ranger station. Along with his driver's license, Mary handed him a ticket for conducting commercial operations without a permit inside a national park. Then the ranger apologized. She had to confiscate his nunchakus as evidence since they were deadly weapons, the possession of which was illegal in a national park as well as a felony in California.

The loss of his weapons seemed to matter little to the martial arts instructor. He shrugged and said, "Will you have dinner with me tonight?"

"Sorry," Mary said. "I'm too busy."

* * *

Collateral duties are common for a ranger. While some rangers are trained to be coroners, others are trained to be critical incident stress counselors. These ranger-counselors conduct critical incident stress debriefings (CISDs) and often function as a NPS liaison and/or counselor for families. Like coroner detail, certification as a grief sponge involves a couple of weeks of additional training and no additional pay. When CISD "peer counselors" lead group "stress debriefings," you can talk about your feelings and cry if you want to. But the rangers with the weather-beaten Stetsons don't say much during these sessions. They appear to be able to walk it off, shrug it off, laugh it off, and forget it. I saw an example of this coping mechanism when I showed up for work the next morning. Tacked to the bulletin board in the briefing room was the photo Mary had taken from the helicopter. On the white border under this snapshot of a corpse at the base of the Lost Arrow Spire, written in black marker, were the words "Canceled Czech."

I, too, relied on jokes to dismiss the many tragedies we saw. I was another ranger who had to learn things the hard way. Rule Number 313: Tombstone humor is a Band-Aid placed over what may become a deep and festering wound.

5

OUR FIRST SUMMERS
IN THE SIERRA

Human bones littered the park. At least, that's what the boys from Stanford kept insisting. But the ranger in charge wouldn't believe them. And who could blame him? Park visitors were always finding human bones while hiking the Yosemite wilderness. Most times these "human bones" turned out to be deer legs, raccoon teeth, or sticks. Yet these Stanford students on summer break were adamant. They had found human bones in the pine needles near the John Muir Trail, near a rocky section the horse packers called the Ice Cut, and somebody needed to do something about it. So with the reluctance you would expect from a put-upon public servant, the supervisor agreed to look into the matter right away. He sent his least experienced ranger, a newbie named Mike Archer, to do the job.

It was the last day of April, Mike's first day on the job, and the start of a rough season. A couple of months later, in June, Mike would do something with such newbie earnestness that the entire Yosemite Valley day shift and half the dispatchers would tease him about it for the rest of the summer. The ribbing wasn't so much for how the ranger would handle the incident as for the way he would report it: "I'm on the Mist Trail," Archer would pant into his radio with the utmost seriousness, "and I am in foot pursuit of a naked man."

With his short crop of curly blond hair and a wiry, athletic frame, Ranger Archer could be much too bright-eyed and way too bushy-tailed to take in more than small doses—especially to the older rangers wearing the weather-beaten Stetsons. They took one look at the necklace of multicolored stones Mike wore around his tanned young neck and thought, *Let's see how long that hippie necklace lasts.*

As the Stanford students led Mike up the trail toward the alleged human bones, he began to wonder if he belonged here. Maybe this wasn't just some bullshit, newbie call. First of all, those Stanford guys were pretty smart. Second, they mentioned that the bones had clothes with them, and Mike couldn't recall the last time he'd seen a deer wearing pants.

When they reached the Ice Cut, the Stanford students refused to go any farther because the bones creeped them out. Mike told them to wait by the trail until he returned. Then he entered the forest alone. A short walk brought him to the boulders in front of a cavelike alcove. At first a mosaic of shade and sunlight camouflaged the white objects scattered among the rocks. Then Mike saw that the Stanford boys had been right. These were undeniably human bones, and they were wearing a nylon jacket. Over the radio Mike asked his supervisor what he should do next—this being a situation more complicated than a newbie like him was prepared to handle—and the supervisor instructed him to protect the integrity of the scene until the criminal investigators arrived.

Within minutes, down in the valley two special agents threw saddlebags filled with investigation equipment over the backs of their patrol horses. Park ranger versions of a street cop's detective, the special agents were sturdy men with sturdy mustaches that they wore long and bushy—cowboy style—so that the hairs covered the corners of their mouths, making it hard to tell if the men were smiling or frowning. They were the type who might laugh at Mike Archer's beaded necklace.

At the death scene, Mike leaned up against a rock and worked on his face tan while he waited for the special agents to arrive. When he heard a snuffling sound, he got up to investigate and was startled to find a bear peering at him from behind a log. It was a black bear, a yearling. The previous summer this bear would have been a cuddly little cub seen sniffing around the campground dumpsters. But now the bear wasn't cuddly—and it wasn't little. It was a big, unpredictable adolescent hoodlum of the forest, and it was growling at the park ranger who had so rudely interrupted what it had been doing: gnawing on a human pelvis!

This is very strange, Mike thought as he watched the bear's front teeth curl shavings off human bone. *Maybe I shouldn't let him do that.* The ranger slapped his ball cap on his thigh and yelled, "Drop it!" The bear lumbered off toward the trees but, like a dog with a shoe, it refused to drop its chew thing. Mike threw a stick at the bear. It shuffled a few feet back. The ranger ran toward the bear. It shuffled a little farther back.

Mike and the bear continued this tango until the animal looked over its shoulder with a mischievous gleam in its eye. *Come on ranger, aren't you going to follow me?* the bear appeared to say before it vanished into the darker realms of the forest, the human pelvis still in its mouth.

That's when Mike decided to give up the chase.

A few months later the DNA forensics confirmed what the mustached special agents had suspected. The bones belonged to a male hiker in his twenties. The hiker had been reported missing the previous spring. An empty bottle of pills found near the body suggested suicide, but the exact cause of death remained a mystery. The special agents typed "most likely" and "intentional overdose" on their government reports.

* * *

Yosemite National Park owes its existence to John Muir, the founder of the Sierra Club and a man dubbed "the father of the national parks." If you are a John Muir fan, however, it may disappoint you to learn that he first came into the area in 1869 as a shepherd's assistant, earning his living by fattening sheep, creatures he later dubbed "hooved locusts," on the lush meadows of the High Sierra. Thirty-five years later, Muir would tour the same territory with the president of the United States, convincing him that the area should be preserved.

Muir's job as a sheepherder allowed him plenty of free time for nature rambles and quiet reflection. He published the notes he wrote during this time under the title *My First Summer in the Sierra*. He writes of an extravagant, joyful landscape overflowing with good tidings. Snowmelt creeks are "champagne water." Bears are "hardy mountaineers." Nature is "beauty loving tenderness." Trees and waterfalls sing and bow in worship. "Let children walk with nature" he writes, "and they will see that death is stingless indeed, and as beautiful as life."

Not quite 130 years later, and a few days after Mike Archer caught one of Muir's "hardy mountaineers" gnawing a human pelvis near the John Muir Trail, the young ranger was inspecting the marks nature's "loving tenderness" had made on an injured female hiker he found lying in a tributary of the Merced River. The lower half of the woman's body had been under the snowmelt water for at least an hour. She was bleeding from a nasty cut on her head. She had a broken nose, a crushed pelvis, and a leg fracture. Yet despite these traumas and the onset of hypothermia, the woman still had the strength to insult her rescuer.

"You're an idiot," she yelled during Mike's awkward and slippery attempts to pull her from the river. "You'd never make it in the real world."

The female hiker had picked an unfortunate time and place to fall. With sunset in three hours and hiking more than a half mile off the trail, she had fallen thirty feet down a steep and rocky drainage and landed in the creek.

Mike Archer reached the woman first and was sorry for it. For nearly an hour he suffered the full impact of the woman's insults and complaints before two ranger-medics, Keith Lober and I, arrived. *Thank God,* Archer thought. *Now she can start yelling at them.*

A rescue helicopter from Lemoore Naval Base was on its way. We hoped to use the military aircraft to perform a short-haul extraction. Short-haul is a rescue technique that involves lowering and/or raising a rescuer and/or victim via a fixed line under a helicopter. Clipped onto a cable attached to the helicopter, the rescuer is at the complete mercy of the helicopter pilot, who inserts the ranger into narrow canyons, moving water, or vertical cliff faces—locations that are extremely difficult or time-consuming to reach on foot. If the helicopter gets in severe trouble, the pilot may have to "pickle" (dump) the load. If the "load" happens to be a park ranger and a patient, well, it sucks to be them. This is why we referred to short-haul-certified rangers as "dopes on a rope." Short-haul rescue is so dangerous, only a dope would do it.

The terrain was tight. In order to extract the woman, we had to first move her through the cascading rapids to a reasonably flat rock in the middle of the creek. We were all crowding one another on this water-sprayed rock when Keith Lober realized he had forgotten to pack his climbing harness. "Everybody dump your packs," he ordered. Only one person had brought a harness—a diminutive volunteer, who tossed it at Lober and said, "You can use mine!" Lober had the seat harness halfway up his legs before he realized it was too small.

As the gods would have it, Lober, who wore a size large, was the only certified "dope on a rope" at the scene. Sunset was on our heels—at which point, like Cinderella's carriage at midnight, our rescue helicopter would transform into a pumpkin. The woman's injuries might kill her if we didn't get her to a surgeon soon. Carrying her across the treacherous terrain in the dark would result in an agonizing all-nighter, delaying her arrival to a hospital by more than twelve hours. Thus we found ourselves in an absurd predicament. The success of our rescue mission hinged upon whether Lober could fit his butt into a climbing harness that was two sizes too small.

* * *

Ranger Keith Lober "thrives on chaos." He is one of the best and most tested high-angle rescue-paramedics in the world. Officially he has been honored with four awards for valor from the Department of the Interior. Unofficially he's earned at least twenty more. Scores of people owe their life to him. But every hero has a flaw, and Lober's is his temper. Whenever a coworker was clumsy or a rescue operation failed to run smoothly, Lober threw a tantrum. He hurled safety helmets. He kicked medical kits. He threatened to strangle people as soon as we returned to the rescue cache. If you handed Lober a normal carabiner when what he wanted was a locking D, if you pulled out a 14-gauge needle when he asked for a 14-gauge catheter, if darkness fell and you brought AAA batteries for the headlamps when they required AA, you had better run for cover. "You imbecile," Lober might say before he hurled something heavy in your direction, "you incompetent piece of dog crap, you intolerable slime around the rim of a frog's ass. You're off my rescue!"

Keith Lober's temper was legendary. The locals called him "Sheriff Lobo," after the main character in a short-lived sitcom in which Claude Akins played a scheming Southern sheriff who routinely berates his bumbling bunch of deputies. Rumor was that Lober had punched another ranger in the nose, knocking him out cold, a few years earlier while he was working at the Grand Canyon. And once, when rafting the Merced River, he slapped a paddle across the head of ranger Chris Robinson when he didn't react quickly enough to Lober's order to "paddle right." Park locals and more than a few park managers viewed Sheriff Lobo as the worst kind of asshole ranger. But if you found yourself severely injured in an impossible place during impossible weather conditions, Keith Lober was the kind of asshole ranger you wanted dropping down a rope to see you.

* * *

That day in Merced Creek, the ill-fitting climbing harness had our tempestuous paramedic fit to be tied. One at each of Lober's hips, Mike Archer and a rescue volunteer were pushing down and back on Lober at the same time they pulled up and out on the straps of the climbing harness. When they failed to gain enough slack to buckle the belt, Lober erupted into an Ahab-like wrath, shaking his fists at the sky while the rotor wash from the hovering helicopter threw creek water in his face. I'm not sure if it was the fear of Sheriff Lobo or the frigid water, but newbie Mike Archer was shivering like a drenched puppy. Even the noise from the helicopter engine failed to drown out Lober's screams, "This fucking harness is too fucking small!"

Our patient observed the whole thing.

"Don't worry." I told her. "He always does this."

Twenty minutes ago, the woman had been constantly bitching. Now she was absolutely speechless. We had strapped her into a metal basket that looked as though an amateur welder had built it out of curtain rods and chicken wire and were clipping this basket to a long rope attached to a military helicopter. After Lober managed to squeeze into the harness, the helicopter would lift her and the ranger hundreds of feet above the ground. Then she would be injured, immobilized, and utterly dependent on a paramedic who was displaying the bedside manner of an ice-cream-deprived five-year-old. *Forget my injuries,* she had to be thinking. *Am I going to survive my rescue?*

As soon as Lober wedged himself into the harness, the helicopter pilot lowered the rope to us. The rotor wash blew icy creek water at us, stinging our eyes and making it hard to breathe. It was like working on the deck of a ship in a storm. We rushed to hook the basket to the cable. Lober's glasses were fogged. A volunteer wiped off the condensation. Somebody gave the Navy pilot a thumbs-up, and the helicopter lifted. The slack left the rope, and Lober and the patient were off the ground. On the way up, a corner of the rescue litter hit a large boulder jutting out over the creek. This sent Lober and the patient spinning like a yo-yo at the end of a twisted string. The sight of it alone was enough to make me motion sick. Later that night, I questioned Lober about the experience. He said, "It wasn't the rock that scared me. It was that awful twisting."

* * *

A Yosemite ranger's job is not always this exciting. There are slow days. Tedious, boring days when, if you have to give any more directions to any more confused visitors or impound any more improperly stored food or type any more fender-bender accident reports or direct any more traffic around any more bear jams or smile politely at any more tourists who call you "rangerette," you swear you're going to drop a gallon of whiskey into your back-pack, hike a hundred miles into the wilderness, and never come back. There are days when you wish for something interesting to happen just to break up the monotony. Sometimes your wish is granted, and you immediately want to take it back.

In 1994 I completed an intensive park medic training program. "Park medics" are rangers qualified to start IV lines and give life-saving medications in the field under a physician's orders and direction. (A park medic is equivalent to an EMT-Intermediate and does not receive any additional pay for acquiring these skills.) Obtaining my certification as a medic involved four weeks of academic classes plus one hundred hours of clinical rotations at hospitals and with urban ambulance crews. I aced the academic requirements, but I was far from being competent in the field. After months of minimal field guidance from Keith Lober and other experienced ranger-medics, I nearly failed to convince a skeptical doctor to sign me off as a full-fledged, independently functioning park medic. But I wanted to be cut loose from the umbilical cord. What I lacked in skill, I'd make up for in ignorance.

One afternoon we received a report of a serious head injury at Hidden Falls. The shift supervisor pointed at me, and I was out the gate. Sprinting up the trail with a rescue volunteer at my side, I weaved through boulders and hurdled low branches. I ran because I was driven by a desire to help the person with the serious head injury. I ran faster because I hoped to beat Keith Lober to the scene.

Unless I reached the scene first and made lifesaving actions on my own, Sheriff Lobo would take charge and be the hero, like always. I figured he ought to let me have this one, but I knew he wouldn't. While I approached the scene on foot, Lober was jumping into a rescue helicopter bound for the accident site. This did not deter me from the finish line. Helicopters are fast, but I once held my high school's record for the girls' half mile. If I hoofed it, I might beat him.

I won the race when I saw a woman walking down the trail toward me. Blood smeared her pale cheek. A slack look hung on her face. *This must be my patient,* I thought. She looked a little out of it, but she was conscious and she was walking. Piece of cake. Then, in a monotone voice, she said. "It's K—. She's dead."

Behind the woman were four people holding a purple towel stretched between them to form a drooping stretcher. Inside the towel something heavy—a body—bounced as they hiked toward me. A misshapen head flopped out of the towel. Black hair hung loosely toward the ground. The name K— began to register. She was a nurse at the Yosemite Medical Clinic. She was my age. She had a thing for strong margaritas. I liked her.

No. Please. I've changed my mind. Give me a shift that's boring.

"Put her down," I said with a blunt voice that I barely recognized as my own. "I'll take it from here." A part of me closed shut in that moment, like a curtain had fallen to the stage in my mind, cutting off my backstage emotions about K— so that I could act. Behind me, a large thing crashed through the tree branches. It was Lober, performing a dangerous rappel from the helicopter into a dense forest. Today, neither of us would play the hero.

The "on-scene death investigation" was a routine Lober could, and probably did, do in his sleep. Take some photos. Make a few measurements. Scribble notes onto yellow notepads. Put the body in a bag. Put the bag in the basket stretcher. Hook it to the line. Give the helicopter pilot a thumbs-up. After the body was off to the morgue, Lober and I remained behind to continue our investigation. We split up. He hiked west on the loop trail that leads to the top of Hidden Falls, and I went east.

Hidden Falls is a short loop, a path more than a trail. During the wetter seasons, it travels under an elfin trickle of water surrounded by ferns and columbine. Then it goes up and around to a three-pronged gusher that lands in a clear pool. From the pool the path traverses a bald slab of granite. It's a pretty little hike only locals know about. They bring beach towels in case they feel like taking a dip. At the topside of the loop, I met Lober. We stood on opposite sides of the rocky slab with fifteen feet of moist granite between us. In his report Lober described this stretch of rock as having a "Teflon-like slipperiness." He pointed to a little divot in the moss—a silver dollar–size patch of green peeling loose from the rock, like a scab.

"That's the spot," he said. The spot where K—'s foot lost friction before she slid off the edge and fell fifty feet. I lifted one leg up and stretched it out, toe pointed, balancing on my other leg like a ballerina. I grinned wickedly at Lober. I was going to step there. I was going to cross over to his side of the slippery slab by stepping on that same deadly spot. To beat it. To prove that it happened to her, but it wouldn't happen to me. To show Lober how brave

I could be. But Lober wore an expression I hadn't seen on him before. "Andy," he said, his voice weak and pleading. "Don't."

When Keith Lober acts sensitive, it scares you. I brought my foot back down to the rock. "I'll meet you down below," I said.

At the base of the cliff, Lober guided me to where he had found the impact site. We took photographs for the file: a bottom-side view of a cliff; a patch of gray rocks; a puddle of clotting blood. To a ranger, such pictures tell a sad story: a woman slipping down a granite slab; her friends watching her disappear over the edge, then running down the trail to find her crumpled among the boulders; the gurgling sounds of her last breath. Panic. Urgency. Grief. Desperate attempts to save a friend's life and then the gloomy task of cradling a body in a purple towel and carrying it out of the wilderness.

Dusk was upon us. We hiked out along the north side of Mirror Lake. The conversation was limited. I worried that Keith Lober, my reluctant mentor, would think me too female if I brought up the emotional impacts of our job. But I had to ask, "Do these things ever bother you?"

"Of course," he said. Death was never stingless.

6

DEAD BEAR WALKING

Ranger Noel McJunkin thought he had the best job in the world. His commute consisted of a four-mile hike into the park wilderness. His office was a canvas tent near a babbling brook. His beat was the backcountry of Little Yosemite Valley. His job was to walk the trails, checking for camping permits and warning hikers of the hazards. How hard could that be?

As a backcountry ranger, Noel met fewer people and responded to fewer calls than the beleaguered frontcountry rangers patrolling the park's busy roads and crowded hotels. Away from their cars, outside the roaming ranges of their cell phones, and at least four trail miles from the nearest beer tap, the hikers in Little Yosemite were friendlier and more relaxed than the average frontcountry visitor. In turn, Noel was friendlier and more relaxed than the average frontcountry park ranger.

But every man has his limits.

Each year, thousands of hikers travel through Little Yosemite Valley during their strenuous eight-mile trek to the top of Half Dome. Many of these hikers camp for at least one night in the Little Yosemite Valley Campground. In the evenings, before the weary trekkers crawl into their tents, a backcountry ranger like Noel McJunkin makes a stop by each campsite for a little chat. Raised in the hills of Tennessee, Noel was the type of ranger other rangers call "low key." He smiled when he asked to see your camping permit. He conversed pleasantly with you while you dug it out of the bottom of your pack. And when you handed him your permit, he ever so politely asked you to turn it over to the back so he could point out your signature, the place where you signed a statement that you did read and understand all the park regulations listed above.

Up to this point in the conversation, Noel's Tennessee drawl was as sweet and smooth as syrup on pancakes. But then, just as he brought up the issue of food, the ranger's voice changed, becoming deeper and more authoritative. "All food must be stored in the metal food-storage lockers provided," he'd say, "except when being prepared and eaten. Then all food will immediately be put back into the metal food-storage locker. This includes all food and everything that smells like food—chewing gum, breath mints, toothpaste, suntan lotion, baby wipes, shampoo, lip balm, and what have you."

When it came to food in the Yosemite wilderness, the normally laid-back Noel McJunkin was extremely serious. Actually, Ranger McJunkin was more than serious; he was downright fascist. And like many hikers, you might wonder, "What is his problem?"

Noel's problem was female. His problem had three babies to feed. His problem had a name, and her name was "the Swatter."

* * *

In July 1993 a bear was attacking so many hikers in Little Yosemite Valley that, like a serial killer, she had earned herself a nickname— the Swatter. So addicted to human food that she was willing to slap around a few humans to get it, the Swatter discovered that snatching hamburgers off picnic tables or pulling apples out of backpacks was much easier than digging for grubs under logs. Heck, to a hungry sow with three cubs to feed, even a bag of freeze-dried vegetarian lasagna was worth fighting for—even if she had to bite or slap one of those spindly two-legged things before it hollered, dropped its pack, and ran away. But humans see things differently. We can't have 250-pound animals bitch-slapping people for their peanut butter sandwiches. Although black bears are less fearsome than grizzlies (a white hunter killed the last Yosemite grizzly in 1895), these animals still kill people from time to time. And if, God forbid, a Yosemite bear maims or kills a U.S. taxpayer, the park superintendent will find his butt in the liability hot seat faster than you can say "early retirement."

Earlier that summer, to avoid any more human-bear conflict, park biologists shot the Swatter up with tranquilizers, strapped a radio transmitter to her neck, loaded the sow and her three cubs in a cargo net, and transported them by helicopter to a remote canyon far, far away. Ten days later, with chin-scratching amazement, the biologists discovered that the Swatter and her babies were back in Little Yosemite Valley, extorting campers and robbing children of their candy bars.

With the Swatter on the loose in Little Yosemite Valley, the pressure was on ranger Noel McJunkin. Every evening he diligently patrolled Little Yosemite Valley, explaining food-storage regulations to campers and acting extremely anal about dirty cook pots, chewing gum, and breath mints. If only he could convince backpackers to store their food properly. Then, maybe, Labor Day would come and go before the Swatter hurt somebody.

Early one evening in July, with visions of dead bears and bleeding hikers dancing in his head, Noel met a young woman and her boyfriend sitting on two backpacks near the top of Nevada Falls. As was customary, the ranger asked the couple to show him their backcountry permit. "I'll show you mine if you show me yours," the young woman replied.

Neither Vanessa Butterfly (not her real name; but the one she gave Ranger McJunkin) nor her boyfriend had bothered to obtain a free camping permit that day, but this was not something they were going to admit to a park ranger. They would not tell the ranger their real names, either. No matter how laid-back he was or how thick he put on that Southern accent. Instead Vanessa Butterfly told Ranger McJunkin that she was born on "Valentine's Day 210 B.C." and "This is a free country, so we don't have to do what you say."

These antics worried Noel. Was he really going to have to do the last thing he wanted to do? On this hot summer evening? When he was three miles from the nearest road and hadn't had dinner yet?

"Oh, ranger," Vanessa Butterfly said. "The only reason you are harassing me is because you had a dysfunctional childhood." Then she grabbed her pack and marched away, ignoring Noel's pleas to come back until he said, "Stop, or you are under arrest." At that, she took off running.

Ms. Butterfly was spry, but she was no match for a backcountry ranger who hiked more than thirty miles a week. Manzanita scrub scratched at Noel's legs and arms as he initiated his pursuit. In the heat of the chase, he grabbed the young woman and pulled one of her arms behind her back in a flustered and sweaty attempt to handcuff her. Meanwhile, Ms. Butterfly made good use of her free hand, pummeling the ranger about the face and shoulders while screaming, "Stop it. You're abusing me!" According to Noel's typewritten report, six hikers, eyes wide and mouths open, witnessed the entire event, thus missing the rare chance to watch the sunset from the top of Nevada Falls.

Ranger Kent Delbon and I were sent up the trail to assist Noel McJunkin. To get to the top of Nevada Falls on the Mist Trail, you hike through a lush natural garden drenched with mist from the spray of Vernal and Nevada Falls. During the day, the soaking feels fantastic and you might see a rainbow. The bad news is that in order to reach the top of the falls, you have to climb three hundred ottoman-size granite steps.

It was a warm evening. The trail was packed with tourists grunting up and down the slippery rocks. I started off at a pace with which Ranger Delbon didn't care to compete. I slowed down once I realized that he wasn't trying to prove anything. This wasn't a race to him; it was two partners on the way to some bullshit call. As we climbed alongside the first waterfall, the humidity fogged up Delbon's glasses. We stopped so he could pull a section of T-shirt out from under his bulletproof vest to wipe off the condensation. I watched him blink and squint before he put his glasses back on. Then he gave me a shall-we-continue smile.

Three target-heart-rate-exceeding miles later we reached a flushed and fatigued Noel McJunkin standing next to a handcuffed Vanessa Butterfly. While Noel was preoccupied with catching his quarry, the boyfriend had made a hasty getaway. The young woman pouted and stamped her feet.

I informed Ms. Butterfly that if she didn't start cooperating, we would strap her down into a rescue stretcher and carry her ass out. This was something none of us wanted to do because six hours later, six rangers would be taking six ibuprofen for six severely cramped backs. It was tempting to let Vanessa Butterfly go. Chalk up the providing false information, illegal camping, resisting arrest, and assault charges to the fit-throwing tantrum of a confused young woman. It was tempting to tell Ms. Butterfly, "You know what, why don't you go on ahead and camp wherever you like. Don't bother with those tiresome food-storage regulations, either. In fact, right before you crawl into your tent and get all snuggly, be sure to dab a little peanut butter behind each ear."

Wisely, this time I let my male partner do all the talking. Delbon told Ms. Butterfly that playtime was over. "It's time to start hiking." Her response to the ranger's request was to drop on her fanny and say, "Not unless I get to smoke a cigarette first."

By now we were all boiling, but Ranger Delbon's voice was cool and collected. "I'm hot. I'm tired. I'm thirsty," he said as a bead of sweat rolled off his nose. Pinching his thumb and finger within a millimeter of each other, he added, "and I have about this much patience." At that, Vanessa Butterfly stood up, shut up, and started following Ranger McJunkin down the trail.

As Vanessa Butterfly and her boyfriend learned that night, camping without a backcountry permit inside a national park can earn you a $500 fine and a free permit to sleep inside the Yosemite National Jail. Yet for some hikers, citations and the threat of imprisonment are weak deterrents. A month after Noel McJunkin's encounter with Vanessa Butterfly, another hiker backpacked illegally into the Yosemite wilderness. He illegally pitched his tent in the Swatter's territory. He illegally fell asleep next to a bag of food. Despite his sins, the camper slept soundly. That is until the Swatter crashed through his tent and ripped a hole in his neck.

Fortunately the Swatter didn't kill the man. Holding a bloody bandanna to his wound, the backpacker hiked back down to Yosemite Village, where a doctor at the park's emergency clinic sewed him up with forty stitches. The man came within centimeters of having his jugular slashed. A park ranger took a report—it was the Swatter's death warrant. Cubs or no cubs, the bear had to go. In the memo authorizing the bear's euthanasia, the park superintendent signed this statement: "There will always be conflicts that arise with four million visitors and approximately 400 to 500 bears in Yosemite. The sad fact is that the bears often end up paying the price with their lives."

Wildlife biologist Kate McCurdy drew the short straw. She grabbed her rifle and tracking equipment and asked her supervisor to assist her with the hunt. A signal from the bear's radio collar led them to the doomed animal. The biologists and their rifles sent the Swatter and her cubs running up a tree. Kate aimed for the bear's heart and pulled the trigger. When the Swatter hit the ground, the earth shook.

What to do with the three cubs? Killing an animal she had dedicated her career to protect was never easy for Kate McCurdy. But without their mother's guidance, the cubs might freeze or starve to death this winter. Killing them now was probably the most humane thing to do. Kate discussed the situation with her supervisor. He reminded her that at this very moment, his wife was at home taking care of a new infant. That day, neither biologist had the heart to shoot three babies. They would leave the cubs to fate. From the limbs of a pine, the three little bears watched the two biologists bury their mother in a shallow grave.

Most likely, on their hike back down to the Valley, Kate and her boss didn't talk much. "It's standard procedure when we euthanize a bear that we don't talk to one another the rest of the day," Kate told a reporter for the *Sierra Star*. "We go home early and get drunk instead."

The night they put ol' Swatter down, Noel McJunkin didn't get much sleep. Into the cold hours before dawn, he lay on the hard bunk inside his Little Yosemite Valley tent cabin, listening to the heart-wrenching howls of three little bears bawling for a mother who was never coming back.

The next spring, Kate McCurdy tracked the movements of the park's bears as they came out of hibernation. Amazingly, the Swatter's cubs had survived the winter. To pull off such a feat, the three beers probably stumbled upon a rich food source as soon as they crawled out of their den. For the bears, finding the carcass of a large mammal would have been fortuitous—a sacrifice of one life to save three. The biologist was pleased the cubs were alive. But the bears ended up being a disappointment in the end. By Labor Day the Swatter's offspring were flying the colors of dumpster-diving, people-swatting outlaws.

7

THE RANGER OLYMPICS

Thanks to the frantic knocking, I was awake. Barely. I had a night-shift sleep schedule, and it wasn't yet nine. In my pajamas and rubbing my eyes, I opened the door. On my porch stood Mary Litell, the tall girl from the day shift, her entire body shaking with fear and fury.

"I am so fired," she said.

To many in the Park Service, Yosemite isn't a proper park. It has four million visitors a year—more than a hundred thousand visitors on one summer day—a golf course, two swimming pools, four bars, and a jail. "That's a town, not a park!" one ranger said when I confessed that I had accepted a job in Yosemite Valley. In the Valley District alone, on a typical summer night there can be more than fifteen thousand employees and visitors, as many as ten campsite-marauding bears, scores of wanted felons, ideally no more than three registered sex offenders, and, if you are lucky, four park rangers on duty to keep them all from killing themselves or one another.

During the 1990s, Yosemite visitation levels were peaking while staffing levels continued to decline. Back then a Valley ranger had to leave her phone off the hook to get a good night's sleep—and had to pack up and leave the park without telling anyone where she was going just to get a friggin' weekend off.

49

So I wasn't as sympathetic as I ought to have been the morning a newbie summer ranger woke me after less than four hours' sleep and stood in my kitchen, worried sick that our superiors were going to fire her over something she had done less than ten minutes ago.

I did, however, understand why the girl had lost it.

In May I had left a supervisory position at Zion National Park to work in Yosemite Valley. Not long after I arrived, the assistant superintendent, the second in command over Yosemite's eight hundred or so employees, called me into his office to discuss the "Valley thing." He informed me that every time a woman worked night shift in Yosemite Valley things went sour. (Many years earlier, a female ranger came to work to find the severed head of a cat sitting on her desk. Few women assigned to this district had lasted more than one season.) The assistant superintendent said that he had pressured the supervisors to hire me—the only permanent, full-time female law enforcement ranger in the Valley District. He told me I was a "test case."

That summer, four women—one full-time and three seasonal hires—worked as law enforcement rangers in Yosemite Valley. We called ourselves "Valley Girls," and it didn't take long for us to compare notes. Women talk. Women exchange knowing glances. Women tell one another things some men would rather we didn't. That summer we shared stories about a ranger who hit on three of us, all within one week. We warned one another about the ranger who, after having too much to drink, wouldn't leave a Valley Girl's room until he was pushed out the door. And we dropped the bombshell: Park managers think female rangers are test cases!

The assistant superintendent was a black man in his forties. Surely he had more than a textbook understanding of what it means to be a test case. I'm convinced he meant well. But when he told me that I needed to prove that women could handle working in Yosemite Valley, it was like squirting lighter fluid on what, up to that point, had been an insignificant grease fire. He might as well have taken a piece of white chalk and drawn a line outside the ranger station door, popped off a starting pistol, brought a mega-phone to his mouth, and shouted, "Let the I-can-do-anything-better-than-you-can games begin!"

The boys added insult to outrage when they said things like, "You were hired because you have breasts," and "Don't get your panties in a bunch—honey," and "Why is there so much tension between us?" drawing out the word "tension" so that it was as much a croon as it was a snarl. You can't begrudge a woman for entertaining fantasies of the boys crying during the girls' victory lap in front of a cheering crowd after one of them said, "Let's make it Boys vs. Split Tails" during a Trivial Pursuit game and you shot back with, "Okay, fine. Split Tails vs. Teenie Weenies it is," but your supervisor turned to you and said, "Settle down Lankford."

To make matters worse, the seasonal rangers like Mary des-perately wanted full-time permanent jobs—jobs that came with health insurance, retirement benefits, and decent housing—jobs the Park Service wasn't handing out like peppermint candies. You had to fight for them. Thus Yosemite Valley became a granite arena staged for fierce battles of competency: who shoots the best, who works the most overtime, who handles the gnarliest body recover-ies, who heli-rappels the most, who saves the most lives, who can run the eighteen miles to the top of Half Dome and back the quick-est, who's the best horseman, who's the bravest rock climber, who makes the most arrests, who solves the most felonies, who can back the ambulance into its narrow garage without knocking chips of wood off the door jams.

On one of my rare nights off, I met Mary on the porch of the Mountain Room Bar to gossip and complain over beer and cigars. At a particularly boozy point in this conversation, the Valley Girl puffed skillfully and blew out a series of smoke rings. Then she pointed her cigar at me. "And get this," she said. "Not long after you arrived, I asked him what he thought of the new lady ranger from Zion and he said, 'Well, she has an awesome body.'" Mary spat out an errant strand of tobacco. "How sexist is that?"

Intellectually I couldn't have agreed more. My peers should judge me by my performance, not my looks. "That is so lame," I said, scrunching my face in disgust and indignation. But God help me, in truth I was thrilled. *Oh. My. God. Someone thinks I have an awesome body!*

My first night on the job, the shift supervisor assigned me to ride with ranger Kent Delbon. Well aware of Yosemite's reputation for being hard on female rangers, I was nervous; but the tall, clean-cut young ranger with the soothing voice put me at ease immediately. That evening, Ranger Delbon revealed his well-developed soft spot for underdogs. He conversed in Spanish with immigrant visitors, communicated in sign language with a deaf firefighter, and swerved to miss a chipmunk crossing the road. He also showed off his ability to coax a patrol car to do his bidding. At the end of our shift, he zoomed into a hairpin turn with a stunt driver's precision, forcing me to push back on his shoulder to avoid landing in his lap. "That's how I get close to my dates," he said with a wink.

The next night I partnered with Jessica Rust, the other female ranger on my shift. Jessica was more Beverly Hills than Yosemite Valley. She reminded me of a tropical beach. Her manicured nails were delicate pink seashells. Her skin was an unblemished caramel, exquisitely contrasted by an expensive bob dyed the color of golden sand. Her perfume smelled as sweet and faint as hibiscus on a breeze. Her eye shadows were layered with the subtle complexities of a Hawaiian sunrise.

The guys called her "the Princess."

I always felt coarse and plain working alongside the Princess, but the nights I partnered with Jessica were the most fun. I never asked the Princess how she felt about her nickname, but I watched her do her best to break the spell of it. Right off the bat, she cautioned me about becoming romantically involved with our coworkers. "The guys are all right," she said, "as long as you don't go out with any of them." I figured she ought to know since, at my best count, she had dated at least four of our male colleagues.

Three weeks later, Chris Robinson, the most hyperactive ranger in the Valley, sent our Chevy Impala airborne over Humpback Bridge. We were responding to a motor vehicle accident with critical injuries and Robinson, a risk-taking lead climber, insisted on driving. He practically rocketed us the twenty miles to the scene. To avoid being shaken like a martini during the "flight," I braced myself up against the passenger door with one arm while the other hand pushed back on the shotgun locked solidly in a steel rack mounted to the floorboard.

"Not too gripped next door are we?" Robinson shouted over the siren.

Oh, yeah, I was gripped all right. But I'd be damned before I let a male coworker know it. Hiding all indications that I was terrified, gripped, or had in any way noticed the hard trunks of western red cedars that lined both sides of the serpentine road, I said, "You seem to be handling your skids fairly well." I must have pulled off an Academy Award winner, because Robinson furrowed his brow. "This car's a sack of shit," he said, pressing down on the accelerator. "The tires are bald. I'm holding back."

When Robinson skidded us to a stop in front of the accident scene, the Impala's headlights lit up a tragic tableau: a mangled motorcycle next to an equally mangled man splayed out in the middle of the road. I walked toward the crumpled body to check for signs of life. "Come help me with this one," said the ranger who had arrived first. "That one's eleven forty-four."

Hearing "1144," the California code for a fatality, I left the motorcycle driver so that I could care for the passenger, who was still alive. Later we learned that these men were concession employees. After a night of drinking, they had decided to go on a long motorcycle ride in the dark over the park's curviest roads. Now the passenger's leg looked as though it had been run through a paper shredder. There were so many ripped strands of blue jeans mixed in with his bones, blood, and flesh, I couldn't tell what was fabric and what was human tissue. Our patient was talking to us, and that was a good sign. But he seemed much too calm for a severely injured man lying next to a dead friend, and that worried me. I was grateful that Robinson, a skilled paramedic, was there. He started an IV while I cut off the patient's blue jeans. The other ranger pressed a large piece of gauze to the patient's bleeding extremity.

According to my female coworkers, the ranger holding pressure on the leg wound was a philanderer of the vainest kind. True to form, during my first week on the job, he deliberately flexed his bicep under my fingers when I grasped his upper arm to tell him something. I liked it—the bicep. It was the right size, plenty firm, and full of promises a man ought to keep. Ah, but this splendid muscle came attached to a super-competitive ranger with political connections and Machiavellian ambitions. A wise woman gives a man like that a wide berth. I, on the other hand, shook a red cape in front of him at every opportunity.

Bullish masculinity aside, we all felt the strain at one time or another. When Ranger Bicep leaned over to hand Robinson something from the medical kit, he exposed the chink in his armor. His knee was pumping franticly—up down, up down—faster than anybody can consciously move. I recognized this as "sewing machine leg" because I had experienced it myself. Not that night, but several times before. Every ranger suffers from a nearly out-of-control adrenaline pump at some point in his or her career. But Ranger Bicep would rather I hadn't noticed. Something about this one had gotten to him.

To place our patient's leg in a splint, Ranger Bicep pulled traction on the motorcyclist's nearly amputated extremity. I heard wet, crackly sounds as flesh and bone fell back into place. The alcohol in our patient's blood system must have been taking the edge off. He was as polite as an English butler asking permission to remove the salad plates when he looked at Ranger Bicep and said, "Excuse me, ranger. But would you mind not pulling so hard?"

After we dropped our patient off at the Yosemite hospital, Ranger Bicep stayed behind to help me sponge off the bloodstains. Once the ambulance was clean and restocked, we sat down across from each other in the back. Right then it all seemed funny— unbearably, hysterically funny. "Oh, ranger, I hate to bother you. Really I do. I know how incredibly busy you are. But I have one tiny request. Could you not pull so bloody hard on my bloody leg?" We laughed away what we could of the night's horrors and rubbed the water from our eyes. Outside the ambulance bay, the pink blush of a new day glowed behind Half Dome. Ranger Bicep made a sarcastic comment about seeing another Yosemite sunrise. It was my first summer in the valley, so I didn't get it. He explained, "When you see a Yosemite sunrise, it means you missed another night's sleep because of another brutal call."

Once we closed the ambulance doors, there was nothing to do but go home.

"So," he said, "I'll see you tonight."

"Yeah," I said. "See ya later."

It was an awkward separation, an abrupt end to an odd intimacy.

A year later we were worse than bobcats thrown into a cage with badgers. One afternoon, Ranger Bicep stood in front of my patrol car and lectured me about my bitchy attitude. In return I offered him my psychoanalysis of the source of his misogynist tendencies. Struggling to hammer home his point, Bicep grabbed the hood ornament of my Crown Vic and proceeded to twist the ornament this way and that, working it to the tune of our quarrel, until the metal piece snapped off in his hand. The sight of it in his palm appeared to wound him. He stopped arguing and handed me the hood ornament before walking away. Instead of turning the hood ornament over to the mechanic, I kept it. "Girl," my pathetic trophy said, "you may be a test case, but, by God, you aren't the only one being tested!"

* * *

Within this mercurial battle-of-the-sexes crucible, Mary Litell was scrapping for her own equal opportunity: the chance to compete for the gold in the ultimate ranger event—the Iron Man of ranger prowess—a high-angle rescue on El Capitan. Mary was a talented rock climber, she was a ranger, and it was the 1990s. If she wanted to risk her tight little tush by hanging it out over the edge of a three-thousand-foot-high cliff, she had the Equal Opportunity Act–given right to do so. But the boys weren't making room for her—at least not on the most glamorous missions. For months she had watched them run out of the rescue cache with backpacks full of rock climbing gear. For months she'd gritted her teeth in the rotor wash while they practically thumbed their noses at her from the open doors of the helicopter. And one morning, just as Mary finished washing her patrol car at the start of her shift, a supervisor drove up with one of the boys in the passenger seat and told her to give the male ranger her vehicle (it happened to be the newest vehicle in the fleet) as soon as she finished wiping it dry with a rag. Then, as if that wasn't infuriating enough, the male ranger smirked at Mary and said, "Thanks for washing my car."

Thaaa-whap! The wet rag from Mary's hand hit the supervisor's patrol car with a violence that made him flinch. Then she reared back with the long-handled scrub brush as if it were a spear, but the male ranger was able to roll up the car window before she could hit him with it. The supervisor said, "What the—?" but he was interrupted by a tirade about discrimination and playing favorites. The Valley Girl's sentences were seasoned with so many "sonofabitches," "m-fers," and "sexist bastards" that the supervisor had to gather up all the authority he could muster before he could bellow, "Settle down, Litell!"

Mary didn't settle down. Not until the male ranger was out of the car, bowing like a Japanese businessman, and showering her with apologies. "But I like you," he said.

After telling me this story, Mary sat down at my kitchen table, let out a fragile sigh, and said, "It's been nice working with you."

"They aren't going to fire you!" I said, laughing at her. "Not over something that benign. Remember the summer ranger who allegedly shot himself in the leg and then claimed he'd been in a gunfight? The only thing they did to him was not invite him back to work the next summer. And everybody says one of the district rangers had an affair with a subordinate, but he still has his job. And what about the ranger they accused of accepting sexual favors from a confidential informant while on duty? Didn't they give that guy a promotion?"

8

A GIRL IN BOYS TOWN

Mary Litell's first Yosemite job, working at the recycle stand, was more than gross; it was disgusting. Four million people leave behind a lot of trash. But she could glance over her shoulder and see her deliverance—Yosemite Falls plunging over the Valley's north wall. The half-mile cascade of water and rainbow was visible from Mary's workstation. With a downcanyon breeze she could see, smell, hear, and taste the fifth-tallest waterfall in the world. For scenery like that, you'll pick loaded diapers and used condoms out of piles of greasy cans and bottles. You'll sling trash bags into the back of a slimy truck while it spits the backwash from beer-soaked cigarette butts at you.

Yosemite Falls helped Mary forget all those things that needed forgetting: the father she lost to a flat tire and a speeding semi; the lover she lost to a tight curve and a cold river; the cramped tent cabin she shared with a bitchy, chain-smoking roommate; her gross job. And when the scenery wasn't enough, she could slap in a cassette, crank up the volume through her headphones, and sing. Her ponytail bouncing to the music, swinging her hips to dodge the splatter, the dirty blond with the hazel eyes had to be the cutest thing that ever hit the recycle stand in front of the Yosemite General Store—even if she did smell like garbage.

At twenty-one and five-foot-eleven, Mary was all legs and arms—more angles than curves—and her looks were the unassuming kind that, nine years later, a newspaper reporter described as "sun-kissed good." Her attractiveness did not go unnoticed by the rock climber who visited the recycle stand each day. When he hung around long enough to make sure everyone knew the new girl belonged to him, it was flattering. Ripped triceps, washboard stomach, and eyes as blue as Tenaya Lake on a sunny day, the rock climber cut a striking figure. And he was a real rock climber— one who lived the life. He had lots of rock climber friends. He had lots of rock climbing gear. He slept in a van. And he was much too talented to be bothered with something like a job.

Unlike her boyfriend, Mary was grateful for her job at the recycle stand. She listened to Madonna's *Like a Virgin* on her tape player. She slung the bags, dodged the trash juice, and grew numb to the smell. She did the time until she could run back to the bathhouse and shower off the filth, shimmy into a tank top, grab her climbing shoes, and head out for Chapel Wall to take advantage of the day's last light.

Once she was on the rock, there was no past. There was only the right here and the right now. There was only this moment and what she chose to do with it. There was only the rock and how it made her feel—like a virgin. Cheek, chest, belly, hips. She was closer to it than she'd ever been to anybody. She clung to it for dear life and begged it to never let her go. Her crotch tightened as she looked down at the air between her and a field of boulders. Her fingers caressed the warm granite, searching for that sweet spot. But she had to sweat for it. And she had to bleed before she found that bomber hold she'd been looking for. The one that lifted her higher. The one that made it all seem easy. The one that saved her.

And when she was done, standing on the cliff—breathless, high, and in love with her precious young life—if the man on top waiting for her to unclip from his rope wanted to believe the pupil dilation and the adrenaline sparks in her eyes were for him, well, there was no harm in that. Was there? Besides, what good did it do for a man to know that it was only when she was with the mountain that she never had to fake it? And what good did it do for a woman to dwell on how a mountain seemed to be the only thing that was never going to let her down?

Before the rock climber, Mary dated a man who seduced her with tales of a magnificent valley inside Yosemite National Park. In the spring she planned to leave Sacramento and join her new boyfriend, a park concession worker, in Yosemite as soon as the Curry Company hired her for the summer season. But Mary's boyfriend was dead before snowmelt. The rangers said he had missed a turn on the treacherous road to El Portal. The rangers said they had to pull his lifeless, broken body out of the Merced River and that alcohol might have been a factor. But it would take much more than one dead boyfriend to quell the pull Yosemite Valley had on her. She arrived in April, and her late boyfriend's friends helped her get a job working at the recycle stand.

* * *

The six years Mary worked for the park concessionaire were happy ones. Curry Company supervisors were good to her, and the employees working at the park's hotels, shops, and restaurants were like a family—Thanksgiving dinners at the Curry Cafeteria; Christmas talent shows inside the Four Seasons Restaurant. The nearest shopping mall was a winding hour-and-a-half drive to Fresno, if you owned a car. Still, if you got creative, there were ways to entertain yourself—rock climbing without the safety of ropes, jumping off high bridges, helping BASE (building, antenna, span, and earth) jumpers elude park rangers.

The housing of a park employee reflects his or her position in the park pecking order. Superintendents, Park Service division chiefs, and concession business managers are on the top. Special agents and supervisory park rangers are somewhere in the middle.

Concession employees who work service jobs for the corporation are the bottom-feeders.

Most times Mary didn't mind living in a tent cabin. But one morning she woke up to find eight beams of sunlight streaming through eight little holes in her canvas tent. A hungry bear had clawed through her home while she was sleeping. On the coldest days, after knocking the snow from the roofs of their tents, Mary and her friends would warm up by the fireplace in the lobby of the Ahwahnee Hotel, lounging in the plush chairs and sipping complimentary coffee meant for the guests.

The Ahwahnee lodge is an architectural beauty. For its patrons the hotel offers a four-star restaurant, a classy bar, an art gallery, and an overpriced gift shop. The shelves inside this and other park gift shops are loaded with hundreds of irresistible mementoes such as Bridalveil Falls key chains, sequoia shot glasses, El Capitan "This park rocks" T-shirts, Half Dome computer pads, a tin of Yosemite sugar-free peppermints, and a stuffed bear wearing a ranger hat. The Ahwahnee and other park hotels were managed by a subsidiary of a large entertainment conglomerate with a permit to hawk wares inside a national park. It was a lucrative arrangement for the corporation. In 1989, while Mary was working for the park concession, the Yosemite Park and Curry Company made an estimated $17 million in profits.

Mary moved up the park food chain when she left the recycle stand to tend bar at the Mountain Room. When there was work, she worked. During the slow winters, when she was laid off, she lived the carefree life of a climbing bum, following the warm weather from Yosemite's gray granite to the red rocks near Las Vegas or the yellow boulders inside Joshua Tree National Park. Her rock climber boyfriend introduced her to some of the most famous climbers in the world. A natural athlete, Mary mastered the sport quickly. Unlike most women prowling the Mountain Room Bar, she wanted to *be* a rock climber as much as she wanted to date one.

* * *

Like most Yosemite climbers, Mary's boyfriend was not a fan of park rangers. In fact, during the six years he and Mary lived together, he initiated more than one shouting match with more than one law enforcement ranger. (The one they called "Flattop" harassed the locals tirelessly.) Like many park residents, the rock climber felt that park rangers were "tools" of the government who "tooled people" by violating their rights and searching their cars for contraband that sometimes wasn't even there.

Many concession workers and some Park Service employees don't see anything wrong with smoking a little dope, catching a few thrills, and blowing off a little steam. *You* try making thousands of beds, scrubbing thousands of toilets, or serving thousands of plates of doughy white food to doughy white people without using something to help ease it all by. *You* try serving and cleaning up after thousands of impatient vacationers. And every two weeks— after the Curry Company withholds money from your Curry Company paycheck to pay rent on your Curry Company tent cabin and then you take what's left of your Curry Company paycheck to the Curry Company store to buy Curry Company food, beer, and cigarettes—who wouldn't want to party a little?

In light of this attitude, it was surprising to learn that the rock climber encouraged his girlfriend's growing urge to work for the National Park Service. But he had seen the upside of having a park ranger for a girlfriend. A seasonal park ranger can work summers in Yosemite and winters in Joshua Tree. He could climb while Mary worked to pay the rent on a hard-sided shelter inside a national park. His girlfriend a park ranger? What an excellent idea!

During the winter of 1991–92, the couple, along with several other climbers, traveled to Italy to work as rope riggers, stunt doubles, and climbing instructors for the movie *Cliffhanger*. In this film a park ranger battles bad guys after a plane full of stolen money crashes in the interior of what is ostensibly Rocky

Mountain National Park but what is actually the Italian Dolomites. The plot is loosely based on a novel written by a Yosemite rock climber. Titled *Angels of Light*, the novel was inspired by an actual event involving a real drug smuggler's plane that crashed in the park in 1976. The only realism to be had in the film *Cliffhanger* is the fiery plane crash and the rangers crippled from post-traumatic stress. The hero, played by Sylvester Stallone, has too much muscle mass to be a real rock climber and gets too much time off to be a real park ranger.

After a long day of working on the set of *Cliffhanger*, the rock climbers, the Hollywood celebrities, and the film crew would congregate in the posh restaurants of Cortina d'Ambezzo—the Italian version of Colorado's snobby Aspen. The rock climbers felt right at home when, by association, the Italians treated them like movie stars. Except for Mary. After a long day on the rock, she walked into a Cortina bar with a sunburned nose, ratty hair, and scabbed knuckles. Compared with the expertly highlighted tresses, designer clothes, and foundation-perfected skin of the women from Hollywood, Mary felt like a lumbering giraffe among a herd of glitzy gazelles. She could see her boyfriend checking out the gazelles. She could feel him thinking that maybe it was time he traded in his giraffe for something sleeker.

When they returned to Yosemite, the rock climber had acquired something he hadn't had in a long time—his own cash. Meanwhile Mary continued to tend bar and pay the bills. She was writing a check to pay off a credit card bill when she noticed a mysterious charge for a hotel room in San Diego. That's how she knew he had done it again. Except this time, he was dumping her for good.

A few months after the breakup, a Yosemite park ranger broke more bad news. As far as he was concerned, Mary was "a paper ranger." On paper she had everything she needed to be a ranger—the EMT certification, the diploma from a six-week ranger law enforcement academy, the CPR and wildland firefighting cards. But when it came to actual job experience, she wasn't worth a whole lot more than the paper her certificates were printed on. When a supervisory ranger called her into his office a few weeks later, Mary was prepared for the worst.

Jim Tucker, the Valley day-shift supervisor, sat in a creaking chair next to a desk piled so high with reports and other government documents that it resembled the relief model of the park inside the visitor center next door. Tucker, a barrel-chested U.S. Army Military Police Corps veteran, saw more in the young female climber than what was on paper. He figured Mary knew the cracks and crevices of Yosemite Valley better than he did, and he had lived and worked in the park for more than a decade. Tucker told Mary he wanted to hire her, but—the ranger raised his hand to his face and massaged his weary, tired and bloodshot eyes for what seemed like a good minute before he continued— he couldn't pay her as much as she made tending bar. It was 1993. Slinging drinks for tourists and park locals paid, with tips, about $11 an hour. Protecting the park from the people, the people from the park, and the people from one another paid $7.35 an hour. However, Ranger Tucker informed her, if she were willing to work for a lower wage, she had a summer job on the Yosemite Valley day-shift patrol.

"I'll take it," Mary said.

* * *

Within Yosemite National Park, at the apex of the curve connecting Curry Village to Happy Isles lurked a massive cedar with an appetite for ranger vehicles. Many years ago, it was said, this menacing tree had eaten the fender of a patrol car and an ambulance, both driven by a ranger named Frank Pentilla, both on the same day. Thanks to the legend of Pentilla's Corner, ranger Mary Litell eased up on the accelerator as she entered the hairpin turn, despite the fact that she was rushing to a very serious emergency—a body in Boys Town, swinging from the center beam of tent cabin number forty-eight.

To the rookie ranger, a foot patrol through Boys Town was a trek into hostile territory. Years ago, only male concession employees lived in Boys Town, hence the name. Fifty or so canvas tents with wooden platforms on a dry patch of bare ground, the compound resembled the mining camps of the gold rush era in more ways than one. Drunks stumbled in and out of swinging wooden doors. Crowds circled rolling duels in the dirt. Angry glares burned through window screens. Shutters came down with a slap. It was a scene from every Western—the unpopular and outnumbered sheriff walks the dusty streets of Rowdyville.

Among the many calls bringing a ranger to Boys Town were alcohol-fueled conflicts, loud music, drug use, and the occasional date rape of intoxicated young women. Sometimes there were hangings.

The first of the year occurred in April. An intoxicated concession employee depressed by his arrest for DUI twisted one end of a bedsheet around his neck before threading the other end through the grated ceiling of his jail cell. It would have been the first successful hanging of the year, but a ranger unlocked the jail cell in time to catch the man as he jumped off the bunk. Six weeks later, Mary rounded Pentilla's Corner on her way to a report of a man swinging from a rafter in Boys Town.

The man's roommate had cut him down before she arrived. A ranger-medic attached electrodes to the victim's chest while Mary began CPR. When Special Agent Jeff Sullivan entered the tent, the ranger-medic pointed out a knife wound on the victim's abdomen. The wound wasn't bleeding, suggesting that the stabbing may have been postmortem. "Treat this as a homicide," the special agent said, directing rangers to protect evidence while performing lifesaving measures. This announcement startled the youngest ranger on the scene.

Athletic, good-natured, and eager to please, Mary had bounded into that morning's shift briefing like a golden retriever, her lanky body wagging from her ponytailed head all the way down to her tap-dancing feet. But now that Mary had her hands placed firmly on the cold and clammy chest of a potential murder victim, the ranger's cheerful self-confidence waned. "Homicide?" she said, looking up at the special agent. "I'm not sure if I can do this!"

The suspected lynching ended up being "only" a suicide after all. An autopsy and the follow-up investigation determined that the stab wound was self-inflicted. Friends said the concession employee had been lonely and depressed. Forensic evidence indicated that he committed hara-kiri with a hunting knife. When that didn't kill him fast enough, he tied a handkerchief around his neck, stuck his head into a loop of hemp rope, tied the rope to the rafter, and stepped off a chair.

The next day, another resident of Boys Town disappeared. A maid found him several days later in a Merced hotel room, hanging from the rod in the closet. A few weeks after that, another park employee dangled from the center beam of another tent cabin in another employee tent camp. This time, Keith Lober arrived in time to shock the man's heart back to life, but the ranger's lifesaving skills were for naught. The man's heart lived for two more days, but his brain died in that tent cabin.

Four concession worker hangings within four months, three of them fatal. If there was any connection between the 1994 hangings, my research failed to uncover it; but it was a trend that attracted the attention of a government agency on the outside, like the Occupational Safety and Health Administration. That year, during an investigation into the living and working conditions of the park's concession employees, a health inspector measured the daytime temperature inside one tent cabin. It was 112 degrees Fahrenheit.

Although the summer rangers like Mary ranked a step or two higher on the park food chain than maids and food servers, many spent a season or two living in a tent cabin. (In Tuolumne Meadows—at 8,600 feet—summer rangers slept inside one sleeping bag and under five blankets in order to stay warm inside their unheated canvas homes.)

The park concession worker and the park ranger have more in common than they know, but once Mary pinned a badge to her shirt, some park locals saw her as a traitor who had switched sides— especially when she made her first arrest. The depressing incident involved a brain-damaged former rock climber (years earlier, he had been injured in a fall and rescued by park rangers). Abandoned by his drinking buddies, he was stumbling around dangerously drunk and bumping into tourists outside Degnan's Deli before Mary took him to jail to sleep it off. Whether it was in the public's best interest or not, once she started arresting people, as far as most rock climbers and concession employees were concerned, Mary Litell became "Ranger LaTool."

9

THE PARTNER

It sounded like the boom of a giant cannon. On July 10 at 6:52 p.m., a mass of boulders and grit the size of a Motel 6 broke free from Glacier Point and plunged two thousand feet to the valley floor. A plume of dust rose into the air, making some wonder if Yosemite Valley had been bombed. It was not the rocks but the wind—a 245-mile-per-hour blast of air pushed out from the force of the falling granite—that leveled a thousand large trees across thirty-two acres, destroyed the Happy Isles concession stand, injured twelve people, and killed a young hiker when one of the trees fell on him.

Yosemite Valley wasn't always the deep gorge it is today. Long ago it was a shallow river drainage. When the earth's climate began to cool, glaciers were born and then grew. As global weather patterns fluctuated, the glaciers pushed and ground the earth, removing anything that either blocked their greedy expansion or got in the way of their reluctant retreat. When the last Yosemite Valley glacier receded some twenty thousand years ago, it left behind a dramatic U-shaped valley.

Today rivers and creeks continue to sculpt the landscape. Rainfall freezes behind joints in the granite. Gravity, lightning strikes, plant roots, and earthquakes also do their part so that over time, the rock exfoliates from the granite like layers peeled from an onion. Occasionally these rock sheets crash to the ground, sometimes with disastrous consequences. Since 1857 Yosemite rockfalls have killed at least fourteen people and injured sixty-two.

The day after the slide, journalists besieged the park. The public information officer directed all media trucks and vans with satellite dishes to a paved pullout under a photogenic view of Yosemite Falls. One morning, the shift supervisor pointed at ranger Bruce Phillips and me. "Lankford; Phillips," he said. "You two suit up for horse patrol and ride around the media trucks."

A park ranger on horseback never fails to attract attention. Cameras click, videotape rolls, parents come running with five-year-olds wanting to pet the horsey. When the hordes of image-hungry reporters and cameramen spotted a pair of park rangers—the only female and African American on patrol that day—riding by on horseback, footage of Bruce and me would show up on all the news outlets.

"Great idea," I said with mock enthusiasm. "Bruce and I will be the Equal Opportunity patrol!"

"Settle down, Lankford."

* * *

I can't blame NPS managers for wanting Bruce to represent the agency on television. His uniforms fitted him perfectly and, on horseback, he was too fine: strong shoulders, honey voice, espresso skin—a girl could just drink him up. Bruce and I saddled our horses at the barn and rode out to the media circus. Before we reached the Yosemite Lodge, I decided to impress my attractive partner with my horsemanship. With a clicking noise and a touch of the whip, I squeezed my legs, sending Junior, my patrol horse, into a dirt-throwing gallop over the trail.

"A real cowgirl never loses her hat," Bruce informed me when I handed him my horse's reins so I could retrieve my Smokey Bear out of Leidig Meadow.

When patrolling Yosemite on horseback, Bruce Phillips was a living tribute to a once-hidden chapter of park history. Prior to the creation of the NPS by the 1916 Organic Act, the burden of protecting the lands set aside as national parks largely fell upon the U.S. Army. Among the first troops to patrol the rugged backcountry of Yosemite, Sequoia, and General Grant National Parks were the Twenty-fourth Infantry and the Ninth Cavalry, otherwise known as the Buffalo Soldiers. Like their white counterparts, African-American soldiers collected fees, eradicated sheep, built roads, and confiscated guns from potential poachers. In 1904, under the direction of Maj. John Bigelow, troops from the Ninth Cavalry constructed the first self-guided nature trail in a national park.

Among the four hundred Buffalo Soldiers assigned to Yosemite and Sequoia National Parks was Capt. Charles Young, the first African-American superintendent of a national park. Despite the prejudices of the time, Young impressed many white commanders. One Army inspector described him as the best instructor on duty in the parks. A lieutenant colonel credited Young's leadership for constructing park roads and trails "in excess of that done in previous years with the same amount of money." Like his contemporary John Muir, Young contemplated the importance of wilderness preservation:

> *A journey through this park and the Sierra Forest Reserve to the Mount Whitney country will convince even the least thoughtful man of the needfulness of preserving these mountains just as they are, with their clothing of trees, shrubs, rocks, and vines, and of their importance to the valley's below as reservoirs for storage of water for agricultural and domestic purposes. In this, then, lies the necessity of forest preservation.*

Proud and ambitious, Captain Young was the highest-ranking African-American soldier of his day. Yet for a hundred years, Young's side of the national park story went untold. As Yosemite ranger Shelton Johnson, an African American, writes in his essay "Invisible Men: Buffalo Soldiers of the Sierra Nevada":

> *When one examines published histories of Yosemite for example, one would be hard put to find more than a handful of references to either the Ninth Cavalry or Twenty-fourth Infantry. These soldiers lie on the edges of an obscure chapter in a forgotten book. They are not, I believe, the victims of overt racism, but rather casualties of a greater society that simply doesn't see them. They are invisible men.*

Thanks to the diligent research of Ranger Johnson, Captain Young and his men are no longer invisible.

* * *

After Bruce and I performed our token appearances in front of the media trucks, it was time to give the horses a break. Like park rangers, park horses are susceptible to burnout. Everybody wants to say Hi and take a picture. Everybody wants to rub their noses and stroke their manes. You know it is time to call it a day when your horse lays his ears back or lifts his head real high so the kids can't reach him.

Communicating with a horse is one of many skills taught at the Yosemite Mounted Patrol School. Bruce and I learned what little we know about horses from Steve "Kid" Ybarra, a world-champion mule packer, and Billie Patrick, a horse patrol ranger with a fantastically long blond ponytail. Horse school was far from glamorous: six weeks of mucking out horse stalls; six weeks of Ybarra humiliating us for having nothing under our hats but hair; six weeks of sore rears, aching backs, bruised egos, and Wellington boots that smelled of horse piss. But I loved it anyway. You can see it in my hokey, flag-bearing graduation photos.

Patrick and Ybarra could rattle off the histories, confirmations, and personalities of every patrol horse that ever came through Yosemite Valley as well as they could recall their own birth date and Social Security number. Billie Patrick said that the horse named Danny was "too touchy" for the less-experienced riders. Once Danny went so far as to kick a Porsche, denting it a little. Billie said Danny needed a confident rider, but everybody knew the real reason she didn't let anybody else ride him: Billie Patrick was in love with the "touchy" sorrel with the heart-shaped blaze on his face.

Danny's penchant for kicking things weighed heavily on Billie's mind the day a little boy with muscular dystrophy motored up in an electric wheelchair. The wheelchair buzzed and clicked. The boy was flailing his arms about in jerking motions. He couldn't help it. He didn't have full control of his muscles, and he was so excited. His parents looked at Billie expectantly. Their son wanted to pet the ranger's horse.

Horses spook easily at unusual sights and sounds. A honking car or a tarp flapping in the breeze can send them running for the barn, bucking and kicking the whole way. Yosemite patrol horses have practiced maintaining their composure in the midst of patrol sirens, angry mobs, and gunfire. But you can never predict how a horse will react to something it has never encountered. Danny had kicked a Porsche for the hell of it. Billie had no clue what the horse would do to a kid in a clicking wheelchair.

Tightening her grip on the reins, Billie slowly maneuvered Danny toward the boy. Danny studied the wheelchair-bound boy for a moment with one of his big eyes. Then the horse dropped his head right in the child's lap. The boy lovingly hit and slapped Danny's face, and Billie blinked back a few tears. He knew. The horse just knew.

Ybarra and Patrick made patrol assignments by matching the personality of the ranger to the personality of the horse. So it makes sense that Bruce ended up with Duke—a handsome prince of a horse. But I'm still trying to figure out why I always got stuck with Junior—the surly beast that made a mule look like Miss Congeniality.

They said Junior took on the personality of the ranger who broke him and that Junior the horse, like Dan Horner the ranger, would argue with you about whether the time was fifteen minutes after or a quarter past. One afternoon Junior started giving me grief. With his ears laid way back, he would run me in circles and kick up a fuss every time I asked him to do something. I'd rein him left, toward Yosemite Lodge, and he'd go right, toward the barn.

To hell with this, Junior was saying. *I'm heading back to the barn.*

Touching a spur to his belly, I reined Junior back to the left. *Somebody call the Humane Society,* I was telling him, *because I'm fixing to commit animal cruelty.* But the damn horse insisted on going right.

Then we got the call: rowdy drunks threatening park visitors in the picnic area. All the road patrol rangers were busy. It was up to Junior and me to deal with it. Once we arrived, a beefy dude, red-faced and drunk, charged at us like an angry bear. He pointed a finger at my face and told me where I could take my law enforcement authority and shove it.

We had the attention of all the picnickers now. Like them, I wondered how the lady ranger was going to handle this one. Why didn't Billie assign me Duke or Danny today? Arresting this Neanderthal was going to be difficult enough without my mutinous horse sprinting for the barn as soon as I dismounted. Then Junior did something unexpected. He stepped toward the guy, stamped a hoof on the ground, and blew a fierce puff of air through his nostrils.

Following my partner's cue I said, "Turn around and put your hands behind your back."

The belligerent man looked into Junior's steely eyes and said, "Okay, ranger, whatever you say."

I dismounted and laid the reins on Junior's neck. While I handcuffed the man, Junior stood beside me, still as a statue. He had a job to do. The barn could wait.

10

THE TELL-TALE
BACKPACK

As one special agent put it, "For a young ranger, Mary had an uncanny knack for making good cases." Every day, as soon as the shift supervisor let the day shift out of morning briefing, she ran out into the park, sniffing the air and rummaging through all the dark places until she hunted down something weird or smelly, clamped her cuffs on it, and brought it back to the ranger station. The Valley Girl captured thieves and wanted felons. She tackled runaway BASE jumpers. She busted dope dealers, violent drunks, and wife beaters. One year she tracked down an arsonist with hundreds of cigarette lighters in his car. Her first summer, she ferreted out a particularly worrisome weenie-wagger.

Earlier that spring a man had exposed his penis and masturbated in front of a little girl wading in the shallows of the Merced River. Long after all the other rangers had forgotten about this incident, Mary caught a glimpse of a man wearing khaki pants and no shirt lurking around the start of the Four Mile Trail. She didn't even see his face. She just knew it was the guy. As soon as she got out of her patrol car, the shirtless man took off up the trail. She chased him up several switchbacks before he stopped. With nothing but a hunch to go on, the ranger snapped an instant photo of the man, wrote down his identification information, and let him go. A few days later, the little girl's mother positively identified the man in the photo as the one who had exposed himself to her daughter.

Another day she spotted two life-size G.I. Joes sitting in the back of a pickup truck parked in the pullout at Cook's Meadow. There's nothing illegal about wearing full camouflage and combat boots in a national park, but you could say it is the kind of thing that might draw the attention of a park ranger. Mary casually strolled up to the two young men sitting in the back of the pickup truck, flashed her friendliest ranger smile, and said, "Hi, there. Nice day isn't it?"

She poured on the Ranger Rick shtick until the G.I. Joes in the pickup truck became fidgety—rubbing their noses when answering questions; not looking her in the eye; sneaking a hundred glances at a red backpack in the bed of the truck. It didn't require a PhD in behavioral science to pick up on it. Those men were looking at that backpack as though the namesake organ from Edgar Allan Poe's "The Tell-Tale Heart" were beating inside it.

"So, it looks like you guys have been doing some hiking?" Mary asked.

"Oh, yeah," one man said. "We've been here before."

"That's a nice backpack," she said, pointing at it. "Whose is it?"

Mary's question could have been a swarm of bees the way those men reacted. They jumped out of the bed of the truck, ran to the cab, slammed the car doors, rolled up the windows, cranked the ignition, and said, "Sorry, we gotta go!" while Mary stood there and watched them drive away, the red backpack bouncing around in the truck bed.

The ranger wanted to grab that backpack and search it like a dog wants to grab a rope toy and shake it, but lacking probable cause to detain these men, she had to let them go. Mary couldn't stop thinking about that red backpack. What was in it? Drugs? That was the most likely thing. But those guys were wearing camouflage. Maybe they were poachers, or archaeological site looters called "pot hunters." Jeez, there was no telling what was in that backpack—jewelry snatched from the Ahwahnee gift shop, a stash of stolen wallets and credit cards, peregrine falcon eggs, rare plants, black bear gall bladders worth a fortune on the Asian black market. Or maybe, just maybe, those two guys were a couple of psycho serial killers and the reason they didn't want anyone looking inside that backpack was because a human head was rolling around inside it!

What was in the backpack? God, it was killing her. That red backpack was not only going to keep the ranger up at night wondering, it was going to haunt her for the rest of her life. *What was in the backpack?*

Back to patrolling the park roads, Mary tapped her fingers on the steering wheel. Maybe she hadn't handled the contact right. Maybe she had made a mistake. Maybe she really did have probable cause to search them and didn't realize it. She was still beating herself up over letting two psycho serial killers escape to murder again when she noticed the car in front of her. Unbelievable. It was the pickup with the red backpack. Those G.I. Joes said they were leaving the park, so why were they back on this road leading into the Valley? Mary eased her patrol car up to the pickup's rear bumper.

When the driver noticed the ranger car in his rearview mirror, he became so nervous he couldn't drive. He wove the truck all the way across the traffic lane until the tires crossed the double yellow. Hallelujah! The driver had given her a reason to pull him over.

Standing at the driver's window, Mary said, "What's going on here?"

"Uh. I uh. We . . ."

"Do you have drugs on you?"

"Uh. . . . No."

As soon as a backup ranger arrived, Mary asked the guy driving the truck if it was okay to search the cab for weapons. "Sure," he said, "no problem." The ranger checked the floorboards. She looked under the seats. She opened the glove box. There she found a little metal tube about the size of a lipstick case. "What's this?" The guy shrugged. Mary handed it to her male partner.

"It's a CO_2 cartridge," her partner said. "You know, an explosive, like a firecracker."

Possession of firecrackers and other explosive devices is illegal in a national park. This was enough probable cause to search the truck and everything in it. The ranger jumped into the back of the pickup and started tossing stuff behind her like a dog throws dirt in pursuit of a bone. As soon as she found the suspicious pack, Mary grabbed it, pulled down the zipper, and stuck her hand inside. Out she came with a metal pipe, six inches long and two inches in diameter. The pipe had metal caps on both ends and a fuse coming out of it. She held this prize up in the air, turned to her partner, and said, "Catch."

The ranger caught the pipe, took one look at it, and said, "Jesus, Mary! It's a bomb!" Not really sure what to do, and still in shock that his partner had tossed him an explosive device as if it were a can of beer, Mary's partner jammed the bomb into his pocket and stood watch over the G.I. Joes, who were now handcuffed and sitting on the curb. The Valley Girl kept searching. She found a fishing tackle box full of bomb-making paraphernalia. She found a book on how to build bombs. She found dated photographs of the two men grinning proudly from the top of Glacier Point.

The NPS special agent arrived on the scene. Good, it's Sullivan. Surely this righteous bust would make up for that day in Boys Town when she grabbed his arm like a scared little girl and said, "Homicide? I'm not sure if I can do this." Mary caught Special Agent Sullivan's eye, nodded to her partner, and said, "Check this out!"

The male ranger pulled the bomb out of his pocket.

"Holy Christ!" the special agent shouted as he dropped to the ground.

Sullivan quarantined the entire area, shutting down traffic on the road. A flak jacket–clad bomb squad from Fresno detonated the bomb. It wasn't a huge bomb, but if you were planning on staying attached to your ass, you would avoid putting it in your back pocket. The special agent warned the Valley Girl to remember that next time she decided to play catch with bombs.

The G.I. Joes went straight to jail, where one of them quickly squealed. He said they had been planning to take the bomb up on one of the popular hiking trails and light the fuse. Days later, rangers and county deputies conducted a raid on one suspect's home. They found bombs in the freezer. They found bombs hanging from the ceiling. They found books on bombs and lots of gunpowder. Investigators wondered if recent visitor reports of explosions on the Nevada Falls Trail might have been something less benign than routine rock falls.

11

MARY, THE SPLIT-TAIL CLERK-TYPIST

If you aspire to become a permanent full-time-with-benefits park ranger with the NPS, you had better pack for an arduous quest. First you must satisfy the requirements of the Division of Human Resources. To satisfy the Division of Human Resources, you must follow guidelines set by the Office of Personnel Management. And according to the Office of Personnel Management, a person may not apply for a permanent full-time-with-benefits park ranger position unless she has "career status" as a permanent full-time-with-benefits federal employee. In other words, in order to apply for a job as a permanent full-time employee, you have to *be* a permanent full-time employee.

This is the park ranger's catch-22.

Fortunately for the brave and the desperate, there are always loopholes. To beat the ranger's catch-22, a devout nature lover has several options. All of them grim. You can compete for an entry-level "open to non-status applicants" ranger position at a big city park like the Statue of Liberty or Independence Hall (where the scenery is scarce and the cost of living–to–wage ratio is punitive). You can accept a job as a federal prison guard, probation officer, or postal worker. You can work for the IRS. You can volunteer your services for two years while exposing yourself to political unrest and exotic diseases in the Peace Corps. You can enlist in the military and hope you become a veteran of a war. Or you can do your time as a Park Service clerk-typist, toiling behind a desk until a ranger supervisor rescues you from administrative exile.

Most park rangers work many years as a temporary ranger before they are deemed worthy of seeking a permanent full-time-with-benefits assignment. But patience wasn't one of Mary's virtues. After laboring two years as a summer ranger in Yosemite, she desperately wanted the benefits and job security of a full-time job. Of all the paths leading to a permanent full-time ranger, Mary figured the least painful was to take the route of a clerk-typist.

Her first challenge was to take a clerk-typist test. She woke up early one morning and drove three hours from Yosemite to downtown Sacramento, where she got in line with all the other people desiring jobs as clerk-typists for the federal government. But before she got in the door, a test administrator turned her away. She wasn't among the first forty people in line. Weeks later, they gave the test again. Mary got up earlier and drove faster. This time she was third in line. She took the test and passed it. In the fall of 1994, at the end of her second summer as a park ranger, Mary started her job as a full-time clerk-typist at Yosemite National Park. Her duties included filling out time sheets, making photocopies, typing letters, and grinding her teeth into a smile every time the district ranger massaged her shoulders when she'd rather he didn't.

It was hell. Sitting in the stale air of the office. Punching numbers into an adding machine. Watching the rangers swagger in, their guns on their hips. By Christmas the guys were treating her like they treated all the other office women: flirting with her when they needed something; ignoring her when they didn't. They seemed to be forgetting that a few months ago Mary had been one of them. They seemed to be forgetting that this clerk-typist thing was only temporary.

* * *

A Yosemite April can be dreary. It may even snow. Indeed, on April 13, 1995, rain, sleet, and snow took turns punishing four rock climbers ascending a route on El Capitan called "the Nose." A classic climb, the Nose is perhaps the most sought-after big-wall ascent in the world. In 1958 three men achieved the first ascent of the Nose. It took them forty-seven days stretched out over seventeen months. Today the average climber completes the 2,900-vertical-foot, thirty-one-pitch climb in five days of "immense physical and psychological drain." The failure rate is high for those who attempt this route. The first rock climber fatality on El Capitan occurred in 1905. Since then more than twenty-six climbers have died on "El Cap"—nearly a third of those deaths related to bad weather.

The weather certainly challenged the four climbers on El Cap that April 13. In their struggle to reach a safe position to hole up for the night, one climber dropped his sleeping bag and watched it plummet two thousand feet to the valley floor. Eventually all four men made it to Camp Six Ledge, a triangular platform of rock smaller than most bathrooms. Six hundred feet from the top and 2,300 feet from the bottom, this ledge offered relief from the cliff face but not from the weather. That night, a waterfall of rain and melted snow poured down the rock wall through a crack at the back of the ledge, soaking the climbers and their gear. A vertical half mile above the ground, the men huddled together and contemplated their predicament. Four men; three wet sleeping bags; two icy ropes; one exposed ledge; zero relief from the weather— and it was getting darker and colder by the minute. Although they were loath to admit it, without help from the park rangers, the climbers might die.

Around 6:30 p.m., tourists heard cries for help coming from the face of El Cap. By the time rangers received these reports, the sky was too dark and the weather too dicey for a rescue helicopter to pluck the men off the rock face. If the climbers were to receive any assistance before dawn, a strike team would have to approach the top of El Capitan on foot.

For this mission, rescue coordinators organized a strike team of twenty-one men. Led by paramedic park ranger Keith Lober, this team consisted of rangers, other park employees, and trained rescue volunteers known as "SAR-siters." In return for their assistance on SARs (search and rescues), rock climbers earned free camping privileges in a designated area (the SAR site) of Sunnyside Campground. The role SAR-siters play on the Yosemite rescue team cannot be overstated. Without the additional talents, manpower, and athletic abilities of SAR-siters, Yosemite rangers would be overwhelmed by the number of rescue missions they respond to each year. A good number of SAR-siters have more technical search and rescue knowledge than your average park ranger.

In 1995 Mary was still "cutting her teeth" as a rescuer. So that night the strike team leader didn't let poor Mary play any rescue ranger games. Instead the clerk-typist strapped snowshoes onto the varsity rescuers' backpacks. She helped load gear into the rescue vans. She watched the strike team drive off into the blustery storm. Then she sat behind a desk and filled in the blanks on time sheets. On that snowy April eve, Mary the Split-Tail Clerk-Typist must have felt like Rudolph the Red-Nosed Reindeer.

The vans drove the strike team from Yosemite Valley (3,900 feet) to Crane Flat (6,100 feet), where they got into the snow machines that would take them to Tamarack Flat (6,300 feet). From Tamarack Flat the team would snowshoe nine miles through the snow to the top of El Capitan (7,500 feet). From the top of El Cap they could lower a rescuer, supplies, and dry sleeping bags to the rock climbers—ideally, before they all froze to death.

It was a doable plan. But the April storm had something else in mind. The snow machines bogged down in sticky snow before reaching Tamarack Flat, leaving the rescuers many miles from their intended destination. I imagine this is the point when the strike team leader cursed the crippled Sno-Cats and threw the snowshoe that made his rescue team flinch. This expedition to El

Capitan was turning unpleasant, triggering an eruption from their leader—Sheriff Lobo.

* * *

El Capitan's name comes from a Spanish interpretation of its Native American name Tu-tok, or "rock chief." Tu-tok's profile is evident in the three-thousand-foot-long slope of granite that forms his "nose." Although El Capitan is the largest granite monolith in the world, it isn't the tallest. To the east sits a granite dome a thousand feet higher and a whole lot prettier. They say that of all the photographs taken by Ansel Adams, including a misty shot of El Cap, it is a shadowy portrait of Half Dome under a waning moon that made the landscape photographer famous.

The Ahwahnee name for Half Dome is Tis-sa-ack. Controversy surrounds the source and authenticity of Yosemite "Indian" legends. At least two tribes claim the Ahwahnee as their ancestors, and several bastardized versions of the Tis-sa-ack story are floating around. Yet the Half Dome legends all have at least one thing in common—a woman with man trouble. In a story documented by Galen Clark in 1904, Tis-sa-ack is a spirited wife who drinks up all the water in Mirror Lake. When her husband tries to beat her, Tis-sa-ack curses and throws her basket at him. For their wickedness, the Great Spirit turns both spouses to stone. Half Dome is Tis-sa-ack. Basket Dome is her dropped basket. North Dome is the angry husband.

Another Tis-sa-ack story includes Tu-tok, the spirit of El Capitan. One day Tu-tok falls in love with the lovely Ti-sa when he sees the angel of Yosemite Valley lounging around on the top of Half Dome. But Ti-sa rejects the rock chief's repeated advances and eventually flees. Devastated, Tu-tok neglects Yosemite Valley. His heartbreak sends rockslides thundering off the mountains. His tears flood the rivers. His apathy allows green leaves to turn brown and flowers to wilt. Eventually the Great Spirit intervenes, restoring the Valley to its original splendor and imprinting an image of Ti-sa on the side of Half Dome for Tu-tok to look at. A dark stain represents her long black hair.

Most people view these scenic rivals from the valley floor. But the relationship between El Cap and Half Dome is best appreciated from their tops. Hike the arduous route to the peak of Half Dome and see that, from Ti-sa's point of view, Tu-tok has his arrogant nose turned away and appears to be snubbing her. But when standing on the top of El Cap, one realizes that Tu-tok's disdain is only pretense. No rock chief can ignore the sensuous swell of Half Dome's backside.

* * *

Snow and darkness obscured the inspiring view from El Cap on the evening of April 13, 1995. In the interest of safety, Lober halted his strike team's death march through the hip-deep snow and ordered them to bivouac for the night. The conditions were miserable. They got worse when Lober discovered that his team hadn't packed enough tents and sleeping bags to go around. On another rescue similar to this one, Sheriff Lobo resolved the same problem by forcing two SAR-siters to spend the night out in the snow. In a desperate attempt to stay warm, one volunteer hovered so close to the campfire that he melted the seat of his GORE-TEX pants.

Lober and his strike team suffered a wretched bivouac near Tamarack Flat, while Mary the Clerk-Typist slept in her warm bed. In the morning she reported for duty at the rescue cache, expecting a shift of restocking gear and finishing paperwork, all the boring stuff, until the incident commander broke the news. The strike team had not reached El Cap. And at this very moment, the storm clouds were parting, opening a "window" of good weather. The commander needed to get rescuers flown to the top of El Cap before this window closed. With twenty-one of the most experienced rescuers in Yosemite Valley stuck under the heavy clouds covering the higher elevations, the incident commander had no choice. The fourth-quarter buzzer had rung. His starting lineup was stuck in a snowbank. It was time to send the bench sitters into the game.

The SAR cache ranger was an obsessive-compulsive recycler. He jammed fax machines with used paper. He crammed packing peanuts into garbage bags and filled an entire room of the rescue cache with them. New rangers and rescue volunteers were warned to be leery of any food offered to them by the SAR cache ranger. He cut mold off cheese, ate fruit others had discarded, and offered rescue workers stale doughnuts in boxes retrieved from a garbage can. Notoriously thrifty, the SAR cache ranger loved a bargain. Instead of GORE-TEX parkas, he had purchased bright yellow raincoats and pants that looked like the kind worn by school crossing guards. No one wanted to wear them, so they were going unused.

Before Mary left the rescue cache, the SAR cache ranger handed her one of these suits. He told Mary to put it on if she went over the edge. The SAR cache ranger was eccentric, but he was also a well-respected rescue guru with an MIT education and a genius IQ. Mary took the rain suit, which was still in the packaging, and promised to wear it.

* * *

Sitting inside the rescue helicopter, Mary's scalp prickled with excitement. The military pilot lifted off, aiming for a blue hole in the clouds. Mary looked out the window. The people standing in Ahwahnee Meadow got smaller and smaller. Then El Cap got bigger and bigger. The wet granite sparkled like a prism in the sunlight.

On top of El Cap, Mary leaned over the edge and peered down—a long way down. In her dorky rain suit, she looked like an idiot. But she didn't care. Mary once told a friend she craved experiences that "make me have to wet my pants," and today she was going over the edge of El-freaking-Capitan, as soon as SAR-siter Eric Rasmussen got the lowering system ready.

With a few more knots to tie and a couple more anchors to check, Mary looked up. Uh-oh. Standing on the ridge above the cliff's edge was Sheriff Lobo, glaring down on her. After dropping off the B team, the helicopter picked up Lober and part of his strike team and brought them to El Cap. As soon as the strike team leader saw Mary at the edge, Lober ran down the knee-pounding descent, waving his arms and yelling. Stop. Hold up. Wait for him.

No way.

"Go. Go. Go." Mary said. "He's coming." The B team scrambled to tie knots and lock carabiners. "We got here first."

Once Lober reached the edge of El Cap, he saw a group of junior rescuers preparing to conduct a time-critical, high-angle rescue operation. The weather conditions were extremely hazardous. The lives of four climbers were at stake. And the "man" they had chosen to send over the edge was a clerk-typist with hazel eyes, a freckled face, and a long ponytail—and she was wearing a ridiculous yellow rain suit.

"McDevitt, you're going over," Lober said, pointing to Dan McDevitt, an experienced rock climber and rescue volunteer.

"But I'm ready," Mary said.

"Give McDevitt the rope."

"I'm already tied in," Mary said. A sheet of ice the size of a sliding glass door slid off the edge of El Cap and crashed down the cliff face, zinging like a missile on its way to the valley floor. What a shitty day to be on El Cap. Yet here she was—fighting for an opportunity to dangle over the edge during a freakish April snowstorm while the only thing that kept her from plunging three thousand vertical feet to her death was a rope no thicker than a roll of string cheese. *If I don't go over the edge of El Cap today, I'll be a clerk-typist forever.* "Keith," Mary pleaded, "I can do this!"

"We are wasting time." A shadow from a fast-moving cloud darkened Lober's face. Their window of good weather could close at any moment. "Mary, I said give McDevitt the rope."

The clerk-typist tightened her grip. *If you can pry it from my dead fingers.*

"Dammit, woman," Lober said. *Have it your way.*

Rescue volunteer Eric Rasmussen took a photograph of Mary as she began her descent. In the photo you see that rescuers have kicked off most of the ice, but the granite is still dusted with snow. The perspective is deceiving. The tiny trees behind Mary are actually one-hundred-foot-tall pines growing on the valley floor a half mile below. Mary wears a climbing helmet, sunglasses, and a chest harness with a radio. Her megawatt smile matches her megawatt yellow rain suit. She is about to become the first Split-Tail Clerk-Typist to go "over the edge" as the lead rescuer during a high-angle mission on El Capitan.

The rescuers on top of El Cap lowered Mary six hundred feet. She used her feet to maneuver herself down the rock and over to where four shivering men squatted on a granite shelf the size of a king-size mattress. Soaked to the bone by the frigid water gushing down the crack behind them, these four rock climbers would not have survived another night exposed to the wrath of the April storm. *Thank God,* they must have been thinking, *our hero has arrived.* A climber reached out, grabbed the rope, and pulled Mary in. When she stepped on the ledge, the climbers got their first good look at the "man" the NPS had sent to rescue them.

"Oh, no," one climber said. "It's a chick!"

"I prefer to see her as an angel," another climber corrected him.

The climber who made the chick comment must have been a fan of Norman Mailer, a writer who famously said a man should approach a woman in the same way he would approach a mountain. On the front of this climber's helmet was a cartoonish work of art—a pair of shapely female legs spread wide. The space between the woman's legs was a mountain. The summit of this mountain, at the peak of the inverted V made by the woman's legs, was the "pinnacle" of female anatomy—a split-tail.

While rescuers lowered McDevitt down a second rope, Mary explained how the rescue was going to go down. All six of them, the four climbers and the two rescuers, would ascend the ropes using hand-held metal devices. They would go two at a time, one on each rope, until they reached the top of El Cap, where a helicopter was waiting to fly them all down to the valley. As soon as McDevitt joined them on the ledge, the first two climbers would ascend the ropes. The two rescuers would go last. The window of good weather could close on them any time. It was dicey out there. "So be careful and keep moving."

The man wearing the sophomoric helmet had opinions— maybe they should do this, and maybe they should do that.

"They wouldn't send her down here if she didn't know what she was doing," another climber said, convincing the first to shut up.

From El Capitan Meadow, Yosemite's chief ranger watched the rescue operation through a telescope. Tourists joined in on the excitement. Through binoculars and telephoto lenses, they squinted at the tiny figures climbing the ropes to the top of El Cap.

On top, Lober cursed a coil of rope for having the audacity to get in his way. This time Sheriff Lobo was mad at himself. He had made a tactical error. To reserve the energy of his exhausted rescue team, he had chosen to have the stranded climbers put out some effort in their own rescue. Now, in hindsight, it was clear that his team should have hauled the four climbers up the cliff face with a modified sailing winch rather than have them "jug up" themselves. Doing it this way was taking much too long. The temperature was just above freezing. Melted snow was turning into ice. A wall of thick, dark clouds were closing in. *Mother of God,* Lober fretted: *Could they be moving any slower?*

As soon as the fourth climber topped out, Lober had the four men and most of the rescuers flown off the mountain. He kept a skeleton crew behind while Mary and Dan McDevitt started up the ropes. The rescuers were now racing against the approaching storm.

Mary sweated off five pounds of water weight inside the rubber rain suit, but her gloved hands and exposed face were freezing. She pushed her ascenders up the rope, but the metal teeth of the devices weren't gripping the rope as well as they should. They kept slipping because her rope was sheathed with ice. It was two feet up, one foot down. Ascending the icy ropes was a frustrating if not terrifying experience. Imagine you are climbing a six-hundred-foot ladder. Imagine this ladder is on top of a skyscraper twice as tall as the Empire State Building and is covered with ice. Sometimes your hands and feet fail to grip the rungs of the ladder and you slide a few feet down before you stop. The higher up the ladder you go, the more frozen it becomes, the more exhausted you feel, and the more distance you have to fall.

Rescuers assigned to be "edge attendants" were clipped to ropes so they could lean out over the cliff. When the exhausted rope climbers finally neared the top, the edge attendants grabbed McDevitt and Mary by their clothes and pulled them over the lip. The rope climbers were fully spent, slightly dazed, and wobbly, like runners at the end of a marathon. But their exertions weren't over yet. To reach the landing zone, they had to sprint a hundred yards up a rocky, snow-covered slab. The thick, dark clouds descended upon El Cap. The storm was shutting the weather window and threatening to ground the helicopter.

"Get up here or I'm leaving you," the pilot announced over the helicopter's external speakers.

"Leave the fucking gear," Lober ordered.

"Thank you," Mary said to ranger Mike Archer when he stepped behind her, put his hands on her backpack, and pushed her up the slope.

Inside the helicopter, someone offered Mary a dry climbing helmet to wear. On the flight down, the rescuers were all smiles.

They slapped Mary on the back, congratulating her on her extraordinary achievement. But the men were also looking at her funny and some of them were chuckling. When the helicopter landed in Ahwahnee Meadow, Mary removed her helmet and inspected the front. She had been wearing the helmet with the pornographic cartoon.

Down in the meadow, the chief ranger was proud of his rangers.

The supervisor standing next to him said, "Did you see the one in the yellow rain suit?"

"How could I miss him?"

"That was Mary, one of your clerk-typists."

"Well . . . I guess we better make that girl a ranger."

* * *

Despite the chief ranger's declaration, Mary was not hired into the next permanent full-time ranger position that opened up at Yosemite. In June 1995 she married another ranger working in another park. Mary Litell Hinson quit her clerk-typist job and became a housewife. Before long, domestic duties had her missing ranger work so much that she "couldn't stand it." Then a female supervisor called her with a tempting offer. Would she consider a permanent full-time-with-benefits job in Arizona, at a park so big and so bad it rivaled even the likes of Yosemite?

Leaving her clerk-typist job to live in the same time zone as her husband had been easy. Leaving her husband for a career as a park ranger was not. Though his words were supportive, Mary's husband was glum the day he drove his bride to the airport. They hadn't even celebrated their first anniversary, for Christ's sake. But it was obvious to Mary. If a girl wanted to be a permanent full-time-with-benefits park ranger, she had to be willing to make some sacrifices.

12

GATEWAY TO THE UNDERWORLD

My intentions were good. We started early. We rode his dirt bike through a maze of dirt roads leading to the trailhead. We packed light and traveled fast down the short but perilous route to the springs. By the time we reached the turquoise waters, I expected us to be tired but not overly so, hot but not overheated, and ready for a swim. Refreshed, relaxed, and rinsed of our sweat, we would then lounge in the shade of a tamarisk. Here I would offer my companion the fringe benefits of warm sand and isolation. Then we would take a nap. But things did not go according to plan. Instead of seducing my boyfriend, I nearly killed him.

They warned me not to come. Not to this particular spot deep within the twisty bowels of the Grand Canyon. Not to this enchanted spring near the geologic abomination whites aren't supposed to see. Not to the place the Hopi call Sipapu.

In photographs it looks benign—a vaguely volcanic mound of mud with a cervix-like hole on top—but the Hopi tribe believe this unimpressive cone of travertine possesses a great power. They believe it is the portal from which their people emerged into this world of light and into which the spirits of the dead return to darkness. The Sipapu is both the Place of Emergence and the Gateway to the Underworld. And such a place is too sacred for human eyes.

Ask any Grand Canyon ranger. He won't dare deny it. People hiking within the vicinity of the Sipapu can choose from a long list of torments: nightmares, ghostly visions, violent episodes of vomiting, madness, lightning strikes, bone-breaking falls, flash floods, and death. As the legend goes, women and whites especially should avoid visiting the area.

Not being the type who spooks easily, I invited my boyfriend to join me on an eighteen-miles-in-one-day trek to see the Gateway to the Underworld. The day I chose for this journey was during an Arizona heat wave. When my boyfriend voiced his concerns, I blew them off. "Trust me," I said. "It'll be fun."

I knew better. I had been a search and rescue ranger at the Grand Canyon for two summers now. I had seen the punishments inflicted upon those who undertook extreme and remote treks on days the mercury hits 112 degrees. I knew how the Big Ditch has her way with the unwary.

My first mistake was not allowing my boyfriend time to acclimate to the desert heat. I met Kent Delbon the year we worked together in Yosemite Valley. After our sweaty trek to help ranger Noel McJunkin at the top of Nevada Falls, I fell for the tall ranger with the cool head and calming voice. In addition to his incorruptible character, Kent's blond hair, well-defined jawline, and steady blue eyes reminded me of Clint Eastwood. Indeed, the NPS still uses his image to represent law enforcement skills on its *Ranger Competencies* brochure. But after we camped in Death Valley, climbed Long's Peak, and backpacked the Sierra, his true nature was revealed. At work the ranger played Dirty Harry. At home he was more Tom Hanks.

From the very beginning I warned him. I am not the marrying kind. But Kent was also the type who didn't spook easily. After a three-year career-induced separation, he had recently left a full-time job with benefits in California to be a ranger again, with me, in Arizona.

But now a nasty case of heat exhaustion had afflicted him miles short of our destination. The last slimy backwash from our canteens had disappeared two hours ago and a partially digested version of Kent's breakfast burrito cooked on a rock two miles back. His cheeks were as ruddy as the sandstone enclosing us like mile-high prison walls. By the time we reached the spring, he was on all fours, panting after gagging up some bile.

I needed to get him cooled down and hydrated immediately. He eased his weakened body into the creek. We swam across the deepest pool to where the spring gushed from the stone. We put our mouths to the source and drank our fill of the chalky water. I directed Kent to the tamarisk and covered him with a wet T-shirt for evaporative cooling. As soon as he could keep food down, I fed him our saltiest snacks. We waited patiently for the sun to drop behind the sandstone. Once Kent was feeling better and the shade had cooled the canyon's oven, we slowly climbed our way up and out of the mess I had put us in.

After a grueling scramble to the trailhead, we had a long and bumpy dirt bike ride in the dark to look forward to. I clung to Kent's waist and rested my cheek on his sweaty back as he followed the headlight up the rocky road. The clock struck midnight before we were safe at home, sleeping inside my two-bedroom cabin a quarter mile from the South Rim.

In the morning I vowed to return. I wanted to see the Sipapu— to hell with the consequences. I wanted to hike to the so-called Gateway to the Underworld, carry a flashlight up to the very top, stick my head into the hole, peer deep into the dark heart of the damned thing, and take a picture. Next time, I decided, I would go alone.

13

SCORPION KARMA

For Grand Canyon volunteer Sjors Horstman, health insurance is a jar of flies he keeps on the windowsill. Sjors (pronounced *shores*) is half Dutch and half Chinese, and people often say he looks like Charles Manson. He hates it, but his wild mane of black hair and the mischievous glint in his dark eyes make the comparison unavoidable. His resemblance to a mass murderer, though, does little damage to the volunteer's charisma. Most people fall in love with Sjors within minutes of meeting him. Retired couples adopt him. Millionaires from Los Angeles hire him to house-sit their mansions. Lawyers from Manhattan mail him presents every Christmas. The flies—they buy him protection.

The NPS calls Sjors a VIP, which stands for Volunteer-in-Parks. He lives inside the Phantom Ranch Ranger Station. Seven hard miles from the nearest road and less than a half mile from the Colorado River, Phantom Ranch is a compound of rustic cabins, mule corrals, and campgrounds scattered alongside Bright Angel Creek and the North Kaibab Trail. Since 1922 the concession operation has provided respite for the more than forty-eight thousand hikers trekking through Phantom Ranch each year. At the cantina you can buy lemonade, cold beer, and T-shirts vacuum-packed to the size of a deck of cards.

The NPS makes good use of its volunteer. In return for his board inside the ranger station and a modest stipend, Sjors does whatever preoccupied park rangers need him to do. He irrigates the cottonwood trees in the campground. He answers hikers' questions. He directs rescue helicopters into tight locations. He holds up IV bags and empties vomit basins. He takes rectal temperatures of heat stroke victims. Sometimes he fishes bodies out of the Colorado River.

Years ago Sjors was a television repairman in Los Angeles. He has traveled all over the world—but the Grand Canyon did something to him. He first signed up as a volunteer in 1986 and since 1988 has spent a majority of his days and nights at Phantom Ranch.

According to Sjors's best estimate, a bark scorpion stings one out of every thousand hikers passing by Phantom Ranch. Bark scorpions (*Centruroides exilicauda*) are tiny creatures. In daylight they are translucent beige. At night, when hunted with ultraviolet light, they glow in the dark. They are the most poisonous scorpions in the United States, with venom that is more toxic per ounce than that of a rattlesnake. Prior to the development of antivenin, these scorpions killed an average of three people a year in Arizona. Today only the extremely old, the extremely young, or the extremely allergic have cause to fear death by bark scorpion. A scorpion sting probably won't kill you: It'll just hurt like a son of a bitch.

Most park rangers at Phantom Ranch have been "scorped" at least once. Many of them take extraordinary measures to avoid being stung a second time. Sjors knew a ranger who slept with all the lights on (scorpions are nocturnal), and he's aware of several who went so far as to place all their bedposts in pickle jars. The theory being that the slippery glass discourages the scorpions from crawling into bed with you. Unfortunately, scorps have been known to drop down on sleeping rangers from the ceiling. Every Phantom Ranch ranger inspects the walls and checks the sheets before getting into bed and in the morning shakes out his or her shorts before dressing. A few rangers who forget the latter have suffered stings in the most appalling places.

Sjors knew a ranger who hated scorpions so much that he stomped them flat with his hiking boots every time he got the chance. But the more scorpions the ranger killed, the more he got stung. "Man," Sjors told the ranger, "you keep killing the scorps, and it's giving you bad karma." So the ranger stopped stomping, and the scorpions stopped stinging. From then on the ranger was a believer. If he found a scorpion inside the ranger station, instead of stomping it he used one of the chief ranger's incomprehensible memos to scoop it out the door.

Sjors Horstman has never intentionally killed a scorpion, and for the better part of seven years, he lived in the Grand Canyon without being stung. Then he made the mistake of boasting about his good karma to a nosy writer researching a story for *National Geographic*. Two nights later, a scorpion dropped off the ceiling while Sjors slept, landed on his chest, and stung him five times. Sjors woke up feeling as though he were being tortured with fire, electricity, and needles all at once. Shirtless, he ran to the bathroom and looked in the mirror. A scorpion sat on his shoulder, taunting him with its pincers! Sjors slapped the bugger off. The little terror hit the floor and scurried under the wall behind the toilet.

One day Sjors spotted a female scorpion carrying a litter of baby scorpions on her back. It was the kind of natural oddity that rangers, especially lady rangers, go gaga over. Sjors intended to catch the mama scorpion, show it off to the lady ranger, and then let it go. No harm, no foul. But in the process of scooping the mama scorpion into a jar, he jostled several babies off their mother's back. With a sweaty brow and a surgeon's concentration, Sjors used a pencil to push the babies back on to the mother's back. Alas, despite his efforts, five of the babies died.

A few days later, while lying in bed and having a midnight phone conversation with a girl, Sjors shrieked. A scorpion was stinging him! He examined his arm and found two red dots. Over the next twenty-four hours, the volunteer suffered. His arm burned. His stomach cramped. His eyes darted rapidly back and forth. His entire body felt as though he were being stabbed with pins and needles. Worst of all was the awareness that he had been stung only twice. Sjors had accidentally killed five baby scorpions. He still had three karmic doses waiting for him.

This is why if Sjors finds a scorpion lurking in the heel of his shoe, he delicately coaxes it onto a piece of paper and carries it outside, bringing along his jar of flies and giving the scorpion a treat before he lets it go.

* * *

Scorpions are well adapted to life in the desert. Their slow metabolism and wax-covered exoskeleton help them retain moisture, allowing them to withstand triple-digit temperatures. However, if you force a scorpion to stay in the sun for over an hour when it is 113 degrees, the scorpion will die. Scorpions survive the desert because they retreat to the shade during the hottest parts of the day. This makes you wonder how we can be so sure we are the most intelligent species on the planet. The scorpion—a primitive invertebrate with a microscopic excuse for a brain—has the good sense to stay out of the sun on hot days while thousands of *Homo sapiens* go hiking in a desert canyon during a July heat wave because we think it might be fun.

Hiking out of the Grand Canyon is not fun. Hiking out of the Grand Canyon is an ordeal. At Phantom Ranch the Colorado River is a vertical mile below the canyon rims. The fourteen-mile trail from the river to the North Rim gains so much elevation that it passes through five of the seven life zones found in North America. Ecologically speaking, the experience is like walking from Mexico to Canada in a day. The South Rim trails are even steeper. Hiking from Phantom Ranch up to the South Rim is comparable to climbing the stairs to the top of the Sears Tower three times. Landmarks along the way indicate the mood the climb puts one in—Devil's Corkscrew, Asinine Hill, Heartbreak Ridge, Skeleton Point. At best, a river-to-rim hike is like having your feet glued to a Stairmaster in Hades for five hours, with the machine set to torment level number nine. At worst, the endeavor is deadly.

Occasionally hikers succumb to the exertion or the heat, collapse on the trail, and die. When this occurs during the peak hiking seasons, rangers must direct hiker traffic around the body. Word travels. I have seen days when this morbid news infects backpackers with a unique hysteria. At their campsites they wring their hands with worry, dreading their trek out of the canyon as if it were a walk up the steps to the gallows. In the evening, when the park ranger walks through the campground to check permits, these hikers grab at her like lost souls seeking a shortcut out of purgatory.

"Ranger, please! I'll sacrifice my firstborn for a helicopter ride to the top!"

"I'm sorry," the ranger says. "Helicopter flights are dangerous and expensive. We use them only to rescue people with life-threatening medical conditions."

"How about a mule?"

"Same deal. We save the few mules we have for the truly ill and injured."

"My God, ranger! Have you no compassion? We'll never make it out of here alive!"

"Yes you will, if you follow my advice: Start before dawn and rest during the hottest part of the day. Drink plenty of water, and eat plenty of salty foods. Wet yourself down when it becomes hot. It's a dry heat. Evaporation will cool you. If you feel bad, stop walking. Get in the shade. Wait for sunset. It's actually prettier in the canyon then, and there's no rule against hiking at night. Here's a flashlight you can borrow. Here's some electrolyte powder. Here's some extra food. If you follow my advice, you can hike safely out of this canyon. Remember, just go slow."

Then the ranger has to move on. There are other campsites to visit, as many as 150 more terrified campers to counsel. Once abandoned by the ranger, these frightened hikers sit at their picnic tables in a state of anxiety. Staring up at the canyon walls, they rock back and forth in rhythm with their feeble mantra: "We'll just go slow. We'll just go slow. We'll just go slow."

The next day, by mile five of the trek, some hikers are offering substantial bribes to park rangers in return for a helicopter ride out of the canyon. Others issue threats: "I'm calling my congressman first and my lawyer second if you don't fly me out of this canyon!" Or they throw accusations: "You should have gates up to keep people like us from coming down here!" A few resort to trickery: "Ranger, you have to get me out of here," the clever ones say while clutching their chests. "I feel the big one coming." And there are the pessimists who plop down on the trail and give up. "Ranger, I'll never make it," they moan. "So why prolong the misery? I'll just die right here. Please tell my wife I love her."

Park rangers call a hiker like this a "Code W." A Code W is a wimp. There is nothing medically wrong with a Code W. He is only tired and sore. His spirit, not his body, is broken. A Code W falls for the Grand Canyon's insidious trap and now wants the federal government to rescue him out of it—on his terms and within his time frame. A Code W does not consider the many real emergencies and depressing tragedies the ranger has dealt with that day.

The park ranger secretly loathes the Code W. The ranger has seen eighty-year-olds, cancer survivors, and one-legged women hike out of the canyon without so much as a whimper. The Code W is the reason the ranger has not slept in twenty-four hours. He is the stabbing pain between the ranger's shoulder blades. He is the fifteenth hot mile the ranger has hiked in one day. He is the missed lunch, the romantic dinner date stood up, and the paperwork piling up. He is the lecture the district ranger has to give and the apologetic letter the superintendent has to sign because a federal employee spoke to a taxpaying Code W in a manner unbecoming of a U.S. park ranger.

But the ranger should remember: Judge not the Code W lest ye also be judged. The Grand Canyon entraps even the hardiest of men. In fact the first Europeans to see the Big Canyon of the Colorado, an intrepid group of Spanish explorers, were also the first (documented) suckers to fall for the ruse.

* * *

Of America's many iconic landscapes, the Grand Canyon shocks and surprises us the most. For example, tributaries gradually lead us to the Mississippi River. The Appalachian mists lift gracefully, unveiling the Smoky Mountains' subtle charms. The smell and sound of the Pacific and Atlantic Oceans warn you of their existence. The Rockies, the Sierra Nevada, and Mount McKinley reveal their immensities miles before you reach them. But the Grand Canyon creeps up on you. The Grand Canyon remains hidden and coy. The Grand Canyon waits. It waits until you step out of the trees. It waits until you walk up to the edge. It waits until you lean out over the cliff for a better view—before the entire world drops out from under you and vanishes into a hole a mile deep, three hundred miles long, and ten miles wide.

This is the first of many ways the Grand Canyon messes with your mind.

In 1540 a group of Spanish explorers set out to find the great river mentioned by the Hopi Indians. After a twenty-day march, García López de Cárdenas and his men peered over the rim. The canyon's immensity skewed the Spaniard's perspective. Cárdenas estimated the rocky spires to be man-size and the Colorado River to be six feet wide. Native American guides warned the Spaniards. The river below is much wider than it appears, they told Cárdenas. Distances are deceiving. It takes several days for a man to reach the water.

These Native Americans are such pansies, Cárdenas may have thought. The river looked close enough to touch. The route to it was downhill all the way. How hard could it be? Cárdenas sent three of his most agile young men over the edge of the cliffs to the river. Tired and thirsty, the men returned much later than expected. They told Cárdenas they had only made it a third of the way down. "What appeared to be easy from above was not so, but instead very hard and difficult," the Spaniards later wrote. The "man-size" rocks seen from the rim were taller than the great tower of Seville. The river Cárdenas estimated to be six feet wide was as immense as the Thames (two hundred feet across).

In 1540 the Hopi gently warned the Spanish explorers. Today the NPS practically assaults hikers with advice. For example, at the top of every major trailhead leading into the Grand Canyon, you may encounter a large and ominous sign, illustrated with a skull and crossbones:

DANGER
EXTREME HEAT CONDITIONS EXIST IN THE CANYON.
HIKING MAY LEAD TO LIFE-THREATENING INJURY OR DEATH!
HIKE AT YOUR OWN RISK.

Every year, hundreds of people start their hikes by having their pictures taken with these signs. Watching a hiker do this is like witnessing someone stomp a scorpion, and the ranger winces every time. Mocking that sign is a fool's amusement. Park rangers find portraits of hikers grinning in front of it when they develop rolls of film removed from the bodies of people who died on the trail.

* * *

VIP Sjors has seen many rangers come and go during his tenure at Phantom Ranch. The volunteer has been there so long, it often seems like he ought to be the one in charge. Indeed, not too long ago the volunteer told a ranger who had transferred there, "You aren't going to be here long enough for me to train you."

Few rangers remain in the Inner Canyon more than five years. The scorpions will unnerve them. The heat or the isolation or the Code Ws will eventually get to them. Or the trails will destroy their knees. But Phantom Ranch will always be home to Sjors Horstman. The volunteer more than survives this harsh and unforgiving environment. He adores it—scorpions and all.

14

PREDATOR-PREY RELATIONSHIPS

The elderly man collapsed as soon as he stepped down onto the tarmac at the Grand Canyon Airport. Pumping on his chest the whole way, park rangers rushed him into the back of an ambulance and then to the clinic. The guy didn't make it. In the emergency room, ranger Chris Fors experienced what he called "a tough moment" when he helped the man's wife remove the wedding ring from her husband's finger. The couple had come all the way from Germany to see the Grand Canyon. Now she was alone in a foreign country with a dead man.

The next morning, Chris drove down to the coroner's office in Flagstaff to observe the autopsy. Watching the procedure was 75 percent fascinating and 25 percent disgusting. *Crack.* The county forensic pathologist used brush cutters to break the ribs. He explained that Arizona's Coconino County couldn't afford to buy the medical version of a tool that did the same thing. *Squish.* He reached into the man's chest and pulled out a heart the size of a large grapefruit. *Clink.* He bounced a dental pick off a large chunk of plaque inside the man's heart.

"Massive myocardial infarction," the pathologist announced. This guy was functioning on borrowed time anyhow. Once he inhaled the thin air here at seven thousand feet, he was a goner. Next the county pathologist and his assistant began to pull out more internal organs. This was where the 25 percent disgusting part came in. Chris jotted down the information he needed for his report, then got the heck out of there.

* * *

The Grand Canyon was a vortex for weird. Hikers tried to hang themselves with shoelaces tied to rafters in backcountry rest houses. Bighorn sheep walked into the Thunderbird Lodge, galloped upstairs, and jumped through plate-glass windows. Tourists got into blood-splattering fights over females and parking spaces. Park visitors routinely asked if the canyon was "man-made." Retired couples kidnapped doe-eyed cocker spaniels without remorse. Elk kept Christmas lights entangled in their antlers until after Valentine's Day. And ranger Chris Fors had thought the perverts and plover haters at Cape Cod were wacko.

In 1990 Chris drove cross-country from Massachusetts to the Grand Canyon. When he arrived, a park housing officer gave him a key to his new government housing—a run-down trailer in a row of run-down trailers in the ranger ghetto on Hopi Street. On the first night in his new home, a racket coming from the trailer next door awakened Chris. The trailers were set close to one another. When Chris looked out his bedroom window, he could easily see into his neighbor's home, where a naked man was running back and forth across the length of the living room, screaming hysterically and waving a broom above his head.

Chris threw up the window. "Hey, what's going on ovah they-ah?" he yelled, revealing his New England roots.

"Bats!" the man shouted. "There are fucking bats in my fucking trailer!"

Thus Chris met his new neighbor and coworker, paramedic ranger Keith Lober. (Lober would transfer to Yosemite in the summer of 1993.)

A ranger assigned to night shifts rarely sees the Grand Canyon while on duty, but he does become quite familiar with the other park environs—the smoky bars; the booking jail; the back of the ambulance; and the employee housing areas, especially the male dorm, Victor Hall. Built in 1936 and designed by architect Mary Jane Colter, Victor Hall's brown wood siding, green window trim, and sandstone boulder foundation exemplified "National Park Rustic." But once Chris stepped inside the two-story dorm, the ranger saw sights he never expected to see in a national park.

Many times he and the other park rangers rushed up the steps of the dormitory to reports of women screaming, vandals breaking out windows, drunks breaking the railings off the balcony, and people getting the shit beat out of them.

One night Chris chased a resident through the hallways who was wielding a knife and threatening to slit throats. Another evening Chris and his partner each grabbed an arm of a 250-pound Native American refusing to leave a dorm room. The intoxicated man swung the two rangers around as if they were rag dolls caught on the blades of a windmill until he became dizzy, lost his balance, and fell forward, putting his head into the drywall. Only then were the rangers able to cuff the man.

Such occurrences were common in all the employee dorms, but Victor Hall seemed to be the worst. Rangers and many locals had a secret nickname for the place. Sometimes slips of the tongue were made over the radio. "Dispatch, I'm on scene at Victim Hall. . . . Oops! Scratch that. I mean Victor Hall."

Late one night a female concession employee sat on the sandstone steps of Victor Hall. She had called a taxi to take her to work. Around midnight a man grabbed her by the arm, pulled her into the bushes, and began ripping off her clothes. The woman screamed. She couldn't believe it. She was being raped by a stranger. Here? In the park?

The taxi driver arrived in time to see a man drag a young woman into the bushes. (A few years later, the Park Service cut down these same bushes because too many intoxicated employees were sleeping in them.) The taxi driver was shocked. A woman was being raped. Here? In the park?

Chris was on a routine patrol when he drove his cruiser into the parking lot of Victor Hall and saw the taxi driver talking into his radio with a look of extreme anxiety on his face. Something bad was happening. Chris got out of his car to investigate. Behind the bushes, a man was attempting to rape a woman. Here? In the park?

Not on his watch.

"Hey, you!" Chris yelled in his deepest voice. "Come out of there." The rapist dropped the girl and ran into Victor Hall. The ranger chased the rapist up the stairs. The rapist ducked into a dorm room and slammed the door. Chris covered the door with his gun. More rangers arrived, and they forced open the door. Inside they found the rapist lying on the bed. He was completely naked—masturbating.

At first Chris liked taking creeps to jail. In time the novelty wore off. As soon as the rangers arrested one bad apple, the park concessionaire hired two more to take his place. Concessionaire wages were puny. In order to fill all their positions, supervisors were forced to hire people with a variety of unsavory pasts. The concessionaire packed these people into the same dorms with the other employees—simple-minded and easygoing working people, good-hearted dopers, down-on-their-luck displaced wanderers, retired couples, and naive college students on summer break. Chris began to see how, by cramming all these people under one roof, the park concessionaire had created a human environment similar to the one enjoyed by the park wildlife: a place for predator and prey to interact.

Rapists weren't the only big bad wolves hiding behind the park's bushes. There were husbands looking for cheap alternatives to divorce. There were surly drunks who stabbed and shot people.

There was a charming but malevolent man who talked several parents into allowing him to bring three young boys on a camping trip. There was a concession worker who killed his girlfriend and stuffed her body under the bed in his dorm room. And there was a homicidal fugitive who got the bright idea to visit the Grand Canyon, hijack a Winnebago, kidnap a few tourists for hostages, obtain a million dollars in ransom in exchange for their release, and then escape to Mexico.

* * *

Chris had a sense of humor like a rattlesnake strike, quick and biting. When supervisors rationalized foolish policies with platitudes, when loyalty mongers attempted flattery, when good friends looked him in the eye and said something sentimental, the ranger threw out witty comebacks like a fighter throws out a forearm to block a strike to the face.

When he called vegetarian patties "lesbian burgers," he said it with a wink of irony. He was a good cook. His homemade pizzas, grilled salmon with garlic, and nachos seasoned with his own improvised spices were often hits at the backyard potlucks. And he had a soft spot for cats. Once he visited the park kennel with the intention of bringing one cat home, but the cutest kitten had a sister, so he ended up with two. Every winter, Chris painted his own Christmas cards—ink and watercolor portraits of snowy New England farms and churches. But this artistic cat lover also had a chesty baritone and an intense personality. Chris filled up more space in a room than was taken by his stocky build. Of all the rangers who worked at the Grand Canyon during the beleaguered nineties, he was the last one you would expect people to beat on.

But beat on him they did. Intoxicated people kicked him, knocked him upside the head, socked him in the ribs, and threatened to slit his throat. During the years he worked as a Grand Canyon park ranger, Chris was scratched up, kicked down, spit on, wrestled down a flight of stairs, and punched in the nose. But these assaults lost their import the moment a fugitive from justice pointed a gun in Chris's direction and pulled the trigger.

* * *

Have mercy on Grand Canyon rangers. Don't ever ask them, "Where's the best place to see the sunset?" One, they are asked this a hundred times a week. Two, it drives a ranger crazy. It's like asking the mother of quintuplets to choose her favorite. There is no best place to see the sunset. The canyon has two rims. Each rim is 277 miles long. For heaven's sakes, just pick a spot and watch it happen. But if you insist on knowing the best place to watch the sunset, the ranger will provide an answer to your question. Keeping the irritation behind his teeth, he'll say, "Hopi Point," before giving you directions to a large overlook with lots of safety railings and a convenient bus stop where a shuttle can easily drop off and load up hundreds of sightseers.

Not long after they move to the Grand Canyon, park employees learn to avoid the park roads and restaurants immediately after the sun goes down. Every evening immediately after sunset, the lines form outside the Arizona Steak House and thousands of tourists get in their cars and leave the park all at once, causing the roads to bottleneck with traffic.

The post-sunset rush hour was peaking the night Danny Ray Horning, an escapee from an Arizona prison, stuck a .44 Magnum Ruger Blackhawk out the window of his getaway car and shot a bullet over the bow of the patrol sedan occupied by Chris and his partner, ranger John Piastick, who was driving. The bullet came very close to hitting the rangers. As the bullet whizzed by, the noise made Chris's ears ring.

"Holy shit!" Chris said. "That son of a bitch just shot at us!"

Piastick spun the 1987 Crown Vic 180 degrees and put the pedal to the floor, hoping to catch up with ranger Donny Miller.

Miller was already in pursuit. Minutes earlier, a terrified boy had waved down the ranger in the Babbitt's General Store parking lot and begged him to stop the man trying to kidnap his family. When Miller approached Horning, the fugitive pointed the Ruger at the ranger, forcing him to take cover while Horning returned to the car with the two hostages and drove away.

When the pursuit reached the traffic gate blocking West Rim Drive, Horning tried to crash through it but failed, shattering the glass in the rear window. In the backseat sat the two hostages Horning had kidnapped at gunpoint in Flagstaff the day before. Over the top of the hostages' heads, Horning shot at Ranger Miller through the back window. Miller dived for the shotgun in his ranger car. When the ranger came back up with a shotgun in hand, Horning disappeared into the woods, leaving his two hostages behind.

Rangers soon learned Horning was wanted for questioning related to the murder and dismemberment of a California catfish farmer. The fugitive had eluded Arizona authorities for more than a month before the thirty-five-year-old convicted bank robber and child molester decided to visit the Grand Canyon, where he intended to kidnap six hostages and hijack an RV. With tourists as hostages, Horning would ask for $1 million in ransom and the release of his brother, who was in prison. Then the RV would transport them all to Mexico. If a cop pulled him over and recognized him, Horning was going to "blow him away."

Horning arrived at the Grand Canyon on June 25, 1992. Over the next two weeks, the NPS, along with the state authorities and the FBI, initiated the largest manhunt in Arizona history. SWAT teams, bloodhounds, and shotgun-rangers swarmed the park's trails, hotels, and overlooks. Roadblocks jammed up all roads leading in to and out of the park. Tourists were waiting five hours before seeing the canyon. Three days after Horning shot at the rangers, he came out of the woods and attempted another kidnapping at Grandview Point. But this couple refused to cooperate. So

Horning stole their station wagon. Park rangers found it the next day, crashed into a tree.

"When we entered the park," the station wagon's owners later complained, "nobody told us to watch out for a fugitive." The incident commander assigned Chris, among others, to conduct surveillance near where the attempted kidnapping had taken place. Dressed in camouflage, the ranger hiked into the woods and hid in the brush near Grandview Point. All night he sat on the pine needles with his M-16 in his lap. Chris had slept little since Horning had shot at him three days ago. By 4:00 a.m., lifting his eyelids felt like bench-pressing 250, and his chin kept dropping to his chest. Later an investigator informed Chris that Horning had come close enough that night to hear the ranger speak into his radio.

The attempted kidnapping at Grandview elevated the blood pressure of the already tense ranger serving as the incident commander. Within four days Horning had stolen and crashed two cars, forced his two hostages from Flagstaff to stay overnight with him in the El Tovar Hotel, attempted to kidnap at least four people, and shot at three park rangers. The potential danger to park visitors was one of many reasons the incident commander and an FBI agent drafted a memo asking the superintendent to temporarily close the park. If they evacuated the entire park, these two lawmen figured, innocent civilians would be out of Horning's reach and authorities could scour the entire South Rim with a dragnet of cops and hounds until they flushed out the fugitive. It seemed like a sensible plan—if it weren't so bad for business.

Not unlike what happened when Chief Brody urged the mayor of Amity to close public beaches in the movie *Jaws*, upper management howled at their suggestion. It's the peak of tourist season for Christ's sake! Fourth of July is next week! The taxpayers will tar and feather us in front of Congress. The park concession will submit a "million dollar a day loss of business claim." Are you daft? Have you gone completely insane? The superintendent can't close the park. Shark you say? Looks like a dolphin fin to me.

Ranger "Brody" was removed from his position as incident commander, the Grand Canyon remained open, and Danny Ray Horning waited for more swimmers to enter the water.

Like Victor Hall, the Desert View Watchtower is the brainchild of architect Mary Colter. Perched on the rim like a stone castle and inspired by Anasazi pueblos, Colter designed the Desert View Watchtower to be exactly what it is: a cool-looking gift shop. In 1932 the first tourists walked through the shelves of knickknacks in order to climb the stairs of the watchtower to see the view. Sixty years later—on July 4, 1992—two female medical students from England drove out East Rim Drive to do the same. The view from the top was splendid. After snapping a few photos, the British women descended the spiral stairway and headed for the parking lot. On their way back to their car, something bad happened. A wild man was pointing a gun at them. He was hijacking their Nissan Sentra. He was taking them hostage. At high noon on the Fourth of July.

Here? In the park?

Welcome to America, ladies. Happy Independence Day!

Horning forced the two women to drive him through two roadblocks. A ranger waved them through the first. At the second, a highway patrolman asked Horning to step out of the car. The petrified hostages watched the highway patrolman compare an emaciated Horning with hair dyed blond to the wanted photo of a well-fed brunette Horning and then let the fugitive go. Outside the park, Horning left the two women tied to a tree. The next day, an Arizona woman reported seeing a raggedy man drinking from her garden hose. A Border Patrol officer found the fugitive sleeping under the deck of someone's house. (In 1994 Horning was convicted of the Stockton homicide and dismemberment. He remains on death row inside a California prison.)

Before Horning was captured, a reporter from a Phoenix station interviewed Chris. The ranger described the fugitive as "a disgusting child molester. A racist. A classic sociopath who murders

111

people, kidnaps tourists, and shoots at park rangers." These quotes didn't make it on the evening news. Instead local papers published "Go Danny Go" letters to the editor, and a reporter stalking the lobby of a park hotel interviewed an attractive young woman wearing a Harvard sweatshirt. "[Horning's] not so bad," the woman said on camera. "He hasn't murdered anybody yet. He's becoming a folk hero."

To Chris it was a slap in the face. Horning had been convicted of molesting a five-year-old girl. He had sawed off the head and limbs of a husband and father. He had shot at Chris and his friends. And here was this cute coed, someone a ranger might like to date, calling the bad guy a hero. What a bitter pill to swallow. Of course the ranger took it personally. He was tolerating crappy housing and accepting shitty pay in exchange for risking his ass to protect the public—only to have them cheer on the creep who had tried to kill him. Un-friggin' believable.

15

CRUEL WORLD

Chris Fors was off duty, enjoying a leisurely drive along the West Rim while listening to Gordon Lightfoot's "The Wreck of the Edmund Fitzgerald." As he drove by the overlook known as the Abyss, he noticed a blue Honda parked there. Chris continued to the road's end at Hermit's Rest. On his way back, he saw the same car parked at the same overlook. It was 10:30 at night. Perhaps the guy was lost, or out of gas. Chris slowed almost to a complete stop to offer his assistance if needed, but the Honda's driver glared at Chris as he passed, giving him the nastiest look.

It was October 1990, near the end of Chris's first summer at the Grand Canyon, but the young ranger already had superb instincts. He would have called this in to dispatch but was afraid he'd sound paranoid or silly when he reported, "Hey, there's a man parked at the Abyss who glared at me when I slowed down my personal car in the dark of night to stare at him."

Early the next morning, the Honda was still parked at the overlook when a park maintenance employee stopped to collect the trash. The maintenance employee found a piece of paper taped to the guardrail. On the paper note someone had drawn an arrow. The arrow pointed down, over the rim. Next to the note was a rope. One end of the rope was tied to the guardrail; at the other end was a rifle. The note asked authorities to return the rifle to a relative. Below the rim, rangers found the writer of the note.

Sometime the night before, the man had stood up on the railing, shot himself with the rifle, and then fallen. The man's leg was caught in the rope, so he fell only ten feet. The man had a handgun in his pocket and body armor in the car. When Chris heard this, he concluded it was probably for the best he didn't call in his observations the night before. The guy seemed like the type who wouldn't have minded taking a few rangers with him.

* * *

In 1993 you could walk into any video store and rent the film *Thelma and Louise.* In this movie two women take a road trip that launches them into a violent crime spree. In the end, Thelma and Louise find themselves caught between an army of macho cops and what Louise calls, with awe and admiration, the "Goddamn Grand Canyon." A sympathetic male detective tries to convince the women into turning themselves in, but Thelma and Louise choose to drive their green 1964 Thunderbird convertible into the abyss. Their suicide is a bittersweet metaphor—a refusal to accept a gloomy existence of compromise and confinement. Many didn't appreciate the movie's depressing end. Others liked it all too well.

* * *

In May 1993 Chris was giving his girlfriend, a blond he met at graduate school, a ranger-guided tour of the park when another ranger spotted something five hundred feet below the rim. Chris dropped his girlfriend off at a point along the rim where she could watch the rangers work. Ranger Keith Lober rappelled down a rope. Five hundred feet below the rim, he found a rental car. The car had landed on its top and it looked as though it had been compressed in a junkyard compacter. The car and the occupant were now two feet tall and had been that way for nearly the entire month of April. Removing the body from the crushed steel required the use of heavy machinery flown in by helicopter. The body was identified as a young male recently diagnosed as HIV positive.

In January 1993 a thirty-six-year-old woman watched *Thelma and Louise* multiple times before attempting to drive her Suburban off the rim at the Abyss. When a rock blocked her dramatic launch into the canyon, the woman walked to the rim and jumped. Then in November a tourist called 911. A man had driven a car off the rim near the South Kaibab trailhead parking lot. The tourist said the man nodded to him as he accelerated his 1967 Pontiac Tempest toward the rim and rocketed it into the canyon.

Some people drive to their death. Others prefer to go on foot. A few bring a long plastic tube and duct tape. They tape one end of the tube to their muffler and put the other end in the car via the driver's-side window and seal it tight. Then they park at some lonely overlook with the engine running. (To Chris this last method didn't make any sense. Why would you drive all the way to Arizona from Ohio to do something you could do in your own garage?)

* * *

Whether or not a rope, a gun, a helicopter, or a motor vehicle is involved, the Sierra Club would agree: Suicide is not an appropriate use of a national park. Yet, although the Grand Canyon is sixty miles from the nearest interstate, it remains a popular natural wonder for those planning to do themselves in. As ranger Patrick Suddath put it to one reporter in 2009, ". . . toward the end of someone's life, when they are feeling a total sense of despondency, they want to return to a place of natural beauty."

Once a week on average, Grand Canyon park rangers receive a BOLO (Be on the Lookout) for a person heading to the park with the intention of committing suicide. Although many suicidal people come prepared with a desperate and elaborate plan, a disturbing number of suicides may be the result of an immediate and impulsive act. According to a University of Houston study, 24 percent of suicide survivors contemplated the act for less than five minutes before doing something drastic. This statistic summons an unsettling question: How many fatal falls labeled accidents are spur-of-the-moment suicides? Can peering into the Grand Canyon enchant or depress you to the point you can't resist the urge to leap into its dizzying depths? In 1993 rangers responded to more fall fatalities than in any other year in the park's history. Three of these falls were unintentional suicides, like the man who jumped from one rocky pillar to another rocky pillar for the benefit of picture-taking tourists. "Watch me!" he shouted just before he missed his target and fell 360 feet.

Local and state governments have effectively deterred suicides by installing barricades, nets, or security cameras at dangerous sites. But the NPS cannot, nor should it, barricade or conduct twenty-four-hour surveillance along both rims of the 277-mile-long Grand Canyon. Thus, once a suicidal person enters the park, the last barrier between him and his sad goal often will be a park ranger.

Although successful suicides garner more media attention, observant and caring park rangers prevent scores of people from killing themselves every year. In January 2009 Grand Canyon rangers stopped three suicidal acts within one month. Occasionally rangers must respond to the suicidal inclinations of one of their own. In 1997 a Grand Canyon interpreter committed suicide by hanging himself on the North Rim. In 1999 park rangers prevented a peer from leaping off Yaki Point.

On March 25, 1994, a seventeen-year-old from Ohio walked to a pay phone near the Bright Angel trailhead and called a friend. He had hiked out of the Grand Canyon, the boy told his friend, and he now intended to kill himself. As soon as the boy hung up, the friend called the police. Minutes later two rangers found a car matching the description of the suicidal boy's silver Hyundai parked at the visitor center. When rangers addressed the boy, he said, "Leave me alone." Then he accelerated the Hyundai, nearly running down ranger John Piastick on his way out of the parking lot.

Three rangers pursued the silver Hyundai as it traveled south on Arizona Highway 64. In the lead car was Chris Fors. Once the chase headed out of the park entrance gate, a county deputy and two Arizona state troopers took the lead. Thirty miles later, the Hyundai ran out of gas. The boy pulled the car into the parking lot of a trading post that was really a gift shop. The trading post sold a plethora of souvenirs, including Native American jewelry (both real and fake) and cattle skulls (both real and fake). Chris pulled his ranger car in behind the silver Hyundai. Heavy-metal music blared from the Hyundai's speakers. A teenage boy with blond hair sat in the driver's seat. He held a .22-caliber pistol in his hand. Before long, a half dozen cops and rangers were standing behind the bumpers of their patrol cars. The cops pointed their guns at the Hyundai and yelled, "Get out of the car. Drop the gun or we'll shoot you."

"I'm not going to hurt you guys," the boy said. "I just want you to go away."

When a hostage negotiator from the state highway patrol arrived, he initiated negotiations, but Chris and Ranger Piastick had built a rapport with the boy, so the highway patrolmen coached the rangers. The boy stepped out of the car and paced back and forth, but he did not drop the gun. Acting as the primary negotiators, the rangers engaged the boy with talk about cars and music until the cops and the rangers began to feel that they were making progress. They were going to save this kid.

"I thank you guys for what you're doing," the boy told them. "But after what my father did to me . . . I've already decided." The boy stuck the barrel of the German Ruger in his mouth.

"Don't! Don't!" The rangers pleaded. "If you do this, it's going to bother us for the rest of our life."

"I'm sorry. I have to do it. I came here to do it."

"Please, son. Drop the gun."

The boy calmed down, and negotiations continued. This went on for three and a half hours. It grew dark—a cold desert night. The highway patrol lieutenant took over for Chris so the ranger could retrieve his jacket from his ranger car. When Chris returned, the boy placed the gun down on the hood of the Hyundai and walked away. Five feet. Ten feet. Twenty feet. Once the kid put thirty feet of distance between himself and the gun, two officers, the highway patrol negotiator, and Ranger Piastick made their move. But the boy was quicker than they expected. The boy pounced on the gun. The ranger and the highway patrolmen pounced on the boy. One shot rang out. The highway patrol lieutenant said, "Oh, shit."

With guns drawn, Chris and the other officers approached. The lieutenant was okay. Ranger Piastick was okay. The boy was not okay. He was on the ground, blood pouring out of his head. Piastick, a park medic, immediately started emergency medical treatment. It was another "tough moment" for Chris. He and Piastick had put their hearts into talking the boy out of it. The boy still had a pulse when he was loaded into a rescue helicopter, but he was pronounced dead at the Flagstaff Medical Center.

Months later, Chris made a grocery run to Flagstaff. When he passed the trading post he saw a kitschy work of yard art at the spot where the boy had shot himself. The art was a large rusty water pipe in which an artist had cut out an image of Kokopelli. A thousand years ago, Native Americans painted Kokopelli on a few sandstone panels. Today the Arizona tourism industry prints the humpbacked flute player's likeness on everything imaginable—T-shirts, bath towels, earrings—making Kokopelli ubiquitous to a nauseating degree. This was enough to ruin Kokopelli for Chris, but the rusty metal pipe scraped away the last vestiges of benevolence the flute player may have represented. From then on, any time Chris drove through Valle, anytime he went to see a movie, do some shopping, or transport a prisoner to Flagstaff, he saw that damn Kokopelli pipe. And every time he saw that pipe, it reminded the ranger of a dead boy lying in the dust in front of a gift shop parking lot.

16

CRASH

Chris Fors snatched the radio mike out of its clamp, brought it up to the soft blond hairs of his cop-style mustache, pushed the button with his thumb, and said, "Copy." This came out more like "Caahpy," but the dispatcher was as familiar with the ranger's Massachusetts accent as she was accustomed to the deliberate lack of emotion in his voice. Despite its urgency, the call did not bring on the adrenaline fix Chris craved. The Grand Canyon airport was the third busiest in the state of Arizona. Rangers responded to emergency landings several times a year. Usually the planes landed safely.

On February 13, 1995, a plane returning to Las Vegas from a trip to the Grand Canyon lost power to one of its engines. A Taiwanese family had chartered the flight as part of their whirlwind tour of several American parks. Eight were on board—the pilot and seven passengers: a father and his three daughters, two sons-in-law, and an aunt. Soon after takeoff from the Grand Canyon airport, the pilot informed air traffic controllers that he was going to attempt an emergency landing in the forest a few miles south of the airport. It was the last radio communication the pilot made.

Witnesses saw the plane disappear into the forest north of the runway. When the park dispatcher passed on this information, Chris grimaced. Chances were, there would be no survivors. Chances were, it would be another damn fatality. And it wouldn't be pretty. The crash site was three miles from the nearest paved road. From the air, a helicopter pilot directed the ground rescuers to the scene. A recent winter storm had blanketed the South Rim with two inches of snow, turning the ground into a slippery, sloppy mess.

* * *

Every winter tropical storms gather moisture from the coast of Mexico and haul it inland, sometimes dumping two feet of snow on the South Rim. At seven thousand feet, the winter nights are bitter cold. In the morning the cold air, which is heavier, sinks— to the disappointment of travelers paying the park entrance fee before they realize their view of the Grand Canyon is obscured by low clouds.

With a New England upbringing and Nordic genes, ranger Chris Fors preferred the winter weather. For one, the slower season allowed time for all the social events he missed during the hectic summer—potluck dinners, holiday parties, short vacations back home to visit family. After the storms, he could ski the trails near the rim on his days off, taking time to contemplate the park's beauty and stopping long enough to appreciate how a dusting of snow made the canyon reds seem even redder.

Sometimes the snows caused trouble. Earlier that winter, Chris responded to an accident involving a family from his home state. A few miles outside the park boundary, a Jeep Cherokee slid across yards of icy road until it was stopped by a pickup truck. Inside the Jeep was a family of four from Massachusetts. Three of them were dead or dying. Someone wrapped a scratchy government-issue wool blanket around the survivor and put her in the ambulance. When Chris stepped inside the ambulance to retrieve something, he saw a five-year-old girl sitting on the gurney. "Ranger," the girl said, looking Chris in the eye. "What's wrong with my mommy and daddy?"

It was another "tough moment." At EMT school they taught him not to lie to patients or their loved ones. So Chris said, "We're doing everything we can to help them." Technically it was the truth.

That was January 4, 1995. Eleven days later, on January 15, a kitchen worker at the Bright Angel Hotel ended an argument with another kitchen worker by stabbing him in the torso multiple times. Then on February 4, rangers saved the life of a local resident after he had been beaten severely by a man with a baseball bat—but not without good cause. Allegedly the beaten man had sexually assaulted the mother of the bat-swinging vigilante. Nine days later, on February 13, the plane crashed.

* * *

Chris drove the Suburban as close as he could to the crash site before getting bogged down in the snow. Then Chris and another ranger trudged in on foot. A quarter of a mile from the car, Chris scolded himself for not leaving behind his flat hat. The brim of the Smokey Bear was as wide as some cocktail tables. The hat was not a practical thing to wear when bushwhacking through tree branches. Following the directions radioed to him from a helicopter pilot hovering over the crash site, Chris climbed a knoll. When he reached the top and saw what was on the other side, he felt a horrible sinking sensation.

The charred and twisted metal below him had once been an airplane. Now the only thing recognizable was the tail. The plane must have burst into flames upon impact, and from the looks of the wreckage, there was no chance of finding any survivors. Chris walked around the scene to survey the situation. Scorched plane parts were scattered everywhere. Smoke hovered above the ground. The air carried the disturbingly sweet odor of smoldering human flesh mixed with the acrid smell of jet fuel. In the cockpit area, a body was still on fire. To put out the flames, Chris and a firefighter scooped up handfuls of snow and dumped them on the burning corpse. An arm hung out the cockpit window. Somehow, the arm had escaped the extreme heat of a jet fuel fire and remained unburned. A male hand with a shirt cuff. This had to be the pilot. Or what was left of the pilot. One hand. Chris stared at it. The image of the unburned hand of the airplane pilot was stamped into the ranger's memory. A happy family vacation to the Grand Canyon and this is what it had come to. What a waste.

A buzzing of voices erupted from the forest near what had been the tail of the aircraft. Other rescuers at the scene had found something. Then Chris heard two words that changed everything. Two words that brought on the kind of adrenaline rush this ranger lived for.

"They're alive!"

Looking at what was left of the airplane, he couldn't believe two people had managed to crawl out of the wreckage. It was a miracle. The energy at the crash site shifted. Now there was something the rescuers could do. Chris ran over to where his colleagues were kneeling down several yards from the tail.

Two teenage girls looked at the rescuers with dull eyes. They were conscious and bizarrely calm. Neither asked about the condition of the other passengers. Chiang-Ju had a crushed pelvis and was bleeding internally into her body cavity. The condition of her twelve-year-old sister, Hsiao-Hui, was worse. On top of broken bones, Hsiao-Hui had severe burns over 85 percent of her body. At this point, however, Hsiao-Hui did not show any signs of being in extreme pain. Third-degree burns often destroy the nerve endings in the skin and can cause deadly complications. A patient with severe burns over 85 percent of her body surface is in major trouble. The prognosis for Hsiao-Hui's survival was bleak. Chris and the other rescuers at the crash site worked fast and hard to get the sisters stabilized and loaded onto a rescue helicopter.

In Phoenix, teams of specialized nurses, doctors, and surgeons worked hard to save the two girls. According to a 2001 Maricopa

Medical Center press release, doctors at the Arizona Burn Center kept Hsiao-Hui in a medically induced coma for six weeks and sedated her for six weeks more.

The day she woke up, the doctors and nurses removed Hsiao-Hui's dressings. The twelve-year-old surveyed the extent of her wounds for the first time since the accident. The realization of what had happened must have come to her by then. With the exception of her mother and sister, everyone in her immediate family was dead. Burn wounds covered 85 percent of her body. A twelve-year-old girl would feel at least a flicker of concern for the future appearance of her growing body. However, when Hsiao-Hui saw her wounds, a doctor noted, "She did not cry, or moan, or look even the least bit despondent." What Hsiao-Hui did was look up at her caretakers and smile.

Later Hsiao-Hui said, "I knew I had to get through it. I knew if I did, I'd get better." She wanted to live and was willing to fight the physical and emotional battles awaiting her. She was a twelve-year-old girl with the will of a warrior. Six years after the crash, Hsiao-Hui returned to the burn center in Phoenix to volunteer five hours a day, five days a week, to help treat and counsel burn patients "and let them know there is life after a burn." In the fall she enrolled in the biochemistry program at the University of Arizona.

* * *

On the night of the crash, Chris didn't know that a brighter future lay ahead for the sisters. He came home after work and tossed his Smokey Bear on the kitchen table. He peeled off his heavy gun belt and carried it down the narrow hall toward his bedroom. He dropped the belt's burdens onto his bed and sat down to contemplate the cheap paneling in his cheap trailer.

Over a year ago, a proactive supervisor had discovered a loophole and hired Chris on as a permanent full-time ranger. Chris now qualified for retirement and health insurance benefits, but his parents "didn't jump for joy" at the news. Their son had an exceptional artistic talent, a college education, and a master's degree in Urban Affairs and Planning—and he lived in a trailer he had purchased for $2,000.

Chris's trailer sat on a concrete pad for which the NPS withheld two hundred bucks rent out of his paycheck each month. The trailer was a dump, and the floor was crooked. Miraculously, this had not discouraged his girlfriend, the blond, from moving in with him. For a while they were happy living together in that piece-of-shit trailer. When Chris began waking up in the middle of the night—sweating profusely, screaming incoherently, and grasping at his sheets—neither of them took it seriously. Perhaps, they joked, Chris was having nightmares because his trailer sat on top of an ancient Anasazi burial ground.

17

A COLD WET ONE

It was midnight and ranger Mary Litell Hinson was having a nightmare. Deep within the heart of the Grand Canyon, she was alone inside the ranger station at Phantom Ranch. The nearest backup ranger was five trail miles away. Something horrible was outside. It moaned like a ghoul and banged on the walls of the ranger station. Now it was knocking on the ranger station door. "Come out. Come out," the dreadful thing wailed. "Someone is going to die."

Mary woke up. It wasn't a nightmare. It was real! She was alone inside the ranger station. There was a bogeyman banging on the wall outside her bedroom window. And he was moving, beating his fists on the sides of the building—*bam, bam, bam*—all the way around to the front. Mary ran to the front door and looked out the window. Thank God. It wasn't the bogeyman: It was an emotionally disturbed person (EDP). Mary decided it was safe to let the EDP inside the ranger station but questioned her judgment as soon as he entered the door.

The EDP was so tall he ducked when he walked through the doorway. His eyes were bloodshot. His chest heaved. His arms flailed. He was speaking gibberish. "You have to come with me," the EDP said as he grabbed Mary by the arm and pulled her outside. Mary pushed the crazy man's grip off her arm and ordered him to step back. It took a minute or more before the ranger saw the man's behavior for what it actually was.

"Take a deep breath and calm down," Mary said, "or I'm not going to be able to help you."

"Oh, ranger, please help," the panicked man cried. "A kid has fallen off a cliff."

"Is he alive?" Mary asked.

"He was when I left him."

* * *

Six months earlier I had offered Mary her first permanent full-time-with-benefits ranger job. In November 1995 she left her husband, Scott Hinson, behind in Hawaii to work for me, a supervisor of ranger operations in the Grand Canyon's Corridor District. My district encompassed more than forty miles of the most heavily used trails in the park. The Cross-canyon Corridor linked, by footpath, the South Rim, the Colorado River, Phantom Ranch, and the North Rim. In addition to the trails, the district had three back-country campgrounds and three ranger stations. Along the Bright Angel Trail, almost five miles below the South Rim, was Indian Garden. At the bottom of the canyon and one mile north of the Colorado River was Phantom Ranch. For hikers undertaking the fourteen-mile North Kaibab Trail, there was Cottonwood Camp, at the halfway point between Phantom Ranch and the North Rim.

During the 1990s Grand Canyon park rangers responded to approximately three hundred rescue missions each year. More than two hundred of these incidents occurred in the Corridor District. From a search and rescue perspective, the Grand Canyon is perhaps the busiest backcountry area in the nation, if not the world. The day Mary started working for me, I had been the district ranger less than six months. I held my own, but my staff knew an entire library more than I did about the Grand Canyon. For the most part, I left it to them to train my new employee.

Pat Suddath was one of the rangers who trained Mary. The youngest permanent full-time ranger in the Corridor, Suddath was bright, interesting, and funny. He was also whiney, cynical, and sarcastic. Suddath reminded Mary of the cartoon character Bart Simpson; in the heat of an argument, a blond cowlick rose from his forehead like an exclamation point. During Mary's orientation at the Phantom Ranch Ranger Station, Suddath engaged the new employee in numerous debates over a variety of controversies, like should you stretch before or after you hike? Are coffee beans best stored in a cool dark place or in the freezer? Which of the canyon's geologic layers was the prettiest, the Tapeats sandstone or the Redwall? Which Colorado microbrew was best, Singletrack Copper or Fat Tire Amber? Who should make the initial heroic blitz to a technical river rescue while the other hauled down all the gear, the rock climber (Mary) or the medic (Suddath)? And most important, which park is the busiest in the service, Yosemite or the Grand Canyon?

No matter how cleverly Mary formed her opening statement, Suddath always took the opposing side. So when he said, "The Grand Canyon chews up park rangers and spits them out," Mary wasn't giving him the satisfaction. As far as she was concerned, Yosemite was the biggest, baddest park in North America.

Seemingly unimpressed with Mary's exploits at Yosemite, Suddath briefed the newbie about all the Grand Canyon back-country rangers who had been trapped underwater by rocks, swept away in flash floods, hit by lightning, knocked unconscious by rock falls, dehydrated to the point of requiring fluids to be administered intravenously, stung by scorpions, impaled by cacti, and head-butted off the trail by bighorn rams. Then he proceeded to tell her about rangers who had fractured their feet, legs, ribs, arms, and skulls.

Although she'd never admit it to Suddath, Mary found this all to be a bit much. She began to wonder if she had the right stuff to be a Grand Canyon backcountry ranger. Could she start a fire without matches? Could she carve fish hooks out of willow branches? If pinned by a boulder below the surge of a flash flood, could she saw off her own leg with a pocketknife? If she ran out of water, would she have to drink her own urine?

Mary doubted her relative abilities even more when she met Bryan Wisher, the ranger in charge of Indian Garden. Tall and tanned, Bryan's legs were so long and so muscular it wouldn't have been a huge shock to see him step over a Honda. And his backpack was ridiculous; you could haul a small microwave, four dictionaries, and two watermelons in it. As they hiked, Wisher called out the scientific names of plants. He identified birds on the wing. He discussed the human body's complex reactions to a variety of electrolyte imbalances. He contemplated the underlying assumptions of the Big Bang Theory, quoted Buddhist scriptures, and predicted the weather.

Bryan Wisher was also the most humble and compassionate ranger Mary had ever met. When they stopped for lunch, Mary gnawed on her cardboard-textured sports bar while Bryan reached into his colossal pack and pulled out an object wrapped in aluminum foil. Always the gentleman, Wisher offered the item inside the foil to his partner. Right then, Mary capitulated. Any attempt to compete with ranger Bryan Wisher would be futile. The guy had hiked in eight pounds of smoked salmon. For a snack!

It was a good thing too. She needed the protein. Rangers on the North Rim had found an abandoned car parked in the North Kaibab trailhead parking lot. The car belonged to a young man who had been reported missing. Mary struggled to keep up with Bryan's pace as they searched for the lost hiker. They traversed under cliffs where the man might have fallen. They crawled beneath rocks his body might be under. They hiked back and forth, up and down, and all around. Two days of this and Mary's feet were raw hamburgers. Her legs were soggy noodles. Her lungs were two pieces of burnt toast. But when Bryan asked, "How's it going?" she said, "Terrific!" So Bryan hiked farther and faster. By the time the incident commander called off the search, the Indian Garden ranger had pushed Mary to hike a hundred brutal miles within four days.

After weeks of searching they had found nothing. From experience, we knew the odds were slim that the hiker was alive. I obtained a heart-wrenching acceptance from the young man's father and the incident commander called off the search effort. Six months later, two maintenance workers set out to inspect the pipeline transporting water from Roaring Springs up to the North Rim. While scrambling along the pipe, they found the desiccated remains of a body below a four-hundred-foot cliff. The body was identified as the young man Mary and Bryan had been searching for in November.

Some concluded that the man was a jumper. I didn't subscribe to this theory. I had searched the man's car and gotten to know his father. I believed the young hiker smoked a joint while enjoying the canyon view and then, in a drug-impaired state, had accidently wandered off the trail and over the edge. The foundation for my hypothesis was the marijuana found in the dead man's backpack. The intoxicating substance was the fatal flaw our death investigations always labored to find. In part such evidence served to protect the NPS from any claims of negligence. But, most important, fatal flaws implied that backcountry fatalities were the result of foolhardy or arrogant behavior and allowed room for a comforting delusion. As long as we were smart and careful, it would never happen to one of us.

* * *

The NPS provided a home for Mary on the South Rim—a compact trailer she shared with a female roommate. The trailer had mint-green aluminum siding, tiny windows, and a boxy shape. Park staff called it "the Green Dumpster," and Mary relinquished a portion of each paycheck back to the NPS for the privilege of living in it. Fortunately, like all rangers assigned to the Corridor District, Mary spent very little time in the Green Dumpster. Nine days out of every two-week pay period, she lived and worked at the backcountry ranger stations.

All the Corridor ranger stations were lovely compared to the Green Dumpster, but Mary preferred Indian Garden. For one, "the Garden" had a stunning view up Bright Angel Canyon. At the time, it also had the nicest kitchen, and Bryan Wisher tastefully furnished the living quarters. When working there, Mary felt as though she'd died and gone to ranger heaven. On slow days she could lie in a hammock on the porch and sip ice tea while watching the sunset glow off Zoroaster Temple.

One perfect Indian Garden afternoon, after the sun dropped behind the Redwall, Mary peeled off her uniform and shimmied into a sports bra and shorts. She hiked a mile and a half from the ranger station to the base of Plateau Point. For Mary, free soloing (climbing without the safety of a rope and a belay partner to catch her fall) a four-hundred-foot route was a relaxing activity. The desert air warmed her skin as she climbed. Forty feet from the bottom, she threw a hand up to a flat ledge above her head—a gorgeous hold. She threw up her other hand and, like a chin-up, used the muscles in her arms and back to haul her body weight up the rock. When her face reached her hands she saw something on the ledge in front of her. Mary froze. She was nose to nose with a rattlesnake.

The snake's dusty pink scales told Mary it was the species *Crotalus oreganus abyssus*, (western rattlesnake of the abyss), but the rangers called them "Grand Canyon pinks." The Grand Canyon pink rattled its annoyance at the rock climber trespassing upon its ledge. Very, very slowly Mary lowered her body back down to her last position on the rock.

* * *

Sometimes the boss made Mary pull a tour at the other ranger stations. This was the case during the early hours of April 13, 1996—the first night of her first tour working alone at Phantom Ranch.

Mary told the park dispatcher a child had fallen off the Clear Creek Trail, and within minutes Bryan Wisher was out the door of the Indian Garden Ranger Station. The accident site was seven miles from Indian Garden and two miles from Phantom Ranch. Mary grabbed a rope and blitzed up the trail while volunteer Sjors Hortsman stayed behind long enough to enlist a team of concession employees and NPS trail crew workers to follow him to the site.

When Mary reached the scene, a group of backpackers directed the ranger to the edge of a seventy-five-foot cliff. The backpackers said the boy had inadvertently stepped off the cliff when he got up to urinate during the night. Mary leaned over the edge and scanned the rocks below until the beam of her headlamp lit up the boy. What she saw made her feel sick. It appeared that after hitting bottom, the boy had lived long enough to crawl fifty yards to an emergency blanket someone had thrown down to him. Now the boy wasn't moving or responding to his name. He wore nothing but underwear and the foil blanket. For Mary, seeing this thirteen-year-old boy curled up into a fetal position on the rocks was the "ultimate bummer."

"Look," someone said, "he moved!" Mary returned her headlamp's beam to the boy. Indeed, he had moved.

Meanwhile, Bryan Wisher felt as if he was in a dream. It was dark. It was raining. He was running down a trail and dodging the rocks the wet soil sent rolling off the switchbacks of the Devil's Corkscrew. His knees were on fire. Carrying a fifty-pound pack, the ranger ran seven rugged miles in sixty-five minutes.

While Bryan ran, Mary rappelled in the dark over the seventy-five-foot cliff. At the bottom, she assessed the boy's injuries. He had blood on his head. His ankle was obviously broken. But he was alive. Mary placed him in a dry sleeping bag.

By the time Bryan arrived, Sjors had scouted a route down the terraces. He guided Bryan to the accident scene.

"Is he shivering?" Bryan asked.

"No," Mary replied, thinking that this was a good sign.

Bryan was a park medic. He had carried a ten-pound machine that measures vital signs to the scene. He pulled two IV bags out of his shirt. (To warm the fluids, he had hiked with them next to his body.) "Someone get a rectal temperature while I start an IV," he said, taking charge.

Sjors stuck a digital thermometer where it would obtain the most accurate core temperature. A couple of minutes later, he read aloud the digital numerals on the screen. "It says 83.6."

"Stick it up farther," Bryan said.

If I stick it up any farther he'll be having it for breakfast. "I can't Bryan," the volunteer said. "It's already at the hilt."

Alarm bells were now ringing in the medic's head. Most of us know that a normal body temperature is 98.6 degrees Fahrenheit (37° C). Fewer people are aware that a core body temperature between 93 (34° C) and 97 degrees (36° C) indicates mild hypothermia. Moderate hypothermia falls into the 86 (30° C) to 93 degree (34° C) range, and a core body temp below 86 degrees Fahrenheit (30° C) puts one into severe hypothermia. If you studied the same paramedic texts studied by Ranger Wisher, you know a patient with mild or moderate hypothermia has a favorable prognosis once treated, but a patient in severe hypothermia will not be shivering, is often unconscious or in a coma, and is at risk for deadly cardiac arrhythmia. When caring for a person with a core body temp of 83.6 degrees (let's say it's a kid—a flaxen-haired, sleepy-eyed thirteen-year-old boy with a broken ankle, a bleeding head, and a fractured spine who lies on a cold slab of rock deep inside the Grand Canyon), you should prepare yourself for the worst. Your patient may go into cardiac arrest. Right here. Right now. Right in front of you.

Up to this point in his career, ranger Bryan Wisher had never had a patient die while in his care. Of course he had participated in many body recoveries and assisted with a few hopeless codes— people whose hearts had stopped long before rangers arrived. But to lose a patient who was alive and talking to you when you arrived, and it was a kid! That would be more than tragedy. That would forever break the sturdy heart beating inside the ranger's chest.

To Mary, Bryan was Zen calm. She had heard the stories. A few years earlier, this park medic had braved a flash flood to save twenty-eight lives in one day. She was confident the medic was going to save the boy.

But Bryan felt a panic rising. He heard it in the higher pitch of his voice when he yelled, "Start boiling water. Now! And don't move him unnecessarily!" (Rough movement or excessive activity can send a severely hypothermic patient's heart into a deadly rhythm.) Bryan directed the others to heat water with backpacking stoves carried up from Phantom Ranch. He told them to pour the heated water into plastic canteens. Bryan wrapped IV tubing around the canteens of heated water, an innovative way to gently warm the fluid entering the boy's bloodstream via the catheters the medic had inserted into the boy's veins.

Within an hour of receiving these warm fluids, the boy began to tremble violently. "He's shivering!" Mary said, worried.

"Good." Bryan said. "He's generating heat now."

Over the next few hours, the shivering got milder and milder until it stopped completely. By sunrise the patient's rectal temp was 90.6 degrees (32.5° C), and the rain had stopped. Thirty minutes before sunrise, a helicopter dropped off more rescue personnel on the mesa above, including a female ranger-paramedic named Tammy Keller.

As the Arizona Department of Public Safety helicopter pilot lowered the hook, Bryan looked at Sjors. *It's been nice knowing ya.*

To the rescuers on the ground, the pilot appeared to be performing the rescue helicopter equivalent of neurosurgery when he lowered the helicopter into the tight canyon. The side canyon was shaped like a bowl, and the spinning rotors came within twenty feet of the rock as the pilot attempted to drop the haul hook to the rescuers on the ground. Bryan and Sjors feared that the rotors were going to clip the walls, causing the helicopter to crash and then explode into a ball of flames, igniting every living thing inside the little canyon.

But the pilot lobbed the hook to the rescuers as nonchalantly as if he were casting a baited hook into a prime fishing hole. Mary let the hook touch the ground to avoid being shocked by static electricity before she grabbed it and then clipped it onto the ropes connected to the basket litter. She clipped another line to the harness worn by a ranger wearing a green flight suit. Tammy Keller was this mission's dope on a rope. Mary was impressed. A woman was doing the short haul. She conducted a "buddy check" of Tammy's system and then flashed the paramedic a grin. *You go girl!*

Bryan Wisher's mind for physics anticipated a problem. The victim was on a slanting terrace of rock, and the helicopter was not directly above the load. Once tension was put on the cable, it would create a pendulum. Once the helicopter lifted them off the ground, Keller and the boy were going to swing into the rock wall on the other side of the canyon! Bryan jumped up to put his body between the rock and the rescue litter but felt a force pulling him down. It was Mary. She grabbed him by the shoulders and used all her 135 pounds to pull Bryan's 200 to the ground. In an instant, the medic knew Mary was right. In fact, she may have saved his life. Putting his body between the litter and the rock wall was only going to get him killed.

Mary grabbed a short line tied to the litter and held on to it until she had to let go. Her doing this decreased the force of the pendulum's swing so that before Keller and the boy slammed into the sandstone, all the paramedic had to do was daintily tap her feet on the rock, pushing the rescue litter back into the air just as the helicopter pulled them out of the canyon and into the rosy sky. Within a minute, they disappeared into the Grand Canyon sunrise.

There was nothing left for Bryan to do. His leadership was no longer needed. The boy was on his way to the hospital, where he would fully recover. The suspense was over. The danger was past. The ground rescuers packed up the gear and started hauling it back to the ranger station. Bryan insisted on being the last to leave the accident scene. As soon as he was alone, as soon as he was certain his coworkers couldn't see him, the ranger sat his weary body on a sandstone boulder, dropped his head to his hands, and wept—just for a minute, maybe two.

18

DRY HEAT

Exhaust-spewing tour buses and rental cars filled the parking lot. Like sheep through chutes, tourists were herded by railing-protected paths down to the overlooks at Mather Point. It was January. Youth counselor David Line Denali had driven up from Apache County to show Cale Shaffer, his new outdoor recreation intern, the Grand Canyon for his first time. Cale followed the railings down the stone steps and out to the end of a peninsula of rock until . . . Whoa! The prosaic atmosphere at the parking lot was forgotten. This was some serious scenery. Struggling for perspective, Cale turned to his new boss and asked, "How tall is Wall Street?"

"I don't know," Denali said. "A thousand feet or so?" Five Wall Streets set on top of one another still wouldn't match the depth of the Grand Canyon. It was craziness. Cale couldn't wrap his mind around it. In his home state, there was a place the locals called the Grand Canyon of Pennsylvania. Now this claim embarrassed him. The Grand Canyon of Pennsylvania. Right.

Standing there at Mather Point, the twenty-year-old Outdoor Recreation intern had no way of knowing how intimate he would become with the mysterious terrain in front of him. A beam of sunlight highlighted Zoroaster Temple, a yellow butte to the north. (He would climb it.) The jade ribbon at the bottom of the canyon was the Colorado River. (He would raft it.) The cluster of buildings in the heart of the inner gorge was Phantom Ranch. (He would live there.) Ten miles away on the North Rim, fir and spruce grew from the snowy ground. (He would recover his first dead body there, a victim of a plane crash.) The Grand Canyon guarded many riches—hidden caves, fossilized creatures, ancient ruins, prehistoric paintings, emerald springs sustaining elfin gardens. (And here, among the park's secret treasures, he would fall in love with more than one girl.)

* * *

Cale grew up in a small house on a small street in the small community of Madisonburg, Pennsylvania. Across the street lived an Amish family. A stone's throw from his backyard, headstones marked the graves of seven generations of Shaffers, going further back than the one who died in 1865 from a wound he received fighting to preserve the Union. When he was younger, Cale's dad, Ron Shaffer, raced stock cars. He named his son after Cale Yarborough, the NASCAR champion. After his son was born, instead of racing cars, Ron fixed them. Cale's mom, Carol, was a stay-at-home mom until her son and his sister were older. Then she took a job that bored her, slicing meats at the grocery deli for minimum wage, so that her two children would have an opportunity she didn't have—going to college.

It was a humble childhood, but it was also stable and happy. At sixteen, Cale bagged a scholarship to a youth camping trip in Grand Teton National Park. In Wyoming he saw bigger deer, bigger mountains, and bigger creeks than you can find anywhere in Pennsylvania. When he returned home, Cale posted a map of the United States on his bedroom wall. With a red Magic Marker he circled all the national parks and monuments he intended to visit—Yellowstone, Devils Tower, Glacier, Yosemite, and the Grand Canyon.

Before coming to the Grand Canyon as an Outdoor Recreation intern, however, he first accepted a camp counselor and rock climbing instructor position in Kentucky. For an Outdoor Recreation major on summer break, it sounded like a dream job. But his work as a Girl Scout counselor at Camp Judy Layne induced more stress than he had anticipated. He worked sunup to midnight, rushing around camp, setting up nature games, building campfires, and resolving urgent camp issues such as bed-wetting, head lice, and homesickness.

Of all his duties, teaching hundreds of Girl Scouts how to rock climb and rappel was the most trying. Whenever the girls peered over the edge of a cliff for the first time, one tearful Scout would spread crippling trepidation throughout the entire group. It would take him an hour to convince the first girl she could do it. All these trials on his patience were forgotten as soon as he saw the smile of a pudgy girl after she did a hundred-foot rappel. Cale was a skilled lead climber, but the biggest rush for this Eagle Scout came from helping others gain confidence and enjoy the outdoors.

After completing his summer internship with the Girl Scouts of America, Cale returned to Lock Haven University. Back on campus, he experienced culture shock. Next to Pre-med majors and football players, the five-foot-five Cale felt self-conscious about his height. The angst of being short-man-on-campus was a recurring theme in his college journals, but Cale rarely wallowed in self-pity. One of his favorite rock climbing routes was called Shorty's Revenge.

At the age of nineteen Cale concluded that all he had to do was have faith in his own intentions, shed all concerns of others' opinions, and ignore those who didn't see him for who he was. Only then would he find true friends.

* * *

After graduating in January 1996, Cale accepted a job as an Outdoor Recreation intern with Apache County Search and Rescue. Six months later, he and his boss, youth counselor David Line Denali, drove their team up to the Grand Canyon for what they had thought would be an easy assignment. As soon as they arrived at Mather Campground, Denali left to meet with the park rangers.

With sixteen "at-risk" youths under his supervision, Cale knew trouble came from idle hands. He kept the kids busy with setting up camp. By the time a female ranger returned with Denali three hours later, the tents were staked, the gear was unpacked, and dinner was ready. Denali got out of the ranger's car with a stack of T-shirts in his hands and a look on his face Cale recognized immediately. The boss was freaking out.

Cale grabbed the T-shirts, inspected them, and frowned. The words "park volunteer" on the front were too small to read from a distance. Also, the hikers wouldn't know they were not regular volunteers but search and rescue volunteers. "So," Cale asked Denali, "how did it go?"

"Wait a minute, Cale," Denali said as he sat down on the picnic table. "I have to get focused." The youth counselor needed to process the last three hours. What had he gotten himself into? These rangers had a situation here. They had a major problem. And they were counting on the Apache Rescue Team (ART) to help. Denali's team consisted of himself, two adult interns, and sixteen kids from one of the poorest regions in Arizona.

Many of the youths had been referred to him by the Apache County Juvenile Court system. Several had been abused by alcoholic parents. Many had been in trouble with the law, and a few even had done time for felonies. The juvenile probation department sent these kids to Denali, whose job was to involve them in search and rescue in order to "straighten them up."

That was the hope, anyway. And with Cale Shaffer's help, Denali had trained them well. These kids knew their way around a camp stove and a carabiner. Their team was now part of the

Mountain Rescue Association, and they had worked an Eco-Challenge event in Utah. But they were still kids. Thus far they had only participated in mock rescues and pounded the ground on a few easy searches. My God, didn't this district ranger woman see that? But Denali didn't have the heart to tell the ranger that, perhaps, he and his team were in over their heads. After what he'd seen today, it was obvious she needed all the help she could get.

* * *

For the rangers it began with a knock on the door of the ranger station. Outside, the Phantom Ranch ranger met two breathless teenage girls. "There's a boy lying face down in the trail," the girls said. The ranger called for help, grabbed a rescue pack, and ran down the trail. The day's high had been 116 degrees. The ranger prepared himself to treat heat stroke. When he arrived he saw the last thing he wanted to see: two bystanders performing CPR on a ten-year-old boy with a blue face and a rectal temperature of 106 degrees.

"Pour creek water on him," the ranger-medic yelled at bystanders. Two more ranger-medics and an EMT were flown in by helicopter. Fifty-six minutes after the first ranger's arrival, the boy was cooled, intubated, defibrillated, placed on a stretcher, carried a quarter mile, and loaded into the helicopter that flew him to the emergency clinic on the South Rim. The rescuers left behind were still catching their breath when a hiker ran up and said, "A woman has collapsed on the trail!"

The rangers ran a hard half mile up the South Kaibab Trail before they reached an unconscious woman lying in the shade. A rectal thermometer recorded her core body temperature at 105 degrees. The woman was dying of heat stroke. The rangers poured water on her and asked bystanders to fan the woman to increase the evaporative cooling. The rangers loaded the patient, a heavy woman, onto their stretcher and ran her back down the trail to the nearest spot where a helicopter could land. Immediately after dropping off the boy on the rim, the helicopter pilot returned to pick up the woman.

Within two hours after the knock on the ranger station door, park rangers had treated two patients dying of heat stroke and evacuated one of them out of the Grand Canyon. The woman's life was saved; the ten-year-old boy was pronounced dead after more than an hour of advanced lifesaving measures.

An hour later, Denali sat down at a picnic table in Mather Campground and told Cale his side of the story. That afternoon, the Corridor district ranger, a woman in her early thirties with a strong Tennessee accent, picked him up in her Jeep Cherokee. She brought him to her cluttered office on the second floor of a rustic ranger station, where she gave Denali the T-shirts and the Park Service radio frequencies. The district ranger briefed him on the recent rash of trail fatalities. Four hikers had already died this year, and three of those deaths had been heat related. The first heat stroke fatality of the summer, on June 6, involved a fifteen-year-old Boy Scout. (Grand Canyon rangers would respond to 482 rescue missions in 1996. By Thanksgiving, eight hikers would die of heat illness or cardiac arrest. To date, the summer of 1996 is still, by a far margin, the deadliest hiking season in the park's history.)

The ranger outlined to Denali the role she wanted his team to play. She called it PSAR, or preventive search and rescue. His team would hang out near the top of the most popular park trails and warn all hikers of the hazards. His team would also respond to minor emergencies on the trail so that the rangers could focus on the critical cases. She apologized. There wasn't much time to orient his team, but she had managed to assign a ranger to help out for a few hours tomorrow morning. Then they would be on their own.

Denali was about to ask the district ranger to define "minor emergency" when their conversation was interrupted by an urgent call. A boy: unconscious and unresponsive at the bottom of the canyon near Phantom Ranch. Denali listened and watched. It sounded as though the kid wasn't going to survive. More calls came in. A dumpster was on fire in Mather Campground. At the entrance gate a park visitor was refusing to pay his entrance fee. Outside the ranger office, sirens wailed and helicopters buzzed. The district ranger coached another female ranger—a tall, lanky blond who was coordinating the multiple rescue operations over the phone and a radio. When the dispatcher reported that a woman had collapsed on the South Kaibab Trail, the district ranger (me) turned to the other female ranger (Mary) and asked, "So, do you still think it's busier at Yosemite?"

After Denali finished telling Cale his story, the intern picked up one of the volunteer T-shirts the district ranger had given them to wear. Pointing to the small lettering, he said, "These T-shirts aren't right."

Denali sighed. He was thirty and, unlike the twenty-one-year-old Cale, he could not care less about the design of the T-shirts. In June the canyon had killed a fifteen-year-old. The boy who died today had been ten. The kids on Denali's rescue team weren't much older. What if one of his charges was killed while running up the trail to do a rescue? What if his kids responded to a "minor emergency" and did something wrong that affected a patient's survival? What if he did something stupid and it tarnished the reputation of his rescue team?

"We better pull our shit together," Denali told his intern. "The rangers want us to start first thing in the morning."

"Cool!" Cale said.

That night, Mary Litell Hinson attended the stress debriefing for the rescuers on the mission involving the death of the boy. As the operations chief from the rim, Mary maintained some emotional distance to the tragedy—until she attended the meeting and listened to the rescuers tell their stories. These were older, tested ranger-medics. But today's tragedy had broken them. Their faces contorted with anguish. Their shoulders shook with grief. A few bawled openly. There was a consensus: The warning signs had been placed at the trailheads that morning, and a ranger had outlined the hazards to the adults hiking with the boy. By the time the medics arrived at the scene, it was too late for miracles. Yet none of these facts made the rangers feel any better.

The Apache Rescue Team was a godsend. The next day, within twenty-four hours of its arrival, the team carried a mother and child out of the Grand Canyon. That summer the rangers were too fatigued and distracted to pay much attention to Denali's kids. But running up and down the steep trails and educating hikers while carrying two gallons of water, an oxygen tank, and other emergency equipment certainly ingrained in them the importance of physical conditioning and a good pair of boots. Some youths in the program were inspired to go into the health-care field. A couple of them joined the military and fought in Iraq.

If Grand Canyon rangers influenced anybody that summer, it was Denali's adult intern, Cale Shaffer. After forty-eight hours as a park volunteer, he called home to his parents and said, "I'm going to work here one day! Whatever it takes. I'm going to be a park ranger at the Grand Canyon."

On his last day volunteering at the Grand Canyon as an intern for Denali's rescue team, Cale held an IV bag while a ranger-medic inserted a needle into a dehydrated hiker's arm. Once they loaded the patient into the back of the helicopter, the ranger said, "Hey, Cale. Isn't this your last day? Why don't you ride shotgun?"

Yes! The ranger was letting him ride the rescue helicopter out of the Grand Canyon! And he was going to sit up front, next to the pilot, where he would see the best view! Like getting into a car, Cale ran over to the right side of the 210 Bell Jet Ranger, dropped his butt in the front seat, and shut the door. When he looked up, the pilot stood outside, glaring at him through the window. The man did not look happy.

"What?" Cale asked.

"Son," the pilot said, "unless you know how to fly this thing, you better get out of my seat."

* * *

143

Cale earned every thrilling minute of his first helicopter flight out of the Grand Canyon. By summer's end, he, Denali, and their team of disadvantaged youths had more than carried their weight and taught park rangers a vital lesson: An army of volunteers trained to perform preventive search and rescue could perform public safety education, decreasing the numbers of heat-related emergencies, easing the rescue burden on park staff, and reducing the park's hiker fatality rate.

Inspired in part by the success we had working with Denali's rescue team, over the winter of 1996–97, and under the leadership of Branch Chief Ranger Jim Northup, a hiker safety task group developed an aggressive Hiking Safety Campaign. Our multi-pronged strategy included a variety of public safety announcements and provided enough funds to employ four summer rangers whose sole focus would be PSAR. In the spring of 1997 we implemented the Grand Canyon Preventive Search and Rescue program and trained our first batch of volunteers. The first PSAR ranger I hired was Cale Shaffer. The first volunteers we used were the kids in Denali's Apache Rescue Team.

Cale's dad, Ron, lived by the motto "The satisfaction of a job well done lives long after a quick fix." During the summer of 1997, Cale brought the work ethic imparted to him by his father to his duties as a PSAR ranger. Each day, thousands of people walked down the park's trails. Cale felt it was necessary to speak with anyone who might have a problem. He woke up early each morning in order to reach the day's first hikers. He ate his lunch on the trail and didn't leave until after quitting time. If you contemplated it too much, PSAR work came with a lot of pressure. If only one person slipped by without hearing your warning, that person might be the one hiker who got into trouble in the canyon and died!

One afternoon Cale was working the Bright Angel Trail when a middle-aged man resembling Jackie Gleason came waddling down the path. The man was sweating profusely, his face was flushed, and he appeared to be one cheeseburger away from a heart attack. Cale abruptly ended the pleasant conversation he was having with two long-legged women from Germany and ran after the red-faced man. He absolutely had to talk to that guy before he hiked farther into the canyon!

"Sir, how are ya?" Cale said. "Do you need some extra water? Do you have some food? How far do you plan on hiking today? Maybe you should take a break here. You know, wait until it gets a little cooler."

"Son," the man said, "do you know who I am?"

"No."

"I'm Rob Arnberger, the superintendent of this park!" the man said. "You work for me! I've been the superintendent here for four years! Are you telling me I look like someone who can't hike safely in the Grand Canyon?"

"Sir!" Cale stammered. "Uh . . . I didn't . . . I was just . . . " The ranger extended a hand to the superintendent. "It's nice to meet you, sir."

* * *

In 2008 two doctors published their review of the Grand Canyon PSAR program and its effectiveness. The data indicated that the average number of rescue incidents had decreased from 9.4 incidents per hundred thousand visitors between 1988 and 1997 to 7.6 incidents per hundred thousand visitors in the six years following. In the *Western Journal of Emergency Medicine,* Kandra Yee and Kenneth Iverson concluded that the PSAR program had "decreased the numbers of visitor illness and injury, thereby decreasing the need for costly and potentially dangerous SAR responses." Today the Grand Canyon volunteer PSAR program is more sophisticated than the one we initiated in the late 1990s. But the foundation of PSAR will always be the face-to-face public education performed by ranger Cale Shaffer during the summer of 1997.

19

THE DEVIL'S CORKSCREW

In 1996 Grand Canyon rangers responded to two hundred heat-related emergencies. The next year we responded to only 150. The heat failed to kill a single Grand Canyon hiker in 1997, and this was all the proof we needed to know that our new PSAR (preventive search and rescue) initiative worked. Despite this success, 1997 ended up being another hard year. Our trial by heat was complete. Now the Grand Canyon would test us with plagues of another sort.

In May a dispatcher called me shortly after midnight. "Respond to the rim behind the Bright Angel Lodge, and be prepared for a technical rescue." I parked my Jeep Cherokee in front of the Arizona Steak House and walked toward the back of the lodge. Pedestrian lamps flooded the lawn with a white light and painted our faces a pallid hue. I walked across the grass toward the rim. A ranger coming from the other direction dragged one end of a climbing rope to anchor it to a tree or a post or a car axle. I searched his eyes for an indication of where I should report. The ranger shook his head at me as if to say, "You don't want to be here and neither do I."

At the hip-high sandstone barrier along the rim, another ranger was belaying an unseen rescuer over the edge. I peered over the rock wall and saw nothing but black. "What happened," I asked.

"A woman fell," the belay ranger said, his tone clipped with annoyance. "She's probably 901." This ranger belonged to a clique of male rangers who disliked me—intensely. I assumed the tension was due to my presence and that my questions irritated him. I silently prepared myself as an edge attendant for the rangers lowered into the canyon and refrained from the idle chitchat two topside rescuers might typically enjoy.

A few minutes later, one of the rangers reached the impact site. A second later, he radioed back, "We have a definite 901." (Nine-oh-one is a radio code Arizona public safety personnel use to communicate a fatality.) From the amount of rope it took to reach the victim, he approximated that she had landed three hundred feet below the rim. He recommended we wait until daylight and use a helicopter to short-haul the body out of the canyon.

When I finally learned the details of what happened that night, I understood why my coworkers had seemed so sullen when I arrived on scene and started asking questions. You can file this story under "A Ranger's Worst Nightmare"—a nightmare that began with too many shots of Yukon Jack. Or you could say it began with the heartaches and hassles that come with divorce. Or you could say it began with a friend calling 911 to report an intoxicated woman behind the Bright Angel Lodge, walking the safety wall along the rim as if it were a tightrope.

The victim, a waitress for the park concession, fell off the wall before the first ranger arrived. She landed on a slanted ledge twenty feet below the rock wall. Drunk, despondent, and terrified, the woman sent rocks rolling as she continued to slip closer and closer to the verge of a three-hundred-foot drop.

The first rangers to arrive were from the night shift patrol in South Rim Village. Patrol rangers do not carry ropes with them. To join the woman on this precipitous ledge without the safety of a belay was nothing short of suicidal, but one ranger did it anyway. He inched down the slope toward the woman's position during the long minutes it took for the other rangers to set up a belay, anchor it to something solid on the rim, and safely send a rescuer over the rim.

I lacked the fortitude to interview any of the rangers there that night. I already knew more than I need to know. All their pulses were quickened by her sobbing, wailing cries for help. At least two of them watched her slowly slide down the slope until her grip on a bush was the only thing between her and eternity. They all heard the screams after she let go of the bush. And they all recoiled at the silence signifying the end of her fall.

I don't recall who made the choice, but it was a wise one. The rangers on scene when the woman fell had no business participating in the recovery mission. My oldest PSAR ranger and I agreed to recover the remains and assist a special agent with the on-scene death investigation. By the light of day we were able to reach the impact zone on foot. We left the Bright Angel Trail and traversed the Toroweap Formation to a steep drainage. We climbed up this narrow drainage until we found a body slumped over a large chunk of beige sandstone.

It was the only time I worked on a recovery team consisting only of women. The twenty-eight-year-old victim was near us in age, and her body, mangled as it was, provoked us with its familiarity. We worked quietly, efficiently, and delicately. I recall only one weak attempt at a macabre pun. "You're so thought-full," the special agent remarked, because somebody had to say something when I, with two hands, scooped up the contents from the woman's smashed skull and softly placed them in the body bag.

Later the same day, after a long shower and a change of clothes, I started down the Bright Angel Trail to begin a nine-day tour at Phantom Ranch. I was about to descend the tortuous switchbacks of the Devil's Corkscrew when a fast hiker coming from the opposite direction accosted me. "Hey, ranger," the man said. "You got any Band-Aids? They aren't for me. But I know some people up the trail who might want some."

"Sorry," I said cheerfully, "I'm all out of Band-Aids today."

This was irrational and lazy of me, I admit. Toss the guy some Band-Aids and be done with it. But I had slept less than two of the last thirty hours and was on the far side of exhausted. That morning I had held a young woman's brains in my gloved hands, and I had five additional hot miles of trail ahead of me. Digging through my backpack to hand out Band-Aids to Code Ws who didn't need them was more than I felt capable of doing at that particular moment.

"You're lying!" The man could tell I was blowing him off, and he was furious. "What is your problem, ranger? You can't give a man a couple of Band-Aids? You know something? The American taxpayer pays you to hike all day," he said, swinging his arms out over the scenery. "You have the best job in the world! In fact," the man poked at the badge on my chest, "you ought to be paying me for allowing you the privilege of working here!"

I narrowed my eyes at the man. "You can have my job if you want it," I said, "but you wouldn't last two days." The venom in this statement instantly changed the man's perception of me. I was no longer a slacker public servant. I was an ill-tempered woman carrying a pistol. Mr. Irate Taxpayer did not dare utter another word.

20

FRIDAY THE THIRTEENTH

It was 7:30 a.m. on October 13 and Chris Fors was the only ranger on duty when the Grand Canyon dispatcher issued the first call of the day—a possible burglary at the Yavapai Museum. The museum employee said the door was locked when she arrived, and Chris saw no sign of forced entry. But inside the museum a large glass door had shattered into pieces with no explanation for the damage. Over the radio Chris and the dispatcher shared a chuckle over the mystery. Of course it was Friday the Thirteenth.

A few minutes later, Chris pulled over a speeder in Mather Campground. The driver of the silver Ford Probe—a young man in his twenties—was alone, his head was shaved, and he didn't resemble the picture on the driver's license he gave the ranger. The driver appeared very nervous. He spoke quickly and was trembling slightly.

Chris noticed a pair of plastic handcuffs in the backseat. He picked up the handcuffs and saw they were toy ones. Strange. Chris called in to his dispatcher and asked for a warrant check on the name listed on the driver's license. A few seconds later the dispatcher informed Chris that the silver Probe had been reported as stolen.

"Do what I tell you," Chris said, pulling his gun out of its holster. "Get out of the car."

"Why, why, why do I have to get out? Why?" the driver responded.

"Relax, son," Chris said, "and do what I tell you to do."

At that, the driver made an explosive move for the passenger seat. Instinct told Chris the driver was going for a gun. With his gun pointed at the driver, the ranger ran, away from the Probe and toward his patrol Bronco.

Chris's peripheral vision showed him two tourists in a maroon sedan. These campers were most likely on their way to breakfast at the El Tovar when they came upon a park ranger in the middle of the road, yelling and running and pointing his gun at a silver Ford Probe. Their shock was apparent through the windshield. The tourists wanted out of there in a bad way. Throwing the gear into reverse, the female driver wove the car around obstacles to put distance between herself and the ranger with the gun. The way she handled that Buick was impressive.

Chris keyed his radio mike to call for backup, but two mainte-nance employees discussing valve sizes had tied up the airwaves. The ranger felt completely alone then, like he might not see his family again. Thoughts of his loved ones raced through his mind. No, not thoughts, feelings—a flood of warm feelings for all his family members back in New England.

Somehow, although he was now behind the bumper of his Bronco, Chris could hear with amazing clarity the driver rus-tling through papers on the floorboard, searching for something. When the driver came up from the floor, there was a gun in his hand. Chris applied pressure with his trigger finger and there was a shot. At first the ranger wasn't sure from which gun it came.

"Get me backup," Chris yelled into his radio, his voice higher in pitch, his words coming fast and frantic. "A kid just shot him-self." The length of time between Chris calling in a warrant check on the driver and the driver shooting himself in the head was ninety-two seconds.

Chris crept up to the car and peered in the window. The driver was slumped forward onto the steering wheel. When Chris asked the dispatcher to send an ambulance, his voice had returned to its usual monotone quality. Ranger Donny Miller arrived and grabbed the .380 semiautomatic away from the driver's hand. Then Chris pulled the man out of the car and laid him on the roadway. Blood poured from the young man's head, and a few pitiful last breaths sighed from his mouth and nose. When Chris pried open the man's jaw to begin mouth to mouth, he saw bits of bone and brain in the back of the man's throat. Within the next hour, a doctor at the Grand Canyon clinic pronounced the young man dead.

Investigators learned that the man was an Army private from Fort Benning in Georgia. A month earlier, on the same day his roommate's wallet and silver Probe were stolen, the private went AWOL because he was "tired of being in the Army." He had been in the service less than a year.

Later that day, Chris called the other ranger who had worked the suicide in Valle to tell him that history had repeated itself.

"No way," Ranger Piastick said. "You're making this up!"

Back home at his trailer in Pinyon Park, his girlfriend was very sympathetic—for the first few hours. After dinner she berated him for not doing the dishes correctly. Certain pots were to be washed with vinegar and steel wool, and Chris had forgotten. After it got dark, he went jogging. The critical incident counselors had told him exercise was a good way to burn off stress. His dog, a mutt named Beckett, went with him. By flashlight he jogged the dirt roads through the forest along the canyon rim. Along the way, a wild panic consumed him. He ran faster and faster until he arrived back at his trailer, where he put his hands on his knees and panted as though he had raced a four-minute mile. The next morning, Chris returned to work another shift.

Chris had been at the Grand Canyon nearly six years. Each summer it seemed the workdays got longer, the days off got fewer, the bad guys got meaner, and the ranger staffing levels were going down, not up. Chris was beginning to feel like a block of cheap cheddar. Weak supervisors grated on him. Petulant coworkers grated on him. High-maintenance girlfriends grated on him. Stupid tourist questions grated on him. Fakers threatening to jump off the canyon for attention grated on him. Obnoxious, disgusting drunks grated on him. Every time someone said, "You rangers are so lucky. You're paid in sunsets!" it grated on him.

After the Friday the Thirteenth suicide, Chris believed his superiors were second-guessing him. In five years' time he had participated in hundreds of arrests and two young men had killed themselves in his presence. Sure, on many shifts Chris was one of two rangers assigned to patrol the South Rim Village when three rangers hadn't been enough to handle all the calls. Still, what were the odds? The ranger must be too gung-ho. He must be focusing too much on emergency services. He must be doing something wrong. How else can you explain why so many terrible things happened on his watch? What a shit magnet!

21

THE GUT OF
DARKNESS

When you often work sixteen-hour shifts and your days off come infrequently, your laundry pile becomes a mountain. By late afternoon on the first day of what I hoped would be a long and partially intoxicated weekend, I was folding clothes when the park's search and rescue (SAR) coordinator called me at home. A few days earlier, disaster had struck near Glen Canyon National Recreation Area, our sister park to the northeast. The rangers at Glen Canyon now needed our assistance with a search-and-recovery effort. Could I drive out with a small team of Grand Canyon rangers and assist our buddies at Lake Powell?

"Sure," I told him, "of course."

"This assignment," he warned me, "is not going to be a fun one."

After the dam was completed in 1966, Glen Canyon was drowned by Lake Powell, which we called Lake Foul due to all the houseboats and personal watercraft buzzing across its waters. In truth, the clear lake is not at all foul; and the remote, red-rock gorges that remain above water are spectacular.

Of the hundreds of isolated and beautiful tributary canyons leading to this reservoir, the most photogenic is the alluring Antelope Canyon. The upper portion of Antelope is typically a dry, narrow, and twisty crack carved out of the sandstone. A trek through this famous slot canyon is a superlative experience.

On August 11, 1997, eleven hikers and one tour guide were negotiating the famous slot when an isolated rainstorm sent a ten-foot-high wall of muddy water down the canyon. Only one person, the tour guide, made it out alive. One body was found right away. Two more turned up several days later. A team from the Grand Canyon was sent to help the Glen Canyon rangers find and recover the eight still lost.

When our four-person search team arrived at Lake Powell, we met a boatman at the NPS dock. He motored us across the dazzling blue lake rimmed by salmon-colored walls of sandstone. The family members of the people killed in the flash flood were never far from our thoughts, but the new scenery offered a respite from our own park. The day was fabulously hot and sunny. I peeled down to my shorts and a sports bra, and the men were shirtless. For a while we forgot the tragedy that had brought us here and enjoyed a pleasant boat ride to Antelope Canyon.

As soon as we entered the canyon's mouth, the water changed color, becoming at first a gorgeous emerald. As we ventured deeper into the canyon's long and twisted throat, the water turned browner and browner until it was a strange and dusty chocolate. Up ahead we saw two NPS boats anchored in a sharp bend of the canyon. When our boatman motored past the larger boats, the canyon's high walls blocked the sun, covering us with shade.

We were in the belly of the beast now, four miles downstream from where the flood victims were last seen. Here the canyon was about twenty-five yards wide. This pinch was choked by debris the flood had pushed down five days ago. Juniper branches, decaying vegetation, mud, and hundreds of bloating frogs and fish were now trapped between the sandstone walls, forming a mat up to six feet thick in places and floating in seven feet of stagnant, eighty-degree water. The boat operators would foul their propellers in the debris if they continued farther upstream. To extend the search deeper into the canyon, someone had created a tenuous walkway across this loathsome mat using seven plywood boards.

As the boatman motored us in, I recognized two of the Glen Canyon rangers standing on this makeshift plywood dock: Chris Pergiel, a supervisor from my years working Yosemite Valley's night shift, and Mike Archer, the newbie backcountry ranger who had tried to shoo the bear away from the human bones found near the John Muir Trail. As we arrived, Mike crawled out of the water. (Those of us who entered this water were later immunized because we were at risk for contracting hepatitis A.) Mike wore a Farmer John wet suit, and the neoprene hugged his body in a flattering way. I was pleased to see him, but my smile of recognition did not soften the ranger's stony face. Dark strands of detritus clung to Mike's muscular arms, and he was wet up to his neck. I noticed that he no longer wore a beaded necklace.

Surveying the scene before me, I congratulated myself for remembering to bring cigars to cover the smell. Caught within this thick mat were two of the five bodies we found that day. Their angulated extremities and purple faces paid testimony to the flood's cruelty. As I considered the empty body bags, the plywood dock, our wet suits, the life jackets, the mud on Mike Archer's face, and the floating mat of death and decay that continued upcanyon as far as I could see, I began to comprehend what this recovery mission would require.

"Lankford," ranger Chris Pergiel greeted me as our boatman cut off the engine and drifted us toward our Glen Canyon friends. "Welcome to hell."

22

THUNDER AND LIGHTNING

A storm cell hovered over the North Rim, Bright Angel Creek had turned brown at Phantom Ranch, and Bryan Wisher was overreacting. In the ranger station on the South Rim, I was trying to discuss something administrative with my peer, Wilderness District Ranger Nick Herring, but Bryan's radio transmissions distracted me. At Phantom the creek had risen five feet. This posed no danger to the campground, but Bryan was running all his bases anyway, nagging the North Rim rangers to update him on the weather and asking dispatch to ring the emergency phone at Cottonwood on the off chance a hiker would pick it up and advise us of the conditions upstream.

Bryan's apprehension stemmed from a rainy night five years ago. He had been sleeping inside the Cottonwood Ranger Station when a flood roared through the entire campground, washing away several tents and forcing campers to the top of picnic tables. (Bryan's actions that night earned him a Department of the Interior (DOI) Medal of Valor for saving twenty-eight lives. Then in May 1995 he pulled a maintenance employee out of a swollen creek below Indian Garden.) Nick Herring and I knew Bryan's history with flash floods. We sympathized with his compulsion to be overly cautious. But thunderstorms and flash floods were routine events during the summer monsoon season, and Bryan was now ordering the backcountry office to pull out all the permits for campers on the North Kaibab Trail.

Herring raised his eyebrows at me. *He's your employee.*

I shrugged my shoulders. I kept Bryan on a long leash.

Right then our radios emitted a series of tones heralding the announcement of a serious emergency. "Report from West Rim Drive," the dispatcher said. "At Mojave Point; two people struck by lightning." Before Herring or I had time to exhale, the dispatcher was back on the air. "Three people have been swept away by a flash flood at the confluence of Bright Angel and Phantom Creeks." I locked eyes with Herring. He looked as stunned as I felt. Two people struck by lightning and three people washed away in a flash flood! Five potential fatalities at two separate locations at the same exact time. You gotta be kidding me. For a split second, I believed the Grand Canyon had chosen this moment to unleash its judgment on us all. As soon as this preposterous idea passed, I got to work.

A ranger-medic arrived at Mojave Point to see a bystander performing CPR on a German national hit by a bolt of lightning. The medic found a pulse, but the man was not breathing. The second victim, a young woman, was alive but had burns over 10 percent of her body. Rangers initiated lifesaving measures, and the man started breathing again. One helicopter transported the victims to the hospital in Flagstaff. Both were released the next day.

A second helicopter flew me and another ranger prepared for a swiftwater rescue to Phantom Ranch. On the flight in, I took an imaginary black marker to the whiteboard in my brain and in big, bold letters wrote, *Note to self: Never doubt the premonitions of Bryan Wisher!* This time the canyon had staked its claim just as Bryan saw it coming. Three people were hiking down Phantom Creek when a flash flood washed them down the canyon to Bright Angel Creek. One of the victims crawled out of the creek, ran down to Phantom Ranch, and called for help. The other two hikers remained missing.

After the helicopter dropped me off at Phantom Ranch, I briefly met the survivor inside the ranger station. I saw a beaten man. He was scratched, bleeding, and covered with pinkish mud. The mud was plastered to his face and caked in his hair. I could tell he knew his companions were dead. His expression was so pitiful. If I thought about it for one more second, I wouldn't be able to do my job. I had to pull myself together. I had to coordinate search efforts for the other two victims. I had to get all the other campers to high ground because the water level was rising.

Four days after the flood, we had not found the bodies. A relative of the victims called for an update on the search efforts. I was articulate when explaining how the search was going and when it might be discontinued. I was honest and professional when revealing that sometimes in these situations, the bodies were found weeks later, if at all. But when it came to what this family member really needed from me, an ability to provide some small measure of comfort, I was woefully inept.

The woman's body turned up the next day, five days after the flood and forty-seven miles downriver from the point she was last seen. Bryan Wisher participated in the recovery mission, which involved a short-haul extraction by helicopter. For some inexplicable reason, for some bizarre disaster-induced insanity, I had to be there when the helicopter set down its netted load at the helibase. I had to see for myself. I had to compare. I asked Bryan to unzip the body bag. He must have thought I was morbid or nuts or both, but I was his boss so he complied with my request. It made no sense, but what I saw helped me cope. In contrast to what I had seen in the tepid tributary below Antelope Canyon, the Colorado River had been kind. Over the last five days the frigid waters below Glen Canyon dam had firmed the woman's flesh and polished it smooth, lending her skin the appearance of white marble.

Two weeks later the second body was found.

Not long after, in October, Bryan Wisher and I reported to the helibase late in the afternoon. A hiker had fallen while trekking from one gorgeous waterfall to another in Havasu Canyon. The accident occurred inside the Havasupai Indian Reservation. The reservation was outside the park boundaries, but we handled emergencies there whenever requested. Usually when we responded to Havasu, it was because the case was clearly a dire situation. In this instance the hiker had a fractured pelvis, a bleeding head injury, and an altered mental status.

I have jumped into a helicopter bound for the inner canyon so many times I've lost count. Yet each rescue flight was a singular thrill. The eagle's perspective. The artist's palette of colors outside my window. The roller-coaster descent into the dark heart of the inner gorge. The urgent nature of my work. The suspense. What waits for me at my destination? How will I handle it? Can I turn this cliffhanger into a happy ending? Or will this be another damn fatality? And why in God's name did I drink that coffee? Will I be able to hold it until the pilot lands?

Bryan and I pondered such thoughts during our long flight across the Coconino Plateau. Once we reached Havasu, the pilot dropped us below the rim and flew up the canyon. The scenery passing under us would satisfy anyone's Disneyland-esque fantasy—a turquoise river interrupted by misty waterfalls cascading over hidden caves and crashing into luxurious pools of blue-green water. But we had no time to slow down for the view. Our NPS pilot, Jerry Bonner, was in a race against the sunset. Pumpkin Time would ground him if he didn't lift off as soon as we stepped out of his aircraft.

We referred to our helicopter as "the ship." The phrase subconsciously symbolized how our helicopter could be a ranger's lifeboat in the immense and rowdy sea that is the Grand Canyon. The NPS pilots brought us help and home, and we adored them. I'm not sure how they felt about us. Pilots are legendary for their consistent heart rates and unruffled voices. But I imagine our pilots hated every time they had to abandon their rangers in the wilderness, casting us adrift with a patient who might die before daybreak.

Fortunately, the Havasu mission allowed us to resort to Plan B. Unfortunately, our patient's reported injuries were critical enough to justify the extreme risk. Plan B, when used, required a pilot to land a helicopter in a tight and treacherous canyon, in the dark, with the aid of night vision goggles.

Motivated by our patient's critical condition, Bryan and I worked efficiently. I pushed ahead to the accident scene while my partner tossed his radio and flashlight to an intelligent-looking bystander and told him to direct the next helicopter to the same landing spot. "Shine the light at the ground, not the aircraft," Bryan instructed, "or you will blind the pilot." A quarter mile upstream we found the victim at the bottom of a thirty-foot escarpment. Bryan dug out supplies and started an IV. I assessed the patient, placed a collar on his neck to protect his cervical spine, and put him on oxygen. The young hiker mumbled the same questions over and over. His hair was sticky from blood, and I felt a crunchy sensation when I palpated his hip. We secured the hiker's legs and pelvis in a vacuum splint, strapped him to a backboard, and commandeered our bystanders to help us carry him back to the helicopter landing zone.

The disappointment and frustration inherent when diverse personalities perform critical work under dynamic circumstances was absent from this rescue. The mission flowed smoothly and ended triumphantly, like a well-rehearsed dance performed by partners who are fond of each other. We were approaching the landing zone as the state helicopter arrived. The Arizona Department of Public Safety (DPS) medic was surprised to see that all his work had been done for him. We had his patient medically stabilized, packaged, and ready to be loaded into the helicopter. This one was going to be cake. They'd be out of this canyon within minutes. With a smile the DPS medic put his radio to his mouth. "Keep your rotors turning," he told his pilot. "The National Park Service is here."

Once the state helicopter was off to the Flagstaff hospital, Bryan and I searched for a nice spot to bivy for the night.

A companion of the injured man approached us. The hiker was the friendly sort. He looked and spoke like a pot-smoking, surfer dude. "Hey, rangers," he said. "I'm like totally starving." He eyed our packs. "You guys wouldn't have something to eat in there, would ya?" We tossed him most of the MREs (Meals Ready to Eat) and sports bars we had. The stoner was beside himself with gratitude. "You park rangers are awesome, man!" he exclaimed. And that night I believed it.

The best part of the day was when we laid our exhausted bodies down on the warm sand beside the warm water and inhaled the sweet desert air. I fell asleep in the middle of Bryan doing his best to educate me on the constellations. The next morning the NPS pilot, Tom Caldwell, picked us up for our long and scenic flight back to the South Rim.

Bryan Wisher agreed. The Havasu mission was the loveliest rescue of our entire careers. But saving lives at the Grand Canyon was like pushing a wheelbarrow filled with precious stones up a steep and bumpy trail. I had been home less than an hour and was drying off from my desperately needed shower when a man collapsed from a heart attack while hiking the North Kaibab Trail. This news infuriated me. A special agent phoned to tell me that another fatality had occurred in my district; I nearly hung up on him.

I'm not proud of how impatient and frustrated I became during my last years as a ranger. Sure, I did a few wonderful things. I protected woods and wildlife from poachers, destructive use, and fire. Brought some bad guys to justice. Saved a few lives. Carried live rattlesnakes away from campgrounds, transported sick pelicans to rehab centers, and coaxed bear cubs out of dumpsters. Changed a bunch of flat tires, resolved a few marital disputes, and helped scores of tourists who locked their keys in their cars. But you can't derive much joy over your good deeds when brooding about all the times you felt incompetent or acted like a jerk.

* * *

The first federal employee to see the Grand Canyon was Lt. Joseph Ives. Sent by the U.S. Army to explore the area in 1857, Ives returned to Washington and submitted his official report to the U.S. Senate. In this report the Army lieutenant compared his first trek into the "Big Cañon of the Colorado" to entering the portals of "the infernal regions." Ives wrote that when he and his men entered the canyon for the first time, they heard harsh screams and imagined that apparitions of goblinlike figures were perched in the hollows of the impending cliffs.

I'm not sure what it is about the Grand Canyon that unsettles me more, the park's indifference to humanity or its stark reflection of my own duality. Like Lieutenant Ives did in 1857, I, too, have heard "harsh screams" while hiking in the canyon. But when I looked up, there were hawks soaring overhead. Any gargoyles I imagined peering down on me from the sandstone ledges were probably the contented ghosts of the Anasazi, revisiting their ancient food caches. And where I had begun to see a chaotic abyss filled with death and violence, young rangers like Cale Shaffer saw the beauty of God's creation and opportunities to save lives. Yet when people ask me to name my favorite national park, I never hesitate; although my relationship with the Grand Canyon will always be a peculiar affair.

* * *

A month after the Havasu mission, I hiked down the South Kaibab Trail after putting in a full day at the office. The late start had me yearning for my backcountry home—the ranger station—where a meal, a bottle of wine, and a bed awaited me. Descending the switchbacks below Cedar Ridge, I saw bright splotches of blood on the sandy boulders alongside the trail. I figured the blood must be from a hiker's high-elevation-induced nosebleed. As I continued hiking I saw more and more drops of fresh blood, which were getting larger and larger. This was some nosebleed. Right then, a hiker ran up the trail to meet me. Panting with excitement, the man pointed to the switchbacks below us and said, "There's a severed ear on the trail down there!"

I was more miffed than shocked. A friggin' severed ear. How do you like that? The paperwork alone was going to take hours. Forget the fettuccini. Forget the Cabernet. Forget the cushy bed. Your night off has officially been fucked.

"Hey, ranger," the hiker tapped me on the shoulder. "Did you hear what I said? There's a six-point deer on the trail down there!" He lifted up his camera. "I got an excellent picture of it."

The poor guy. He had no idea. The only response the grim-faced lady ranger could give him was better left unspoken. Something was seriously wrong with me.

23

PINE PIGS

On the South Kaibab Trail, six tough miles from the nearest road, the night skies were black. Until a rescue helicopter could fly in at dawn, I was on my own. I poured orange Gatorade powder onto a saltine cracker and held it to my patient's lips.

"But I'm thirsty!" she said.

"Salt is what you need, ma'am, not water." I was under the impression that my fifty-two-year-old patient and her daughter didn't like me. If so, I understood why. I despised my stiff, patronizing tone as much as they did. Still, the ill hiker desperately needed my help. She nibbled on the cracker and, to my relief, was able to keep it down. When I tested the woman's blood sodium, my portable machine had blinked up a shocking number. Maybe this seemingly perverse snack would balance out the woman's electrolytes and we would get through the night without her seizing on me.

Sometime after midnight my patient said, "I need to pee. Right now!" She didn't have the strength to walk or stand. Her daughter and I lifted her 180-pound body by the arms so that she could lean backward over a ditch alongside the trail. She let loose her bladder and the fluid splashed off the sandstone, showering my calves and hiking boots with urine. But I was delighted to see all the excess water leaving the woman's body.

Once my patient fell asleep, I turned off my headlamp to conserve the battery. Northern Arizona's clear skies had made it easy to pick out the fuzzy tail of Hale-Bopp. This comet had kept me company on many all-nighters during the spring of 1997. (I had worked mostly twelve-plus-hour shifts for the entire month of March without a day off.) I pulled my knees to my chest and leaned back against a sandstone boulder. I was going to rest my eyes. Just for a minute. Around 3:30 a.m. I awoke with a jolt. My patient was snoring. I had dozed off long enough to dream of a crashing helicopter and mauling grizzlies.

By dawn the woman felt better. She asked me if she could apply lipstick before she met the rescue pilot. "Sure," I said, "why not?" It had been a long night. We were covered in dust and smelled of urine. Lipstick might be just what the doctor ordered.

After breakfast and a shower at my house on the rim, I put in a full day at the office, catching up with my administrative duties as the Corridor district ranger. Among the many supervisory tasks on my list was a closed-door session with Cale Shaffer. The other PSAR rangers had complained. Cale's high expectations of them were a pain in the ass. I advised Cale to pull back and let his peers fend for themselves. If they were slacking off, I would see it.

Cale had disappointed himself, believing that he'd let me down, and it showed. This broke my heart. The whole thing was my fault. I had placed more responsibility on his shoulders because I had so much faith in him. Though I did my best to act impartial, it must have been obvious to everyone but Cale. He was my favorite temporary ranger. All my permanent employees, especially Bryan Wisher, treated Cale like a beloved mascot, and my superiors adored the newbie nearly as much as I did.

Surely his peers were jealous. Packed into Cale's tight little body were enough brains, brawn, and work ethic for five rangers. His sincere smile and compassionate demeanor had even the most stressed-out park visitors eating out of his hand. By luck or fate, I had hired the perfect ranger, one with an idealism that appeared bulletproof. But this backstabbing business from his peers worried me. Could the Grand Canyon turn a guy like Cale into an asshole like it had the rest of us?

Later, Mary Litell Hinson phoned me at the office. It was great to hear her voice. I had missed my hyper, goofball, adrenaline-addicted employee since she had left the canyon last December. Mary transferred to Yosemite as soon as her husband was hired on there. That was four months ago. Today Mary had called to confess.

"I'm pregnant," she whispered, "but don't you dare tell a soul." Mary wanted to keep her pregnancy a secret because she believed her superiors would confiscate her gun and law enforcement credentials. Yosemite managers had done this in the past, once they discovered a female ranger was knocked up.

"It's going to become obvious to them at some point," I told her.

"I can still work," Mary said. "I'll wear a shoulder holster."

That night, when I finally settled in for a good night's sleep, it had been thirty-nine hours since I'd seen a bed. After two delicious hours of unconsciousness, the phone rang. The dispatcher directed me to the booking jail—a small cinderblock building where rangers processed prisoners before taking them to a county facility in Flagstaff. Inside, I reported to the arresting ranger, Chris Fors, who was completing his paperwork. Through the bars of their holding cells, three intoxicated Park Service employees yelled their obscene protests.

"Come on and get me you fucking ranger," they taunted. "Yeah, I assaulted that security guard, but the fat power freak deserved it. I'm going to sue. I'm going to have your job! You gung-ho motherfucker."

Chris and another ranger worked silently inside the cramped booking room. The other ranger was Chris's roommate, and they weren't speaking, on or off duty. Their spat began when Chris asked out a dispatcher the other ranger had dated weeks earlier.

The roommate told him you shouldn't date your friends' ex-girlfriends. Problem was, in a western national park, when it came to romance the gender ratio was often in a woman's favor. Chris argued that under the circumstances, if you were going to mount the entire available female population in the park, it didn't leave your "friends" any options. This didn't go over as well as Chris had hoped.

The conflict mushroomed when, after a few too many post-shift beers, Chris left numerous inebriated 3:00 a.m. "cat-calls" on their answering machine while the other ranger was trying to sleep. The roommate was creative in his retribution. When Chris returned from his booze-fest early that morning, he couldn't use his toilet because the other ranger had pulled the mattress out from Chris's bedroom and stuffed it in the bathroom.

The cursing drunks and feuding roommates injected more hostility into the booking room than I could tolerate after only two hours' sleep. I suggested that Chris leave while the other ranger and I took the prisoners' mug shots and got their fingerprints. "You rangers are nothing but a bunch of fucking pigs!" one of the drunks screamed at Chris as he stepped outside. In case I believed I was somehow excluded from this insult, the drunk added, "You, too, Andy."

When we were done, I walked over to the adjacent office to retrieve Chris so that he and I could transport the prisoners to a jail in Flagstaff. Chris sat at the desk where he was supposed to be filling in all the tedious blanks on all the tedious federal forms. Instead of completing his paperwork, the ranger had his hands flat on the desktop as he stared at a wall less than three feet in front of him. Although he was inside, away from public view, Chris still wore his Smokey Bear, which was weird. The ranger hat is nothing if not iconic, but it gives you a headache when worn longer than twenty minutes. I had heard the rumors: arguments with supervisors; fights with girlfriends; all-night drinking binges; flashlights hurled across parking lots. People said Chris was losing it, and here I had found him wearing his flat hat indoors and in an apparent catatonic state.

"Hey, Chris," I said, carefully. "We're ready."

Chris kept his eyes on the cinderblock wall in front of him. After a worrisome delay he spoke. "I hate this fucking job."

During our ninety-mile drive to Flagstaff, Chris turned the commercial radio volume all the way up. The music softened the tequila-powered personal attacks the three men in the backseat were hurling at us. We dumped off our glaring burdens at the county jail. Then we slid into a booth inside the only restaurant open at 3:00 a.m. Before our omelets arrived, Chris brought forth his troubles and wrung them out in front of me.

Chris had ambitions. He got a master's degree because he wanted to be a superintendent some day. But those dreams were crumbling almost as fast as the sandstone foundation of the ranger station. Recently they had given away a job he desperately wanted—a supervisory position at Yellowstone—to someone Chris felt was less qualified, and he was carrying around this disappointment like a man diagnosed with a mass in his liver. "If I don't escape the Grand Canyon soon," he said, "the park is going to kill me."

As much as Chris bemoaned his stagnant career, his romantic life fared no better. A year ago he had broken up with the blond from grad school, and now the state of Arizona was experiencing a drought of women willing to date shell-shocked park rangers who lived in singlewide trailers occupied by bats and shared with moody roommates. If he was going to turn his life around, he needed a job that paid well. He needed a job that earned him some respect. He needed a job that allowed him to own a house and please a wife. He needed a job that brought him home each night. He needed a job that didn't give him nightmares. He needed a job that was so safe and secure it bordered on boring. So, Chris confided in me, the park ranger had made a bold career move. He had filled out a job application and mailed it to the FBI.

24

DANGEROUS TYPES

It was a gorgeous Sierra day—a warm October afternoon. Showy milkweeds cast their feathered seeds.
into fall breezes. Red-winged blackbirds bobbed up and down
on yellowing blades of grass. Rainbow trout gorged themselves
on insects floating down gurgling streams. A hundred and fifty
people, some carrying banners and flags, stood at the edges of a
meadow below El Capitan and chanted, "It's our park too!" and
"Let them jump!"

A few Yosemite locals among the increasing crowd heckled
the park rangers who were doing their best to keep traffic flowing.
Families on the way to campgrounds and hotels saw the people
and the media cameras. They pulled their campers and rental cars
off to the side of the road to determine the cause of all this excitement. "What's going on?" they asked. Someone pointed to the
top of El Capitan and said, "A woman is about to jump off that
mountain."

Park ranger Mary Litell Hinson was somewhat relaxed. The
protest was going so smoothly. Three jumps down, just two more
to go. Then the last BASE jumper would be on the ground; all the
protestors and looky-loos would head for their hotel rooms, campsites, or bar stools; and the deer and the red-winged blackbirds
could have their meadow back. Months ago Mary had become

the ranger in charge of the Valley day shift, a shift of park rangers responsible for patrolling one of the busiest national parks in the world. She was the first female in this job, and 1999 had been one of the park's busiest years on record. Despite the heckling from the protestors, Mary viewed this event, watching the rainbow-colored parachutes float down to the meadow, as a pleasant diversion from her normal duties.

The first two jumpers were cool, but the third one, a dentist from Indiana, let loose with the "Nazi Punk Service" rhetoric when Mary handcuffed him. *Give me a break,* the ranger thought. *What does he think this is— Tiananmen Square?* Then someone told her the next jumper was a woman. Mary handed the dentist over to the nearest male ranger before walking into the meadow to wait for the next jump.

On top of El Capitan, Jan Davis counted three-two-one and then ran off the New Dawn "diving board"—an overhanging rock that served as the perfect launch point for jumping off a cliff. Someone caught the moment in a photograph. Davis wore a black-and-white-striped body suit. Her parody of a prisoner's uniform was a joke on the rangers waiting to arrest her at the bottom. Arms outstretched, blond hair blown by the wind, Davis flew out over a spectacular view of Yosemite Valley. It was a flawless jump. She was smiling.

Three thousand feet below the top, journalists, a Park Service employee, and Davis's boyfriend, Tom Sanders, were filming the event. In the film, the BASE jumper's body is an anonymous black figure in contrast to the light-gray granite of El Capitan. Two seconds went by. Davis twisted in the air, wiggling in an apparent attempt to reach her parachute cord. Another second went by. Then another. Everyone was excited. A woman had jumped. "Yeah!" The crowd whistled and cheered. "Whoo-hoo! Go baby!"

Five seconds had now gone by since Davis stepped off El Capitan, and the ranger wasn't cheering. Over the crowd noise, Mary heard Davis gaining velocity as she plunged toward the earth at a speed of more than one hundred miles per hour. The wind whipping at Davis's clothes sounded like someone thumbing through a deck of cards, only louder. Much louder. It was a sound Mary would never forget—the terrible *flut-flut-fluttering* sound made by a human body in free fall.

* * *

Immediately after Mary jumped off her first bridge, she thought she had killed herself. Within two seconds the rope caught her, and the relief was euphoric. She swung back and forth in the darkness until the pendulum motion stopped. Then she climbed back up the rope to her boyfriend, who grinned at her and said, "I saw the fear in your eyes!" Mary's fear seemed to excite the man, but he must have also been relieved. Because Mary had developed a reputation for being fearless, and there is something unsettling about a woman who has no fear.

People said that Jan Davis was a woman who had no fear. People said that after her first husband died of an accidental overdose of blood pressure medications, Davis had developed a death wish. Others said that Jan Davis was a risk taker. She knew how to celebrate life. And some said that Jan Davis was an idiot. There is one thing about which most agreed. Even at fifty-eight, Jan Davis was a pretty hot babe.

"I believe life is about action and passion, and you can't truly begin to live life until you overcome your fear of dying," Davis said. She lived to jump off things; and her boyfriend, extreme photographer Tom Sanders, loved to film her doing it. She jumped off the world's tallest waterfall, earning her the title "the first lady of Angel Falls." She jumped from an airplane wearing lacy red lingerie, high heels, and a parachute. She chronicled many of her BASE jumping adventures in a children's book.

* * *

The differences between bridge jumping, rope jumping, bungee jumping, skydiving, and BASE jumping may seem subtle to those who would never consider stepping off anything higher than a sidewalk curb, but the risks associated with each of these sports are not the same. Rock climbers and rescue rangers like Mary place a lot of faith in their ropes and anchors. "In Gear I Trust," was Mary's motto, and if it were not for her faith in a climbing rope's ability to stop her fall, she would have never have walked on that bridge, climbed over the metal railing, checked her harness, tugged the rope, looked at the rocky river bottom below, counted one-two-three, and let go.

"BASE" is an acronym for buildings, antennas, spans (bridges), and earth (cliffs). These are the four things other than an airplane that you can leap from with a parachute strapped to your back and survive. Considered by many to be the most extreme of all extreme sports, BASE jumping is more dangerous than skydiving because there is less room for error. Sky divers typically have thousands of feet to fall and almost an entire minute of time before they must find and pull the cord that lets loose their lifesaving parachute. If the main chute malfunctions, sky divers often carry a reserve chute that gives them a second chance to avoid becoming a pancake. In contrast, depending on the height of the jump, a BASE jumper only has three to ten seconds of free fall before she must pull her chute. Pull too soon, and she slams into the cliff wall. Pull too late, and she's made her last jump. Two seconds to clear the wall and two to eight seconds to pull her chute does not leave a BASE jumper much room for error. The sport is illegal in many places. This adds to the excitement—especially in Yosemite, where the rangers aggressively enforce the rules.

* * *

During Mary's bridge-jumping days—back when she was single, childless, and working at the recycle stand—she hung out with a few Yosemite BASE jumpers. For them eluding the authorities was a game of cat and mouse. A game played at dusk, dawn, or by the light of a full moon. A game centered on El Capitan.

When standing on top of El Cap, you are 7,569 feet above sea level. The largest granite monolith in the world offers an inspiring view of many High Sierra peaks. To the southwest is the Leaning Tower. Half Dome lies to the east. If you venture down the rocky slab and then crawl on your hands and knees to the very edge, you can peer over a sheer vertical drop of three thousand feet. In comparison, the dizzying view from a New York skyscraper isn't so imposing. If you put a clone of the Empire State Building on top of the original and then climbed to the top of the second building, you still would not be as high off the ground as you are when you stand atop El Capitan. For the thrill-seeking BASE jumper, El Cap's dare is impossible to resist.

Five years before she became a ranger, Mary knew a military guy who BASE jumped off El Cap. The military guy loaned his support crew infrared night vision goggles and two-way radios before he had them drop him off at the trail leading to the top. Then the support crew drove back down to the meadow and, with the aid of their high-tech toys, kept a lookout for park rangers. Sitting in the grass that night to watch, Mary heard the sound—the horrible flapping sound of a BASE jumper in free fall. The sound scared her. Right then and there she decided that although she loved rock climbing and enjoyed jumping off bridges, there was no way in hell she was doing that!

A few seconds later came a loud *ka-pow*—a noise many compare to a rifle shot. Mary described it as sounding more like a giant umbrella being forced open by a gust of wind. This was followed by a chorus of "Whoo-hoos" as the jumper floated down to the meadow. Within seconds of landing, the jumper gathered up his chute, sprinted for the getaway van, and dived in. The support crew slammed the door and the driver sped off—but not too quickly. The last thing you want is to have a ranger pull you over

for speeding when you have a parachute billowing in the back of
your van.

* * *

Since she knew how BASE jumpers eluded the authorities, Mary
turned out to be exceptionally good at catching them after she
became a ranger. In fact, she'd only been a ranger for a couple of
months when she caught her first.

After receiving a tip, a shift supervisor assigned Mary and
ranger Lane Baker to surveillance beneath El Cap. In "plain
clothes," the women spent the last hours of daylight hanging out
in the meadow. Pretending to be tourists got real boring, real fast.
They were about to call it a night when Mary heard the fluttering
sound. "We've got a jumper," she yelled to Baker. The women ran
toward the center of the meadow. *Ka-pow!* There went the chute. It
was dusk, but Mary could see the jumper as he glided down. "Park
ranger!" she yelled, pointing her finger at him. "You're busted."

As soon as he hit the meadow, the jumper dumped his chute
and took off for the forest. Mary and Baker were on him like two
hounds on a hare. Now it was full-on dark. If it weren't for the
occasional headlights from cars driving down South Side Drive,
Mary wouldn't have been able to see the jumper well enough to
chase him. Afraid she was about to lose her man, she shouted,
"Stop! You're surrounded." It was a lie, but it worked. The jumper
halted short of the Merced River, and Baker pounced on him. Mary
watched her partner straddle the guy's back and cuff him. Then
the women exchanged high-fives above their quarry. Two Valley
Girls had captured a BASE jumper—all on their own. The guys
would be jealous. While Mary broke into a brief victory dance, the
jumper whined. Caught by two chicks! "If my buddies hear about
this," he said, "I'll never live it down."

* * *

Although she had befriended BASE jumpers in the past, once Mary became a ranger she suffered no inner conflicts with her switch in loyalties. BASE jumping is against the law. If you're willing to do the crime, you should be willing to do the time. That's how the game works.

Frank Gambalie III played the game. He had BASE jumped more than two hundred times and enjoyed the company of other risk takers, such as Dan Osman. Also known as "the Master of Gravity," Osman pushed the limits. He free-soloed (rock climbing without the safety of ropes). He had been arrested for cocaine possession, and in 1998 he was spending a lot of time jumping off cliffs. But not with a parachute. Osman wanted more time in the air, and he could achieve a longer free fall by cliff-jumping while attached to ropes.

Osman wanted to break his own rope-jumping distance record by jumping from the top of a Yosemite spire known as the Leaning Tower. After making several successful leaps, Osman left his anchor/rope system set up on the Tower between jumps. One day, two rangers hiked up to see if some sort of violation was transpiring atop the Leaning Tower. The rangers inspected Osman's anchor system, but they couldn't find any language in the regulation books that prohibited people from jumping off cliffs while attached to ropes, so they left the system the way they found it.

A couple of days later, sometime during the evening of November 22, 1998, Dan Osman used his cell phone to call Frank Gambalie III. He told Gambalie that he was going for the record books—1,110 feet and eleven seconds of free fall. Another friend, on top of Leaning Tower with Osman, watched the record-breaking jump. The friend heard the sound of a rope cutting through the air. Then he heard Osman scream just before he crashed through the trees. Then silence. This time, gravity was the master.

The cause of the system failure remains controversial. One independent expert in rope mechanics inspected the rope and concluded that Osman's rope failed because it had rubbed against itself during the long free fall, which had caused the rope to burn through and break. Mary believed Osman's anchor system failed because it had been left out in the inclement weather for too many days. Or perhaps it happened because Osman had used a hammer to loosen a tight knot. Some accused the rangers of killing Osman, suggesting that the rangers had messed with Osman's anchor system the day they inspected the ropes.

Osman's death did not stop Frank Gambalie III from jumping off El Cap seven months later, on June 9, 1999. When Gambalie hit the meadow, a ranger was waiting for him. The ranger yelled at Gambalie to stop, he was under arrest. Gambalie released the chute canopy from his chest harness with a flick of his hands. Then he turned to the ranger and smiled. The race was on.

The ranger and Gambalie ran over the meadow and into the woods, jumping logs and weaving through trees. The ranger was gaining on Gambalie as they approached the Merced River. Fed by snowmelt from the high elevations, the Merced ran at dangerously high levels. Gambalie had dumped his chute in the meadow, so it was already lost, but there was the $2,000 fine and the issue of who wins the game. Gambalie considered the raging rapids of the Merced as he stood at its edge. Stuck between a frigid, swollen river and a handcuffs-wielding ranger, Gambalie chose the river. He jumped into the water and was immediately carried away by the current. The ranger knew better than to jump in after him.

The Merced held on to Gambalie's body for twenty-nine days.

Voices in the BASE jumping community blamed the rangers for Gambalie's death. To them, the Park Service's overrestrictive regulations and overzealous law enforcement had forced Gambalie to take drastic measures to avoid getting caught. If BASE jumping were legal, they argued, Gambalie would be alive. To these critics, it had only been seven months since Osman's death and the rangers once again had blood on their hands. "Enough is enough," they said. "It's time we did something about this. It's time we fought for our rights. It's time we organized a protest."

One BASE activist went so far as to compare their cause to the civil rights movement.

Calls for a protest on a BASE Web site unsettled Park Service officials. If there was going to be a large-scale demonstration, the NPS wanted it to be controlled. An NPS special agent contacted a BASE jumping activist. The activist agreed to cooperate during the protest as long as the rangers promised to wait until after the protest jumps were completed before they arrested anyone. Then the jumpers would willingly surrender to the rangers waiting for them at the bottom, where they would be cuffed, searched, and have their chutes confiscated. Later the protestors would appear in court to fight the criminal charges against them. Five would jump—four men and one woman. The event was planned for Friday, October 22, 1999. It turned out to be a perfect Indian summer day. Jan Davis was jumper number four.

* * *

At a conservative point in her jump Jan Davis reached with her right hand for the small of her back, the normal position of a BOC—"bottom of container"—style pilot chute. When pulled from its pouch, the BOC catches air and then pulls out the main canopy. A video recording of the jump indicates that after Davis failed to find the chute cord with her right hand, she reached with her left. Then she reached with both hands at once. Then she glanced over her right shoulder, perhaps to look for the chute cord that she expected to be at the small of her back.

Davis's pilot chute wasn't at the small of her back. It was on her thigh. Not wanting to give up her own chute to the rangers, she had borrowed equipment for this protest jump. Unlike her own equipment, the borrowed chute had a thigh-mounted pilot chute.

Twelve seconds had passed since Davis had stepped off El Capitan. Instead of "Go baby go," the crowd was now chanting "Open, open, open."

Thirteen seconds. Jan Davis fell at a rate approaching 120 miles per hour.

Fourteen seconds. Fifteen seconds. Jan Davis had both her hands at her sides, putting her body in what sky divers call "the boxman position"—a belly-to-ground position ideal for free falling.

Sixteen seconds. Seventeen seconds. Davis rolled slightly to the left.

Eighteen seconds. She covered her face with both hands.

Nineteen seconds. Mary Hinson and a crowd of more than 150 spectators heard what sounded like an explosion. The ground shuddered. There was a brief moment of silence before a car alarm went off. The irritating honks and wails pierced the air. In her peripheral vision, Mary saw Davis's boyfriend slumped over his video camera. A child began to cry.

Mary ran to the ambulance and climbed into the back. She dug through the packs until she found the heavy-duty rubber gloves. Then she ran to the impact site. When she saw the blond hair, Mary thought, *This isn't so bad.* Then she looked down. She was standing in fat. She looked up. Body tissue hung in the trees. It was a mess, and now somebody had to clean it up. The spandex suit that Davis wore as a joke had kept her legs intact so that a pair of black-and-white-striped legs stuck out from the two-foot-deep crater the impact had made in the decomposed granite. The mind of the special agent on the scene produced an unavoidable comparison. The black-and-white-striped legs reminded him of the *Wizard of Oz,* when the Wicked Witch of the East was flattened by Dorothy's tornado-tossed house.

Mary had never felt comfortable with body recoveries. This time, as she worked, she worried about the young rangers and volunteers participating in the day's mission. She worried about Davis's family. She worried about the park visitors who saw what happened. And she worried about her agency, the National Park Service. What would people say? *We permitted this, didn't we?*

25

THANKSGIVING LEDGE

The day Jan Davis hit the rocks, Jim Fisher and Scott Earnest were anchored into the side of El Capitan, ascending a route called "Lurking Fear." The climbers heard sirens echoing off the valley walls and saw fire trucks parked on the roadside along the meadow, but they had no clue that a woman had performed her last free dive off the very mountain they were climbing. Five days later—on day eight of what was supposed to be a six-day climb—Earnest, a twenty-seven-year-old from Colorado, fell seventy feet while leading the last pitch. Fisher heard crunching and snapping as his climbing partner hit a bulge in the cliff and went "rag doll" limp. Fisher believed he had just watched his friend die.

Fisher unclipped from his anchor in the granite 2,000 feet above the valley floor to reach his injured partner. It was no easy feat. Earnest was hanging upside down, bleeding profusely, and mumbling incoherently. His helmet was in two pieces, but he was alive. With care, Fisher lowered his partner down to the Thanksgiving Ledge, a shelf in the granite the size of a couch. Then he dug a cell phone out of the bottom of his haul bag, and dialed 911.

A dispatcher in his home state of Colorado picked up, and Fisher explained the situation. She transferred him to a 911 dispatcher in California, and Fisher explained the situation again. The California dispatcher transferred him to a dispatcher in Yosemite National Park, and Fisher explained the situation a third time. At 4:30 p.m., when the NPS dispatcher transferred Fisher's call to a park ranger at the rescue cache, the cell phone's low battery alarm started to beep.

At 5:00 p.m. on October 27, 1999, Mary Hinson stood in El Cap meadow once again. The nice weather from five days ago had retreated, leaving in its wake a bruised sky and a winter storm warning in effect for the evening. The setting sun gave the Yosemite search and rescue (SAR) team only one hour to get a six-member rescue team to the top of El Cap and two heli-rappel rangers to the injured climber.

On a short-haul operation, a rescuer is attached to the end of a rope connected to a helicopter and transported to a desired location. On a heli-rappel, the pilot maneuvers the ship to an accident scene and the rescuer rappels down the length of the rope to the victim. Mary preferred heli-rappel to short-haul because heli-rappelling gave the rescuer the illusion that she was in control of her destiny. But most rescue experts believe heli-rappelling is more dangerous than short-haul insertions because heli-rappelling requires more concentration from the rescuer.

During a heli-rappel, rescuer errors can be deadly. A heli-rappeler's clothing or equipment may snag in her rappelling device, stranding her midrope. Worse, if the heli-rappeler hits a rock and loses consciousness, she may loose control of her brake hand and zip all the way off the end of the rope. Or if she becomes entangled in a tree, the helicopter pilot may be forced to "pickle" (release the weight of) his human load to avoid crashing.

Wearing a green flight suit and a white helmet, Mary walked through the grass to where her husband held the hand of their two-year-old son. Mary hugged and kissed her family before she climbed into the helicopter. Several times that summer, Mary's husband had brought their son out to watch his mother take off in the helicopter. On an earlier rescue mission, they were observing the operation when Mary's husband overheard a group of tourists talking about the brave "men" performing the rescue on El Cap. When someone said, "How can that guy do that?" he couldn't hold back any longer. "That guy," he told them, "is my wife."

"Wow," the tourist replied, with a glance at Mary's son. "How do you feel about that?"

Mary's husband was proud of her. He supported his wife's career "100 percent." However, not too long before the Thanksgiving Ledge incident, Mary was heading out the door to another rescue while his wife's sister was visiting. That day he admitted to his sister-in-law, "I wish she'd quit doing this."

The rescue pilot started his engine and the rotors began to turn. The chief ranger walked out to the helicopter. "We need to find you another job," he said to Mary. "A mother shouldn't be doing this kind of work." Keith Lober was also on this mission. He had a wife and a stepson, but the chief directed his concerns only to the female ranger.

Mary wasn't sure how to take this. Did he view Lober's life as more expendable? Was this some misguided form of chivalry? Or was he thinking she couldn't keep her wits about her because she's a mother? Did this mean that, after all these years of proving herself worthy, she was still a "test case"?

Regardless of the intentions behind the chief ranger's comment, it messed with Mary's head. Something bad was going to happen. She grabbed Lober by his flight suit, pulled him closer, and yelled over the helicopter noise. "It's windy. It's late. We're rushing. These are not ideal conditions."

Lober said, "We're going for it."

* * *

Inside the helicopter Mary and Lober did their "buddy checks." Ear protection? Check. Eye protection? Check. Fire-resistant flight suits zipped and collars turned up? Check. Sleeves down and gloves on? Check. Pants down over leather boots? Check. Radios operational and secured in chest harnesses? Check. Climbing harnesses tight, with the straps followed back through the buckle? Check. Rope-cutting knives within easy reach? Check.

Buddy checks were now an intimate routine between Mary and Lober, like a husband zipping up his wife's dress after she straightens his tie. This was the fourth heli-rappel rescue these two rangers had done this year. By now Mary and Lober had worked so many rescue missions together, they could almost read each other's minds and finish each other's sentences. Once one of their patients asked, "Are you two married?" and Mary snorted, "God, no!"

"Well," the patient said, "you sure act like it."

If the pilot sneezed, they were all dead. He hovered the helicopter 2,500 feet above the ground. The tips of the rotor blades were within ten feet of solid granite. The rotor noise forced the rescuers to communicate through body language, hand signals, and lip reading. The spotter, a rescuer who remained in the aircraft to assist the heli-rappelers and the pilot, clipped the rope to Lober's rappelling device and released the ranger's seatbelt. Lober stepped down onto one of the helicopter's skids and looked down. Even for Lober, this was not a routine heli-rappel. Later he described this mission as one with "major pucker factor" that was "just plain fucking dangerous!"

Mary tugged on Lober's flight suit to get his attention, but he ignored her. He was too focused on the target, a couch-size ledge 250 feet below them. Mary wanted to stop the rescue. The helicopter blades were too close to the cliff. The chief ranger thought it was too dangerous for a mother. There was a winter storm warning for tonight. The winds were too squirrelly. They were feeling too rushed. As soon as the paramedic-ranger met his partner's eye, Mary dragged her hand across her throat. *Cut the mission!*

What? Lober was about to rappel. *We are already committed.*

No. Mary shook her head. *Let's not do this.*

Under the visor, Lober's lips parted in a maniacal laugh. He had one hand on the rope. With the other hand he waved bye-bye. Then he stepped off the helicopter and disappeared.

The spotter was looking at Mary. *Are you ready?*

The spotter went through the same process of hooking Mary to the rope as he had with Lober. Mary stepped out onto the helicopter skid. She had seen salamis that were larger in diameter than the skid she stood on. In between her legs, the spotter lowered a haul bag containing fifty pounds of climbing gear and medical supplies. The haul bag was attached to her climbing harness. The weight of it was trying to pull her off the skid. It spun violently in the same way Mary would if she slid down the rope.

Of the eight rangers certified to do a heli-rappel in Yosemite, Mary was the only woman. Two years ago, while she was pregnant, they had tried to remove her from the heli-rappel team, but she fought them. Back then heli-rappelling was too much fun for her to give it up because she was pregnant. But now Mary didn't think heli-rappelling was fun. She thought it was going to kill her.

What was it about this one? Was it her son and her husband down in the meadow, watching? Was it because this was the fourth time in six months she had done a hazardous heli-rappel and everybody knows there's only so many times you can get away with doing this kind of stuff? Was it the chief ranger's unsettling remark? Or was it because it had been only five days since she had scraped another woman's body off those very rocks waiting for her 2,500 feet below?

The spotter gave Mary another thumbs up. *You can go anytime now.*

One hand maintained a death grip on the door jam of the helicopter. The other, her brake hand, held the rope behind her back. Mary looked down and saw that her knees were pumping up and down uncontrollably. She had sewing machine legs.

Please, God. If I don't regain control, I'm going to get myself killed.

Mary leaned back and, not unlike a diver from a boat, inverted off the skid and into the air. Immediately she started spinning. The only way to stop the awful twisting was to slide farther down the rope, but her rappel rope was sticking in the device. It would be easier if Lober would pull tension on the rope from the bottom. She looked down at her partner. He was searching for a place to set an anchor. "Grab the fucking rope!" she screamed at him, but Lober couldn't hear her over the helicopter. Once she was a hundred feet down the rope, the rappel became easier. She landed on her back in a manzanita bush. At first she was too dizzy to move. Lober was anchored into the rock now. He made his way over to Mary. "Are you all right?"

"You bastard!" Mary expelled all her tension in Lober's direction.

"What is your problem?"

"Why didn't you grab the end of my rope?" Mary screamed, now more angry than afraid, more motion sick than terrified. "I was spinning out of control, you asshole!"

"Sorry," Lober said. Then he stood there and watched his cursing partner fight to untangle herself from rope and manzanita.

Jim Fisher would later describe the two rangers who "rapped down" to rescue his friend as "consummate professionals." He could tell that Lober, who kept the mood light and made jokes, had been in the rescue business longer. But "the pretty blond" who did the "crazy" heli-rappel appeared confident. Fisher saw no evidence in Mary's demeanor that minutes ago, she had been nearly petrified.

Fisher introduced the rangers to his injured friend, and it was like meeting the Phantom of the Opera. One side of the climber's face was an oozing mosaic of black, fuchsia, and magenta, and a mangled arm dangled at his right side like a pathetic mutation. Lober's primary concern was the possibility of a "closed head brain injury." A bleed trapped inside the patient's skull can put unbearable pressure on brain tissue, causing brain damage and killing the patient within hours—or minutes. If this patient was stuck on El Cap and had what physicians call "walk and die syndrome," saving the climber's life might require a surgeon to direct Lober to bore holes into the patient's skull in order to drain the hematoma and relieve pressure on the brain. Keith Lober was a damn good paramedic, but he'd rather not attempt neurosurgery by proxy while anchored to El Cap during a lightning storm.

Lober grabbed his radio and yelled to the incident commander, "We need to short-haul this patient out of here. Right now!"

"No can do," the incident commander said. The wind was picking up. Dark clouds were approaching. Sunset was five minutes ago. It was pumpkin time. The helicopter was grounded in the meadow. You're on your own. Good luck. Have a nice night.

Lober, Mary, and Jim Fisher quickly moved the injured climber across a sixty-foot traverse to a small alcove (they called it a cave) before the storm hit. Once settled inside, Lober discussed the situation with a doctor over a cell phone. The doctor gave the paramedic orders to start a morphine drip (via an intravenous line) to ease the pain caused by the broken arm. Mary had finished the park medic training program less than a year ago. She begged Lober to let her push the morphine this time. Lober supervised Mary as she drew up the fluid into the syringe and then plunged it into the patient's IV line. Lober instructed her how to titrate the dosage every two hours.

The storm arrived. Wind and rain beat at the tarp the rangers had tied down over the cave entrance. At all times, the rangers remained tethered to anchors crammed in cracks at the back of the alcove. Fisher wrapped a porta-ledge cover around him and sat anchored to a nearby tree outside the cave. Lober got out his backpacker stove and began to boil water. He had brought instant coffee and little containers of Irish Crème–flavored creamer that he had pilfered from the coffee counter in Degnan's Deli. Before too long, he and Mary were downright cozy in that pinched little cave a half mile above the ground. Lober brought his partner a cup of hot coffee and some treats from his food bag. Then he told Mary he was going to teach her something they don't teach you in medic school: The ranger who pushes the morphine is the ranger who stays awake all night to monitor the patient. With that, Lober pushed his backpack into a pillow, laid his head on it, and said, "Good night."

In the morning, the weather broke. The injured climber was short-hauled down to the meadow. At a hospital in Modesto, tests confirmed that Earnest was bleeding in his brain. He also had twelve face fractures, three arm fractures, and two fractures in his foot. But as soon as Earnest healed, he and Fisher were climbing again. In 2001 they reached the summit of Mount McKinley. In 2002 they attempted Mount Everest. However, by 2004 Earnest had stopped climbing. According to Fisher, after the fall Earnest lost his confidence as a climber, along with 50 percent of his ability to taste and smell.

* * *

In 1999 Yosemite park rangers, pilots, firefighters, and volunteers conducted 164 search and rescue missions, recovered twelve bodies, and saved forty-seven lives. The total cost of providing this service to American taxpayers visiting Yosemite was $526,719. This seems quite reasonable when you consider that Congress recently gave the NPS $2.5 million to convert a railroad station into a fancy visitor center in Thurmond, West Virginia—a town with a population of eight.

In the early 1900s Horace Albright, the agency's second director, complained, "Congress has always been stingy with the parks." To Albright's declaration I would add, "And the NPS has always been stingy with the park ranger." Many park employees labor for less than they are due because they work for what they believe is a righteous but cash-strapped federal agency. But when it comes to fleecing American taxpayers to pay for absurd programs, the NPS can shear its fair share of sheep. In Ohio officials at Cuyahoga Valley National Park invested more than $425,000 on a private vineyard and winery. Delaware Water Gap is home to the infamous $333,000 outhouse. Grand Canyon officials have spent millions to build a trainless train station and a Canyon View Information Plaza with no canyon view. Now they are asking for more money ($42.6 million in a 2008 document) to "fix" these failed projects.

Such bloat has critics crying "National Pork Service," while the big park superintendents squeal that too many "pork barrel parks" are feeding from their troughs. In response, agency directors throw the blame at Congress and pray that it sticks. Meanwhile park rangers and other frontline park employees are told to do more and more with less and less. These same employees are sent memos instructing them to avoid using the phrase "budget cuts" and instead say "service level adjustments" when talking to the media or the public.

Only 10 percent of the approximately twenty thousand NPS employees are law enforcement rangers. Park rangers are not the only park employees who risk their lives in the performance of their daily duties. In 1989 a park interpreter fell off a cliff while leading a nature walk in Zion National Park. In June 1995 an avalanche killed a Yosemite bulldozer operator clearing the road for tourist traffic. In 1996 a four-hundred-pound rock killed a Grand Canyon maintenance employee repairing a park trail. In 2007 a NPS wildlife biologist contracted a fatal case of pneumonic plague while conducting a necropsy on a mountain lion.

Nearly all rescue missions put the rescuer at risk of death or injury. Of the 164 Yosemite SAR operations conducted in 1999, two stood out as being extraordinarily dangerous. The first was a heli-rappel on El Cap that was similar to the rescue of Scott Earnest on Thanksgiving Ledge. The other required rangers to rappel down frayed ropes alongside an icy waterfall in the inner gorge of Yosemite Falls. Rangers Mary Litell Hinson and Keith Lober were principal players in both of these hazardous operations.

In 2000 Mary and Lober were awarded two Department of the Interior (DOI) Medals of Valor for displaying "unusual courage" while undergoing a "high degree of personal risk" to save lives during the above incidents. (Lober was awarded a third medal for a 1998 incident.) For two rangers to each earn more than one such medal within a year's time was a phenomenal achievement. But officials in D.C. weren't impressed. The Yosemite rangers were told that the government would pay for only one medal for each ranger. Apparently that was all the NPS could afford.

The medals must be made of gold then, Lober concluded, *or at least be gold plated.* Mary didn't care what the medals were made of or how much they were worth. This one-medal-per-ranger concept didn't sit right with her. If you earned two medals you should receive two medals, or at least receive a bronze oak leaf cluster for the second medal and a silver leaf for the fifth, like they do in the military. And for sure if you earned additional medals because you risked your life more than once on two separate occasions to save more than one human life, you shouldn't have to pay for the second one yourself. Should you?

The rangers' supervisor and peers were dismayed. They "passed around the ranger hat" for funds to purchase the additional medals their colleagues had earned. Collection letters were posted on staff bulletin boards inside several national parks. Eventually word reached D.C. that park rangers were collecting money to purchase Medals of Valor for their peers. Shamed into generosity, a high-level manager said, "Okay, okay, we'll pay for their damn medals"—or something to that effect.

In October Mary and Lober flew to Washington, D.C., to receive their DOI Medals of Valor. They shook hands with Secretary of the Interior Bruce Babbitt and posed for photos. Outside the Interior Building, Lober polished the face of one of his medals against his uniform and held it up to the sun. The eagle on the medal glittered brightly. Outstanding!

After the ceremony Mary paid a visit to the Fallen Firefighters

Memorial at the National Fire Academy in Maryland. Jerry Litell, a Sacramento firefighter killed by a speeding semi-truck in 1983, would have beamed with pride during his daughter's Medal of Valor ceremony. Mary scanned the bronze plaques until she found her father's name. Then she lowered her baby daughter down to the monument, leaned her up against the stone foundation, and took a picture.

When Keith Lober returned home, he handed his medals to a jeweler in Fresno, California, for an estimate of how much they were worth. The jeweler glanced at one of them and laughed. "These are made from pot metal," the jeweler said.

"What do you mean, pot metal?"

"Go down to the thrift store, buy yourself a used cook pot, melt it down, pour it into a mold, and it'll be worth as much as these medals."

"The cheap bastards," Lober said.

26

STUCK IN THE FEE BOOTH

Collecting fees at the park entrance gate benefited Brittney Ruland in many ways. It gave her status as a permanent full-time-with-benefits employee of the U.S. government. It supplied her with a modest paycheck after the federal government withheld rent and taxes. It gave her access to a choice of health insurance plans. And it allowed her to live in park housing. But working in the fee booth—sucking in the exhaust, performing mind-numbing cashier duties, and fending off the complaints of stingy park visitors—eight hours a day, five days a week—also came with one major drawback. It killed her spirit.

In exchange for working in the fee booth, the park housing office assigned Brittney to a room in a wing of the Grand Canyon Clinic. Finding a creative solution to the park's ongoing housing problem, the NPS had converted eight hospital rooms into employee homes. In return for the rent park employees paid to live in the clinic dorm, the NPS provided many "luxuries": The cinder block walls were painted in muted colors. Some rooms had a view of the dusty courtyard where there was a picnic table or two. A cramped nurse's station had been remodeled into a shared kitchen. Rolling hospital tables served as nightstands. The bathrooms were wheelchair accessible. And one pay phone was mounted to the wall in the hallway.

When Brittney returned home after a particularly long shift in the booth, a dorm mate yelled at her from down the hall. "You got a phone call," he said.

"Who was it?" she asked.

"How should I know?" the dorm mate replied. "He didn't leave his name."

Brittney's last relationship had ended in disaster, but there was this other ranger she had danced with at a recent party. So she called him. "Hey, Cale. It's Brittney. Did you just call me?"

"Uh . . . yeah," Cale said.

"Then why didn't you leave your name?"

Cale laughed. He wasn't going to get anything past this woman. "I was embarrassed," he said. He wanted to ask her out on a date. "I have to patrol down to Indian Garden tomorrow. Would you like to join me? We'll hike down and have lunch at the ranger station."

After a week in the entrance station, it was an offer she could not refuse.

* * *

If you want to be a backcountry ranger, you must be willing to add the weight of a gun, a badge, and a ticket book to your backpack. To qualify for seasonal law enforcement ranger positions, you need to complete a ten-week academy like the one Cale attended in North Carolina. The course cost him around $600, and the instructors taught him, among other things, how to arrest people, shoot guns, and drive a patrol car. Although he viewed law enforcement in the parks as a necessary evil, Cale took his studies seriously. At the graduation ceremony his instructors and classmates honored him with two awards some might view as paradoxical: "Most Friendly" and "Top Ranger."

From day one of the academy, Cale made an impression. "Okay, class," instructor Glenn Martin said after introducing himself to the fresh batch of trainees, "I have an important question for you, and I want you to think long and hard about it before you answer." Ranger Martin scanned his finger across the faces in the room until it landed on his first victim, an achingly earnest young man sitting in the front row. "You there, what's your name? Cale Shaffer? Now tell the truth. Why do you want to be a park ranger?"

Cale scratched his chin, contemplating the question for several seconds, before he said, "To meet women."

It didn't take him long to figure it out. National parks were a chick magnet for a certain type of girl, and preventive search and rescue (PSAR) duty provided a guy a great excuse to talk to them. In the Grand Canyon he met the coolest girls. Girls who were unimpressed by dance clubs and fancy restaurants. Girls who wanted boyfriends to take them hiking, kayaking, skiing, mountain biking, and rock climbing. Girls like Kate, one of David Denali's interns, who was so smart and so cute that Cale envied the climbing harness hugging her tiny waist and cradling her taut hips. Girls who, after a grueling day enjoying nature's elements, were happy to stay in bed all morning with hot chocolate and warm blueberry muffins. Girls who could appreciate a little guy with a trail-honed body, romantic sensibilities, and a muddy Toyota pickup loaded with camping gear.

Several times a week, Cale's PSAR duties crossed paths with the naturalist rangers guiding park visitors down the South Kaibab Trail. One day he saw a female ranger leading the morning nature walk to Cedar Ridge. The lady ranger was a natural blond with pale skin and gray-blue eyes. Cale was certain he hadn't met this one yet; if he had, he would not have forgotten. At the long switchback in front of the pale Coconino sandstone, the lady ranger stopped and turned to her charges, pointing out the delicate webs clinging to the cracks in Black Widow Wall. The tourists gawked at spiders while Cale inspected the girl. A skinny pair of legs connected her green shorts to her hiking boots. A soft ponytail fanned out from under her Stetson. Exertion flushed her ivory cheeks. Perhaps, Cale concluded, the lady ranger could use a little PSAR.

"Hi there, Ranger Ruland," Cale said, taking a peek at her nametag. "Can I offer you a few tips on hiking safely?"

Brittney studied Cale. *Great, another arrogant ranger.* Then the PSAR ranger's goofy smile and good-humored disposition won her over. This was a guy she would like to know better, if she didn't already have a boyfriend.

* * *

A year passed before Cale and Brittney went on their first date. At the start of their 4.5-mile hike down the Bright Angel Trail, he said, "I can't wait for you to meet Bryan Wisher. He and his wife, Kim, are like second parents to me." Brittney got the message. If she wanted another date with Cale, she needed the approval of the Indian Garden ranger.

Cale described Bryan as the smartest guy he knew. The middle-aged ranger was also super-fit and towered over her and Cale. At Indian Garden, Bryan played the perfect host, but as soon as she crossed the threshold into his immaculately kept ranger station, Brittney became so nervous she couldn't stop talking.

"The high hit 85 degrees? Wow. It's only March. The canyon is so pretty this time of year. I love it here. I've hiked by this ranger station many times, but I've never been inside it. It's cozy. It's modern. On the way down we saw a beggar squirrel sitting on top of a DO NOT FEED THE WILDLIFE sign. We joked that the squirrel couldn't read. Cale says there are endangered Kaibab amber snails in the springs and that the only other place they live is a meadow in Utah and at Vassey's Paradise. Cool. I hear you are battling the exotic Himalayan blackberry that smothers the creek. Good luck with that. Yes, the pasta is fantastic. Oh, no, I can't possibly. I'm stuffed." (Cale gave her a look. *You're insulting him.*) "Okay, maybe a little."

It was late afternoon by the time Cale and Brittney "topped out" on the South Rim. They had hiked nine arduous miles. At the trailhead the couple shared a shy hug before parting. The sweat stains on Calc's uniform shirt were ringed with delicate white crusts of salt from his body. *Whew,* Brittney thought, *that was a lot of work for a first date*.

"So," Cale asked Bryan Wisher the next time he saw him. "What do you think about Brittney?"

Bryan didn't know what to say about Cale's date—she had jabbered nonstop during lunch. It had made him nervous—but he kept his reservations to himself because Cale answered his own question. "She's intelligent!" Cale told his friend and mentor. "She's fascinating! I think we are going to end up together."

Most of their dates were hikes into canyon country. They searched for obsidian chips on the Hermit Trail. Cale showed off his climbing skills on the red rocks near Sedona. At Phantom Ranch, Brittney revealed she could juggle. One warm April evening they sat on a rock jutting out into the Colorado River and picked out constellations. Their spring courtship bloomed alongside the pink-and-yellow flowers of the beavertail cactus. Then, about two months after their first date, they reached the stage afflicting nearly every ranger relationship—the long-distance separation. Cale had been offered a job as a law enforcement ranger at Wonder Lake in Denali National Park.

If he wanted, Cale could keep his PSAR job at the Grand Canyon, but his supervisor discouraged him. "Go," I told Cale when he called. "Go to Alaska. The Grand Canyon will still be here when you get back." He knew I was right. Only a fool would turn down a summer of adventure in Alaska.

While Cale enjoyed his exhilarating road trip to Denali by way of the Canadian Rockies, Brittney remained at the Grand Canyon and agonized over her next career move. To some, six months in the fee booth sounded like a prison sentence. Brittney believed she might "die of boredom." But if she quit her permanent job with the NPS, her professional reputation might suffer. She definitely would lose her place on the park housing list, and her benefits, including health insurance, would vanish.

Living without health insurance didn't faze Cale. "Do what you want to do," was his advice. "Life is to be enjoyed, not survived!" When Cale's mother called to give him grief for working a job that did not offer retirement benefits, he said, "Mom, with the things I'm doing, I'm not going to live long enough to need it."

A bit of a worrier, Brittney was less cavalier. Seasonal jobs were more fun, but without health insurance, one broken bone could bury her in debt. What do you do? Accept a job of quiet desperation, or try to live without affordable health care? For some rangers this felt like a decision one made while looking at the wrong end of a gun.

27

WHAT'S SO WONDERFUL ABOUT WONDER LAKE?

At first it was funny. At first it was cute. Rabbits were gnawing a ring around the bottom of the Wonder Lake Ranger Station in Denali National Park, not unlike the one beavers chew around a tree in order to bring it down. But by June it wasn't funny or cute. It was maddening. The snowshoe hare population had exploded. Their hunger had devastated all edible vegetation within rabbit reach. Their droppings had turned the campground into a minefield of bunny poop. And every night, while Alaska's midnight sun penetrated the curtains, the incisors of ravenous rabbits were crunch, crunch, crunching into the ranger station.

Cale Shaffer lived and worked deep in the heart of Denali Park at the end of an eighty-five-mile kidney-busting excuse for a road. The ranger station was small, more of a hut than a house, but the scenery was big. From his front porch he could see Mount McKinley rising behind the placid waters of Wonder Lake. With a view like that, Cale didn't mind hauling in his drinking water, the chilly morning walks to an outhouse, or cooking his meals on a propane stove. He had no problem with the federal government taking $200 a month out of his paycheck to pay for such rustic accommodations. He could learn to live with the mosquitoes, the steady rain, the ever-present threat of grizzly attack, and the stupid "What's so wonderful about Wonder Lake?" tourist questions. But having animals eat his house? That was something else entirely.

Some nights the rabbit munching was so loud, so grating to the ears that Cale couldn't sleep. All night he tossed and turned in his bunk and wondered about his luck. Why did the snowshoe hare population have to experience a seven-year boom the summer he came to Denali National Park?

It was 1999. A bus trip to Wonder Lake had become the American version of the African safari. The Alaska tourism business was flourishing. A half million people from all over the world were coming to Denali National Park to take a gander at what the tour guides called the Big Five—caribou, Dall sheep, moose, wolf, and grizzly—the biggest and most dangerous mammals in the United States.

Cale's job was to ensure that nobody was eaten in the process. He kept aggressive photographers from pissing off grizzlies. He prevented tourists from putting their children on the backs of caribou. He patrolled the twenty-eight campsites in his district, enforcing food storage regulations in every one.

The job gave him many opportunities to view wildlife, and he made a scrapbook of photographs to prove it. He took photos of moose, bear, and caribou. Not being a megafauna snob, he also took pictures of wildflowers, beavers, marmots, and birds. He even snapped a portrait of one of the rabbits chewing on his house. In the scrapbook, under a photo of three foxes trotting down the park road in front of a tour bus, Cale wrote: "We have laid claim to almost every other square foot of wilderness and killed it with pavement and shopping malls. But not here. This land belongs to the animals. Forever."

The joke was on Cale: Denali rabbits took these sentiments literally.

* * *

Not long after Cale left the Grand Canyon, Brittney made a decision she would never regret. She quit her job at the fee booth and planned a July trip to Alaska. Brittney stayed nearly two weeks inside Cale's rabbit-chewed hut. During her visit, Cale drove her around in his ranger Suburban, taking his girlfriend to all the best wildlife-watching spots and showing her his favorite moose. The ranger Suburban was a dusty beast of a vehicle, beaten and battered by years of traveling the rugged roads. Once when the tires of the Suburban hit a bump, the shotgun held by a rack mounted on the floorboard bounced out of its locked gate and fell into Brittney's lap. Cale reached across her legs and pushed the gun back into the rack. "It does that sometimes," he said.

One day a female backpacker knocked on the door of the ranger hut. A bear had stolen her food cache, she said, and she was too afraid to return to her campsite to retrieve her gear. Bringing Brittney along, Cale drove the backpacker to the trail leading to her primitive camp. He parked the Suburban on the side of the road, grabbed the shotgun out of its rack, and headed into the high brush on foot, with the two women following him.

The shotgun loaded with rifled slugs was a security measure. A grizzly brave enough to steal food from a human might be aggressive enough to attack and eat a human. Once a bear associated humans with something good to eat, bad news was not far behind. That's why Cale took pains to educate campers to keep their food stored in hard plastic bear-proof containers and then place these containers at least one hundred yards from their tents. That's why if people disregarded the park regulations, Cale would do something he hated to do—write tickets.

A ranger carrying a shotgun startled three hikers on the path. Cale asked the hikers if they had seen a bear. The hikers said no, they had not. Concern grew on their faces. "Why are you carrying a gun?" one hiker asked. "What are you going to do? Shoot the bear?" The accusatory tone of the hiker's questions rubbed Cale the wrong way. They seemed unconvinced that he might need the gun to defend himself. They seemed disgusted that a park ranger might use a gun, a tool of violence, against an innocent bear.

Cale didn't want to shoot a bear. Heck, he didn't even have the heart to pepper spray the rabbits eating his house! But if a bear attacked, he would have no choice, would he? A renegade grizzly was not a thing to be complacent about. Grizzly bears killed people every year in Alaska. Two years earlier, while walking home from work, a female park employee had spooked a sow with two cubs. The grizzly had bitten the woman. Luckily she survived her wounds. Cale had entered the Alaska bush with the intention of guarding park visitors from animal attack. He had two young women with him needing his protection—one of them his girlfriend. Would he shoot a bear? Why were they even asking such a question? Of course, if he had to, he'd shoot the bear.

But it sure would be nice if he didn't have to.

"Hey, bear," Cale shouted, hoping to avoid spooking the grizzly as he and the two women pushed through the head-high willow. Staying together for safety, Cale and the women searched the backpacker's camp for the bear-proof food canister. Eventually they found it. A black cylinder placed on the ground, one hundred yards downwind from the woman's tent, right where park rangers suggest a backpacker should place it. "Oh," the backpacker said. "I guess there's no bear." Turned out a bear hadn't stolen the food canister after all. The woman had forgotten where she had stashed it. Like a mall shopper convinced that someone has stolen her car when she can't find it in the parking garage, the backpacker had come to the nearest man in a uniform for help.

That spring, Cale had left the warm deserts of Arizona and driven three thousand miles to seek adventure in Jack London's "savage frozen-hearted Northland." But at the end of this wild bear chase, as he stood there holding a shotgun that was nearly as long as he was tall, Cale didn't feel at all like a brave park ranger capable of facing down a thousand pounds of angry, man-eating bear. He felt like a parking lot security guard who was being terrorized by bunny rabbits.

* * *

When seen from Wonder Lake, Mount McKinley, the mountain the Athabascan Indians called Denali—the High One—dominates the southern sky. The summit is only thirty-seven miles distant. On clear days, Denali's peak looks close enough to touch. Perhaps the party of miners who failed to notice Wonder Lake had their eyes on Denali when they passed through the area for the first time. When these same miners returned years later, they stumbled upon the glacier-fed lake. Standing at the shores of the second largest body of water in what would one day become a national park, one miner turned to the other and said, "I wonder why we didn't notice this lake before?" Since then it's been called "I Wonder Lake."

* * *

Many times that summer, Cale dusted off the ropes and carabiners stored inside Wonder Lake's rarely used rescue cache, with his eyes on the mountain and his ears on the crackled radio transmissions coming from Denali's base camps. When there's a rescue under way on Denali, "the whole mountain listens." Among the intrepid mountaineering rangers using the park airways that summer, one stood out: the bold and unshakable voice of ranger Billy Shott.

Billy Shott worked "on the mountain." Billy Shott had seen the world from Denali's summit many times. Billy Shott was a lifesaver. Billy Shott was a hero. Billy Shott had a cool name, a cool job, and a cool head that he kept shaved and shiny. And whenever Billy Shott entered a bar in Talkeetna, he was attacked by outdoors groupies with heaving chests; breathless questions; and mountains, men, and mayhem sparkling in their eyes.

Denali's mountaineering rangers earn their prestige the hard way. That May, two months after Cale arrived at Wonder Lake, Billy Shott saved the lives of two climbers, performing two extraordinary rescue missions within two days. Both rescues were stunning feats.

The first was the highest and longest short-haul rescue ever conducted on Denali. A climber had fallen off Denali Pass and was suffering from an open leg fracture, dehydration, altitude sickness, and severe frostbite of his hands and feet. With the weather worsening and while attached to a one-hundred-foot-long line under a Lama helicopter piloted by Jim Hood, Ranger Shott was short-hauled from Kahiltna base camp at 7,200 feet directly to 17,500 feet. Shott's 10,300-foot elevation gain within thirty minutes time subjected him to air pressure changes and rapidly decreasing oxygen levels. It was a death-defying accomplishment.

The very next day, another climber fell two hundred feet on a nearby mountain. The climber's legs and ankles were broken, and he was anchored to a ledge above a 2,500-foot vertical cliff. Dangling at the end of a two-hundred-foot line, Shott was short-hauled to the scene. While still attached to the hovering helicopter, the ranger had to climb forty feet up a slippery slab of slanted ice to reach the injured climber. Shott clipped the man into his harness, and then the Lama pilot, Carl Cotton, backed away his helicopter, swinging the ranger and the climber off the wall and hauling them back to base camp.

By the time fall dappled the tundra with sienna red and burnt umber, Cale envied the life of mountaineering rangers like Billy Shott. On the mountain, rangers didn't have to take stolen lawn chair reports from forgetful campers; they were too busy rescuing the manliest of men from the icy jaws of death! On the mountain, rangers didn't wake up at night to the sound of motor home generators; they lived at a glacier base camp, in a tent hunkered down in a pit dug into the snow. Best of all, on the mountain there were no bunnies.

On the latter, Cale was mistaken. There were rabbits on the mountain, as the Hudson Stuck Expedition discovered in 1913 when they set out to become the first men to summit Denali's highest peak. Along the way, Hudson Stuck and his party encountered a snowshoe hare at a most improbable place—the head of Muldrow Glacier. Following the men up the mountain, the lone rabbit climbed as far as ten thousand feet and subsisted by chewing bark off the willow wands the mountaineers used to mark their trail in the snow. In his narrative of the climb, Stuck wondered if "the ambition for first ascents (has) reached the Leporidae."

* * *

At season's end in November, Cale returned home to Pennsylvania. When Brittney informed him that she had scored a winter job as a park naturalist at Death Valley National Park, he promised to visit her in California on New Year's Eve. "I bet the sunsets are incredible," Cale wrote to her in a letter. "Tell me if you climb Telescope Peak. It goes from sea level to 11,000 feet. Wow! But . . . " the ranger had to let the naturalist know, "the greatest vertical rise in any national park is Denali (from 2,000 to 20,000 feet)."

28

SEPARATION CANYON

Cale played around in kayaks and canoes, but he had never rowed a raft before he grabbed the oars of the *Zambezi,* an eighteen-footer loaded with a thousand pounds of gear and named for the fourth-largest river in Africa. The trip leader, Tom Martin, had reluctantly invited the novice rower to join his river trip party after ranger Bryan Wisher convinced him that Cale was up to the task. Martin's permit allowed them thirty-five days on the Colorado River through Grand Canyon National Park, but Cale could only commit to thirty. Inside the glove box of his Toyota truck was an airline ticket dated February 8 for a noon flight out of Phoenix to Anchorage, Alaska. Martin told Cale he could do the river trip and still make this flight if he left the group at Diamond Creek.

On January 1, 2000, Cale helped Brittney rotate the tires on her car in Death Valley before leaving for Arizona. Four days later he shoved *Zambezi* into the frigid water at Lees Ferry—Mile 0 of the Colorado River's 277-mile course through the Grand Canyon. Within hours the river party sighted ducks flying upriver and a bighorn sheep that sent rocks rolling down a sandstone terrace as it scampered up the cliffs.

Seven miles into the trip they stopped to scout their first rapid. Martin recommended that they take the line flowing between a large pour-over and a large rock. The first rapid unnerved Cale, but Guy, his swamper (an assistant who scouts rapids and bails out the boat while the oarsman concentrates on the rowing), stood in the bow and pointed out the obstacles; Cale rowed *Zambezi* through Badger Rapid without incident. Martin's group of sixteen people in five boats continued downriver, stopping to see waterfalls and ancient ruins while bald eagles spiraled through the skies overhead.

On day two Cale rowed through several rapids. His runs were far from perfect, but he was getting through the difficult whitewater intact and, for the most part, dry. On day five Cale and three of the men arose at dawn to climb Kwagunt Butte. At the summit they left a note in a film canister under a cairn. The days were sunny and warm, but the nights were often chilly. One evening the group gathered up some rocks to heat in the campfire. The heated rocks were piled under a tarp "roof" held down by oars. Inside this sauna they poured water on the hot rocks and enjoyed a sweat.

From the start of day nine, apprehension dampened Cale's mood. Today he had to run one of the canyon's most infamous rapids. "Hance. Hance. Wet your pants," the river runner's refrain had tormented him for days. They stopped to scout several rapids that morning. On what he believed was Mile 75 Rapid, Cale took the left line around Muffin Rock with Jocelyn in his boat. His female passenger held tight when *Zambezi* hit a series of monster waves sideways. Wet but still aboard, Cale rowed the boat into the downstream eddy. As soon as he met up with the other river runners, one of them asked, "How does it feel to have four of the canyon's most difficult rapids behind you?" Cale believed his friends were teasing him. "Cale! I'm serious," someone said. "You just ran Hance!" The entire group was laughing at his ignorance before he realized it was true. He had just run Hance! Cale jumped on the nearest rock and performed a well-earned dance in the end zone. With Hance and Sockdolager behind him, Cale felt ready for anything the Colorado had in store.

Day eleven included a stop at Phantom Ranch. Cale hiked up to the ranger station to call Brittney in Death Valley. Over the phone Brittney expressed her desire that they both work at the Grand Canyon that summer. Cale reminded her that he planned to volunteer on Denali in the spring. But Brittney still hoped they could be together. She had applied for a permanent full-time back-country office position at the Grand Canyon, and Cale's former boss had revealed a way for him to beat the ranger's catch-22. Cale's grade point average put him in the "Outstanding Scholar" category, and outstanding scholars can apply for most jobs listed as "closed to non-status applicants." If Cale put in for the first permanent full-time-with-benefits ranger position that opened up at the Grand Canyon, he might get it.

Cale's phone call to Brittney was brief. A few passengers on Tom Martin's river trip were leaving at the midway point, and a new group of passengers had hiked down the Bright Angel Trail to replace them. Among the new additions to the group was a young woman named Amanda.

On day fourteen they reached Crystal Rapid. Crystal has claimed at least five lives since 1983. The canyon's deadliest rapid, it eroded the confidence Cale had built up over the past two weeks. But he ran it without difficulty.

On day fifteen Cale, another young man, and two women left their camp at Bass for a trek to Merlin Abyss. The hikers never made it to their intended destination. The traverse over to the Shinumo Creek drainage took much longer than they had anticipated. Cale spotted a new route down to the creek. Amanda fell, but she recovered quickly and kept on smiling. They hiked up Shinumo until a waterfall blocked their progress. The sun was very warm. They swam in the huge pool under the waterfall and dried out on the rocks.

As they walked downstream through the narrows, Cale spotted a granary across the creek. He wanted to check out this archaeo-logical relic, but the other couple preferred to continue. In January the sun sets quickly, and they were more than a half mile from camp. Cale looked at Amanda. "You go on," she said to the other couple. "We'll catch up later."

Below the granary they discovered a small arch. Potsherds, broken bits of ancient pottery, were scattered underfoot. Since the Anasazi often stored food in their stone granaries, they built them in hard-to-reach places. The climb to the granary was challenging. Cale had Amanda wait by the arch while he scouted for the best route. A ten-foot scramble over loose rock brought him to the site.

The granary was in fine shape. The dried mud caulking between the stones had preserved the handprints of the maker. When Cale peered inside the granary, he saw something that took his breath away. Inside the ancient storage compartment was a woven basket. The cone-shaped basket was about eighteen inches high and woven out of grass. Cale estimated it to be at least eight hundred years old. He yelled for Amanda to join him. The rush of finding an intact granary brightened the girl's eyes. Cale had known her all of four days, and he was smitten enough to kiss her. He settled for sitting beside Amanda on the ledge as the last blush of day glowed off the Redwall.

The ranger and the young woman silently watched the sunset, just as a granary mason and a basket maker may have done more than a millennium before. Then the moon rose, almost full, casting shadows across their path back to camp. Their friends were waiting for them. The river party ate dinner, had a sweat in a makeshift sauna, and drank whisky around the fire. Before they retired to their tents, Cale made a joyful announcement. Today was one of the best days he'd ever had in the canyon, or in his life.

The perils of distraction were toying with him. The day before his hike with Amanda, he ran Crystal, the canyon's deadliest rapid, with finesse. Now, on a short and nameless rapid, Cale hit a wave sideways, lost an oar, and nearly fell out of the boat. During his near ejection from the raft, he landed on an oar and probably fractured a rib. It hurt, but only when he carried things or took a deep breath. Later that same day he shoved *Zambezi* off from shore but failed to jump into the raft quickly enough and ended up in the icy water. A few days later while running Lava Rapids, a monster wave sent him airborne and then under the boat. The rapid tossed him around like a sock in a washing machine. When he came up for air, the boat went one way and Cale went another. Someone threw Cale a line while *Zambezi* ran the rest of Lava Rapids without her captain.

Unlike some river guides, Tom Martin did not run his river trips as though they were a "twelve-step program," but his trips were such that his team members formed tender and trusting relationships. One night the group formed a human circle in the sand, each person with another's head resting on his or her abdomen. As soon as one person began to giggle, it sent a jiggling hilarity throughout the group. On the lazy layover days they sang, painted, drummed, or played backgammon. One night they gathered around the fire and asked one another profound and intimate questions, such as "What are you most afraid of?"

Over the next week Cale fought to keep sadness at bay. Soon, on day thirty, he would have to leave the river party at the Diamond Creek takeout. He considered Alaska, his plans for the summer, and how much he loved the Grand Canyon. It was a shame to abandon the journey before trip's end. He pictured himself standing on shore while Amanda and his new friends waved at him from a raft taking them farther and farther downriver until he couldn't see them at all.

At the Diamond Creek takeout, they derigged three boats and rearranged the gear. When the time came for Cale to climb into the pickup that would take him out of the canyon, he couldn't do it. "I don't want to go," Cale said to no one in particular. "You can't make me." He would skip the training at Denali and eat the cost of his airline ticket. His friend Zander was leaving the trip at Diamond. Cale asked Zander to make a few calls for him when he reached a phone. He'd sort the rest out later.

Jumping back on the boat felt more than right. That afternoon Cale rowed through some fun, splashy rapids. At camp a fabulous sunset led into a terrific dinner eaten by a cozy fire. His life was going to get back on track. And it was going to happen here at the Grand Canyon. Cale crawled into his tent and drifted off to a peaceful sleep.

The next day they arrived at Separation Canyon. Here, on River Mile 239.5, Capt. John Wesley Powell, a Civil War veteran maimed at the Battle of Shiloh, experienced the most heartwrenching moment of his famous 1869 expedition. Powell's team consisted of eight men and four boats. By the time they reached what we today call Separation Canyon, Powell had been on the river for nearly one hundred days. Two months earlier they had lost one boat and a third of their rations while running a rapid in the Green River. What little remained of their food was now spoiling.

Three months of fear and hardship had soured Powell's men. Fights broke out, curses were thrown, and the air held whispers of mutiny. After scouting the frightening whitewater at the mouth of Separation Canyon, three of Powell's men decided that another terrifying run through another vicious rapid was more than they could endure. They were no longer committed to the one-armed captain's obsessed determination to lead the first voyage down what he called "The Great Unknown."

The night before the men planned to part, Powell could not sleep. On the morning of August 28, 1869, the mood at breakfast was "as solemn as a funeral." In *The Exploration of the Colorado River and Its Canyons,* Powell writes, "Each party (believed) the other (was) taking the dangerous course."

That day Powell and four of his men shoved off and headed for what is now called Separation Rapid, while the other three men began their escape from the canyon on foot. It was a little spooky how this agonizing separation at River Mile 239 mirrored the inner conflict Cale felt during the hours leading up to his fateful decision at Diamond Creek. But in the end, the story validated his choice. The four men who ran Separation Rapid with Powell survived. The three who left the canyon on foot were murdered by unknown assailants.

At noon on day thirty-two, while his flight to Alaska lifted off the tarmac without him, Cale sat on a rock with Amanda. There they spent a lazy afternoon, reading books, painting with watercolors, and talking about life. Their ledge provided a sublime view upriver to Separation Canyon. It seemed a fitting time and place to expose one's true feelings.

A month on the Colorado River and you begin to forget. No televisions. No radio signals. No cell phone service. No Wi-Fi. An atomic bomb could start WWIII, an earthquake could send California into the Pacific, an alien mother ship could have landed and you wouldn't know it. There was only the Grand Canyon of the Colorado and its inhabitants. The people and obligations waiting for you topside seemed to be concerns from another lifetime. Here, as Cale said, "Life is Grand!"

A day on the river overflowed with whitewater, wildlife, and waterfalls. Your fellow species included shirtless river runners and bikini-clad women willing to wallow in warm mud. A night at camp glowed with moonlight, campfires, and whiskey. The isolation conspired with the scenery, and mischief ensued. Yet the canyon cast a fleeting spell. Though river romances were sweet and plenty, they rarely survived the real world.

The girl probably knew this instinctually. Or perhaps it was because she was a drama major, and girls who major in drama are not the kind of girls who date park rangers. Whatever the reason, Cale confessed his infatuation and she rebuffed him. They were near their journey's end, and the Colorado River was changing, becoming more domesticated as it entered the lake created by Hoover Dam. Powerboat operators from Lake Mead could travel this far upriver. Cale saw the trash they had left behind on the beaches.

On day thirty-five they took out at Pearce Ferry. They dragged the boats to the trailers, jumped into the pickup trucks, and were gone. Hours later, Tom Martin and his river runners met in downtown Flagstaff for a farewell dinner. After many long hugs and solemn good-byes, Cale stepped outside the restaurant. A starry sky and crisp mountain breeze sent him back to the canyon—the views; the warm sun; the smell of desert air. He sensed the void, the open space that was all around, and it overwhelmed him with bittersweet emotion. Then a train roared by, jerking him back to the rush and rattle that was life above the rim.

Back on the South Rim, Cale had some facts to face. He had missed the required yearly law enforcement refresher in Alaska. The girl on the river had rejected him, and Brittney was hurt. The permanent full-time ranger job at Grand Canyon position he had counted on was going to someone else, and all other prospects for a summer job were dwindling.

Over the phone, Cale spilled his guts while Brittney listened. She couldn't have been more annoyed. It had been a month since she last heard from him, and she had worried. Then she received a cryptic letter from him a few days after a friend told her the man she loved had fallen prey to the river's charms and all their friends knew about it. She had every right to curse and cry. But Cale's heartbreak over the girl he met on the river melted Brittney's anger. Instead of scolding Cale, she comforted him. By the end of their conversation, his optimism returned. Like always, new friends and new adventures would come his way. He just knew it.

A week or so later, Brittney received a much anticipated call from the Grand Canyon. "Guess what?" she said, phoning Cale with the news. "I just got a permanent full-time job in the backcountry permit office at the canyon!"

"Guess what?" was Cale's response. "I just got a mountaineering ranger job on Denali!"

29

PLACE OF EMERGENCE

It happened right in front of me. I didn't see it, but I heard the muffled pop when it hit the ground. Someone said, "A helicopter just crashed," and my first thought was egocentric. *The Grand Canyon will not let go of me.*

The South Rim was less than two miles from where the aircraft went down. I could see the pink gash of the rim from where I stood. I ran up the knoll blocking my view of the crash site. What I saw from the top gave me that heavy bad-news feeling. The bottom half of a white helicopter was crushed on the tarmac, its contents leaking out like the yolk leaks out of a cracked egg. Later I learned that the engine had failed after takeoff because someone forgot to clean the snow out of an air vent. But as I looked down on the mangled mess of man and metal, as far as I was concerned something big and mean had slapped that sucker out of the sky.

Seven people were on board—the pilot and six passengers. The passengers had traveled from places as far as Germany to see the seventh natural wonder of the world from the air. Each year 750,000 people enjoy fifty thousand scenic flights over the park. The Grand Canyon scenic air tour business is a $100 million industry. The helicopter tour industry, the bane of the National Park Service's crusade for "natural quiet," currently funded my paycheck.

Fifteen months earlier, in the summer of 1998, sitting in my supervisor's office I had said, "I quit" through clenched teeth. I felt beat up by the Grand Canyon. I feared for the safety of my employees. I was too tuckered out to suffer a less-than-supportive boss without complaint. Still, leaving the NPS was the emotional equivalent of chewing my arm out of a gilded trap. The prolonged, agonizing incident certainly left an appalling mess at the scene of my escape. I spent most of my first year off recuperating on the Appalachian Trail. After living out of a backpack during my 2,200-mile trek from Georgia to Maine, I found myself in the mood to accept work of any kind. As long as it was easy. I returned to Arizona and accepted a job fueling tour helicopters three days a week. The pay was suitable. The work kept me near my boyfriend, Kent Delbon, the ranger I had met in Yosemite, who now worked on the South Rim. Best of all, the job was far removed from the chaos inside the park. Or so I thought.

I walked around the crashed helicopter to survey the scene. I heard moans of pain. I saw blood and angulated extremities. I began to triage the victims. The German lady with lower back pain and a rapid pulse might have internal hemorrhaging. The pilot with a foot pointed in the wrong direction could be a future paraplegic. I kneeled down by the pilot. I didn't like it when he told me he couldn't feel his legs. I didn't like it one bit. I was reminding myself to take it slow moving this one to avoid sending a bone shard into his spinal cord when I sensed fluid oozing through the knees of my jeans.

At first I thought it was blood. Then the cool feel of it on my skin told me the fluid soaking into my clothes was something much more terrifying than blood. It was jet fuel. In my mind I saw a rescuer pull a piece of metal away from the aircraft, dragging it across the asphalt and setting off a spark that could ignite the growing puddle of highly flammable liquid. More than once I had seen what remains after a jet fuel explosion. It was not something I cared to experience firsthand. With the help of volunteer firefighters, we picked the pilot up and ran with him, away from the aircraft. On my way back to grab another patient, I saw green-and-gray uniforms pouring out of patrol cars, fire trucks, and ambulances. Although this crash site was two miles outside the park boundary, NPS emergency personnel responded to help, as they always do.

After it was all over, I was pleased with the way I had taken charge on the scene. I had fallen back into emergency work like a goldfish falls back into a fish bowl. I'd been gone for more than a year, but my former colleagues still acted as though I was one of them. The helicopter didn't blow up. The injured pilot would regain the use of his legs. After a few surgeries and a few nights in the hospital, everyone would make it. Other than the lawsuits that haunted the helicopter company, this one had a happy ending.

Later that day, back at my cushy job loading tourists into helicopters, I eased the minds of the fearful. "You don't stop driving your car because you've seen a crash on the interstate do you?" I told them. Despite this logic, the stench of jet fuel followed me around like a shadow, and a pit of anxiety behind my sternum began to grow tentacles. I retreated to the women's restroom. When I reached for the faucet, I saw that my hands were trembling.

A few days later Cale Shaffer called me from Alaska. Would I join him this June for a month of living and working on Denali at the base camp on Kahiltna Glacier? In February Cale and I had climbed an eighteen-thousand-foot peak in Mexico. I handled the elevation with no ill effects and reached the summit right behind Cale. He knew I wasn't ready to chain myself to the Park Service full-time, but a three-week tour on the highest mountain in North America might recharge my dedication to the good fight. I told Cale I would think about it and call him back.

I loved to travel, and I figured my relationship could survive a month of living apart. Indeed, my boyfriend said the opportunity on Denali sounded like an interesting assignment. But unconsciously Kent was doing another one of his Clint Eastwood impressions. A squint in his eye and a clench of his jaw told me something was going unsaid.

A few days later Kent invited me for a walk out to Inspiration Point. It was a lovely April day. A thousand feet below us, the redbuds were blooming. Desiring a better view, I leaned as far as I dared over the cliff. Kent grabbed me by the shirt and pulled me toward him and away from the edge. "If I had a house here on the rim," he said, "with a view like this you could never leave." Then he asked me to marry him.

* * *

Cale was waiting for me to call him with my decision about Alaska, but I kept putting it off. Not sure what I wanted to do, I decided to go hiking on it. Besides, before I left the Grand Canyon for good, there was one more sight I had to see.

Off to visit the Gateway to the Underworld, I fell twice on the way down. On the second tumble, my knee was the only thing stopping me from toppling into a ravine. Cursing, I pulled myself together. A canyon wren mocked me with its descending trill. I ignored the trickle of blood running through the dust on my shin and continued my descent.

At the Colorado River I set up camp while a raven supervised, squawking and glaring at me from his perch in the gray branches of a dead mesquite. Gazing up at the rim, the canyon walls appeared more intimidating than beautiful, and the word "awesome" seemed pretty close to the word "awful."

That night, a downcanyon wind sent my tarp flapping. I got up to cinch the lines in the dark and stubbed my toe. The throbbing pain kept me up most of the night. The next day I reached my second camp before noon. Near the confluence of two rivers, I dumped the weight of my backpack on a slab of sandstone at lunchtime and went for a quick swim. The turquoise waters were warm and welcoming. A better woman would have stayed and relaxed, made a backcountry spa day out of it. But I am nothing if not goal oriented. I do not dally. It was time for my trek upstream, to the cursed Sipapu.

The closer I got, the harder the terrain worked to impede my progress. The bleached and twisted remains of flood-tossed junipers clogged the riverbed. A tamarisk stabbed at my eye before raking the sunglasses off my head. I strained to pull out my leg when it was sucked thigh deep into the quicksand that wanted my hiking boot as a souvenir. Wading upstream looked much easier than fighting the mud and the brush, so I put on a pair of sandals and made my way up the river.

Less than a quarter mile from the Sipapu, a dense cloud shrouded the canyon with a violet shadow, bringing with it a trepidation that implored me, "Turn around. Now." But I had come so far, endured so much. The Gateway to the Underworld was within field goal range. Surely my forebodings only proved the power of suggestion. Standing knee deep in the chalky blue river, I stopped to gaze upstream, inhaled deeply, and contemplated my next move.

I turned around. A 180-degree change in direction, and the canyon seemed to approve. I waded downstream and emerged from the dread into a brilliant day. On the way back to my camp, I was granted several epiphanies. Let the Sipapu keep its secrets. Stop all this striving to prove yourself, to see everything. Stay here at the Grand Canyon and marry the ranger who loves you.

Alaska could wait. Cale needed to find younger, more idealistic partners for his June tour on Denali.

30

ON THE MOUNTAIN

In the summer of 2000 a small group of mountaineers paced and fidgeted at the Talkeetna airbase. Waiting for their flight to Denali, they packed and repacked their gear. What a relief it was when the weather finally cleared and the engine of the Cessna began to whine.

They happily folded their parka-laden bodies into the cozy cabin of the cramped little plane. Leaving the mosquitoes and the trees behind, the pilot gained altitude quickly, aiming for one of the "weather windows" that would offer him passage through the gauntlet at One Shot Pass.

At One Shot the teeth of the Alaska Range came within 150 feet of the Cessna's wings. The airplane graveyard below went unnoticed by the climbers as Mount Foraker filled the windshield. Impact with the granite appeared to be inevitable, but then the pilot tilted back, bringing Denali into view. The mountain was magnificent, intimidating, enormous. The pilot dipped the nose toward a ribbon of ice that went into forever. A bumpy landing on the longest glacier in the Alaska Range ended the gut-sloshing bounces and bladder-emptying thrills.

The climbers' first steps on Kahiltna Glacier were so sweet, some of them got down on their knees and kissed the snow. Even the mountaineers with Himalayan résumés were overwhelmed.

Forty-five minutes ago they had been claustrophobic in green and balmy Talkeetna. Now they were insignificant specks lost in a frigid world of white. They stood dumbstruck before the granite fortress guarding Denali's summit. The mountain announced its intentions by sending avalanches thundering down its slopes, and the noise boomed across the glacier like drums of war.

* * *

Coming toward them across the glacier was a very short ranger, perhaps the shortest guy on North America's tallest mountain. But his "Welcome to Kahiltna Base Camp" was so warm and his smile so genuine, his height was soon going unnoticed. He was not your typical surly mountaineer. Nor was he one of those climbing rangers who come to Denali to climb more than ranger. This ranger was extremely happy just to be here, living on a glacier in a city of tents and teaching climbers how to poop and where to pee.

To ranger Cale Shaffer most new mountaineers looked lost. Every time an air taxi unloaded a fresh load of climbers onto the glacier, it was as though he was the kindergarten teacher on the first day of school. The climbers had to be potty trained.

"A bear may shit in the woods," an older Denali ranger might say, "but a mountaineer should poop in a plastic bag. Then he should throw the poop bag in a very deep crevasse—or he'll get a ticket. And if he really respects the mountain, he'll pack that poop bag into his backpack with the rest of his garbage, carry it all down the mountain, load it into the plane, and throw it in a trash bin as soon as he returns to Talkeetna. Who wants to climb a mountain flowered with turds? Take nothing but pictures. Leave nothing but footprints. Kahiltna Glacier may seem so wild and isolated that you might as well be on Mars, but you're not on Mars. You're in a national park. While in base camp, all climbers will haul out their own trash and use the public urinal like good citizens. We melt snow for water. Remember? Do you want yellow ice in your cook pot? I didn't think so. So follow the bamboo stakes in the snow—the ones with the little red flags on them. At the end of the line you'll find a 'pee hole.' Aim for that. When all the urine begins to melt, creating a yellow crevasse so deep someone might fall into it, let me know. I'll close it down and mark a route to a new spot."

This was the gist of "sanitation education." Except Cale Shaffer did it better and nicer, with less editorializing and more earnestness, fewer sarcastic remarks and more gentle advice. "You know guys, we should respect the mountain," Cale said, and the mountaineers wished all park rangers were like this little dude who smiled a lot.

* * *

Cale was twenty-five. It was his first tour on Denali, and Kahiltna base camp at 7,200 feet was his rite of passage. Maybe, if he didn't screw up, the summer ranger would prove himself worthy of loftier assignments. For now he was married to the air taxis. He checked to see that every climber had purchased a $150 climbing permit. He warned all mountaineers of the potential hazards and pretended not to notice when the more arrogant ones rolled their eyes. (*Who is this kid to tell me how to climb the mountain?*) When the climbers returned to camp, he would weigh their garbage to ensure that nobody had left any trash behind on the mountain. He would charge radio batteries and dig latrines, occasionally looking up the mountain toward the higher camp.

All the really exciting stuff happened at the 14,200-foot camp. That was where the permanent full-time-with-benefits rangers worked. Less than 50 percent of the climbers attempting Denali reached the summit, and so half the people at the 14,200-foot camp would end up failing. A knock on the ranger's tent might be anything from five people coughing up blood to news of a guy falling into a crevasse to a report of "my buddy is in our tent and he won't wake up." At fourteen thousand feet, death from HAPE (high altitude pulmonary edema) becomes a real possibility.

The higher camp was where the action was. Up there a ranger might have a chance to bag the summit. Up there a ranger might earn himself a shiny medal.

* * *

While life at the 14,200-feet camp was more dangerous, Kahiltna Base Camp was far from a luxury resort. Food and water were in short supply on the glacier. Every day Cale or a volunteer took a turn as "the kitchen bitch." The kitchen bitch cut chunks out of snow, dropped the chunks into two huge pots set on a propane stove, and then poured the melted snow into canteens. To collect enough drinking water, the kitchen bitch spent most of the day chained to the communal cooking tent, where radio batteries were charged and meals were prepared. On Kahiltna there were no hot showers, no running water, no fresh fruits or vegetables, no television, and very little contact with the outside world.

For twenty days Cale lived in a tent set up inside a hole dug out of the snow. For twenty days, due to the hidden crevasses, he couldn't walk a city block outside camp without roping up to his two assistants. Yet despite these hardships, Cale felt fortunate to be here. They don't give Denali mountaineering ranger jobs to anybody. In February when District Ranger Darryl Miller called to say, "I'd like you to come work for me as a mountaineering ranger," Cale had felt lucky.

* * *

Approximately 10 percent of Denali mountaineers are women, most of them climbing with boyfriends or husbands. One of the few females on the mountain was "Base Camp Annie." A trekker not a climber, Annie Duquette had no desire to summit Denali.

Nine years ago she had flown to Kahiltna for the first time with her boyfriend. He had climbed Denali, touched his toe on the summit, and left. Annie made friends with the air taxi pilots, got offered a job at base camp, and stayed. On her first day she walked out to use the base camp latrine, a twenty-foot-deep hole in the snow with a box on top. The latrine was built on a snow ledge facing Mount Hunter and Mount Foraker and in full sight of the planes landing on the runway. Too self-conscious to sit on an open-air toilet, Annie decided she'd hold it until dark. Around midnight she remembered: During an Alaska summer, it never gets dark. Eventually Annie got over her shyness and waved at the people walking by while she sat on the pot.

The Kahiltna Base Camp manager was a ticket agent, customer service rep, dispatcher, weather reporter, and air traffic controller all rolled into one. Base Camp Annie coordinated seven hundred flights a year, most of them occurring within a ten-week period. It could be stressful work. On sunny days planes could buzz in every fifteen minutes. On the days camp was socked in by clouds, there might be no flights at all.

After days, even weeks, spent on the mountain, most climbers were anxious to leave. Annie saw it in their red, wind-burnt, frostbitten faces. They would push themselves in a mad dash from the 14,200-foot camp down to the 7,200-foot camp only to find out there was a long line of climbers ahead of them, all waiting for their turn to board a plane. The base camp manager had to deal with these impatient customers. "Some days it gets so bad," Base Camp Annie said, "you want to throw yourself into a crevasse."

The air taxis and the NPS are often at cross-purposes. The former wants to make a profit, while the latter wants to protect a "wilderness experience." When the NPS asks the air taxis to haul climber feces back to Talkeetna, the pilots bellyache. But on the glacier, the NPS ranger and the base camp manager are partners and friends. Cale strapped on snowshoes and helped Annie pack down the landing strip whenever a fresh layer of snow covered it.

Annie grabbed a shovel and helped Cale dig a new latrine when the first one overflowed.

* * *

In May Cale's first tour on Kahiltna included several rare sightings. A songbird made its way to the glacier, limp and cold but amazingly alive. He and Annie put the warbler in a box and sent it out on the next flight to Talkeetna. Even more unusual was the bear several climbers encountered on their way to the 14K camp. Grizzlies have been known to trek across the Alaska Range, but some likened seeing a grizzly near the 14K camp to a Bigfoot sighting.

The scary part was that a bear might discover the food caches that climbers buried in the snow and then left behind because they were too fatigued to dig them up. There were hundreds if not thousands of food caches along the route to Denali's summit. If a grizzly ever found this trail of easy meals leading to base camp, the rangers could have a dangerous situation on their hands. Cale and another ranger called their supervisor down in Talkeetna and suggested that he send a gun up on the next flight, just in case. "You've got to be kidding," was the district ranger's response. "I'm not having any guns up on the mountain."

* * *

Sunny days on the glacier warmed spirits as much as bodies, making base camp a fun place to be. One day a climber stepped off an air taxi with a guitar in his hand. Cale befriended him. The two hung out in the ranger tent, practicing chords and attempting to put a friend's poem to music. One sultry afternoon a pilot dropped off three cold pizzas, a case of beer, and a copy of the *Anchorage Daily News*. Annie, Cale, and two volunteers—a mountaineering couple from Seattle named Jim and Lisa Osse—sat outside in camp chairs, eating cold pizza, drinking warm beer, and reading the paper. It was so hot, they might as well be in Florida, one of them said. "Next tour," Cale announced, "I'm going to bring up some palm trees, sand, and a wading pool . . . with little rubber duckies to float in the water! We are going to have our own little Miami Beach. Right here on Kahiltna Glacier."

"Sure," Annie said. "Good idea." You can't find tropical stuff in Alaska, the base camp manager thought but didn't say. NPS volunteer Jim Osse put it this way. "You don't want to stand in front of the moving train that is Cale's enthusiasm and try to stop it."

Before and after Cale's three-week tours at base camp, there was "training, training, training," including practicing short-haul rescue while attached to a long line swinging under a Lama helicopter. Cale also squeezed in some off-duty adventures. He went mountain biking with a girl he met. One weekend he and another ranger skied several miles to a frozen waterfall, climbed it, and then skied down the other side of the ridge.

* * *

Cale's second tour on Denali was set for June 19. Outfitting for such an assignment required days of preparation and long equipment checklists: "Coffee grinder. Plane extrication kit. Paperwork box. Sleds. Oxygen bottles and regulators. Five shovels. Antibacterial soap. Body bags. Antacids." Cale also had to train and outfit his two volunteer assistants. Menus needed to be planned and groceries purchased and packed. The hours leading up to the flight were spent rushing to complete errands—double-checking the food and gear inventory, paying bills, mailing letters, and calling home.

At the Grand Canyon, Brittney Ruland had stepped out when Cale phoned. He left a message on her machine. "I'm getting ready to fly. I've sent you a birthday present in the mail, but don't open it until your birthday. I'll call you when I get back down." Brittney missed the call by five minutes.

"Tomorrow I fly up to the land of ice and snow," Cale wrote in a mass e-mail to his friends. He "thoroughly" enjoyed his job and everyone he worked with. Once all his loose ends were tied up, the ranger and his two assistants would be on the mountain. Cale had chosen Adam Kolff from Seattle and Brian Reagan from Anchorage as his two volunteers. Like him, Adam and Brian were young, energetic men eager to do some good. All three of them were living lives guided by their "passion for mountains and nature conservation."

The May patrol had been great fun. What would the June tour have in store for him? Perhaps they would save a life or two. Perhaps he would get an opportunity to summit Denali. Cale couldn't wait for Annie to arrive at camp later in the week. She was in for a big surprise. In the cargo hold of the Cessna, packed among the food and gear, were a blue wading pool, paper palm trees, and rubber duckies.

On June 19 the moody weather at base camp was making landing on the glacier problematic. The forecast called for "obscuration and turbulence" over the area, but another pilot reported that Ruth Glacier was "open" at the moment. At 5:10 p.m. pilot Don Bowers decided to go for it. Bowers was a U.S. Air Force Academy graduate with a master's degree in Aeronautical Engineering. He steered his Hudson Air Service Cessna 185 for One Shot Pass, but the visibility over Kahiltna Glacier was soup, and "nuclear" winds were prowling the slopes. Bowers radioed another pilot attempting to leave base camp. There was no safe way to fly in or out of Kahiltna, the other pilot told Bowers. Low clouds obscured the Icefall, Big Bend, and Pica Glacier. One Shot Pass was closed.

A pilot motto is "Leave your backdoor open and a stairway down," which means you don't let the clouds box you in to the point that you can't find an escape route back to God's green earth. When Bowers saw a beam of light hitting Lacuna Glacier, he headed for that "stairway" down to safety. It was the long way back to Talkeetna, but 90 percent of the time you can "jump over" to Yetna Glacier and follow it home. The other pilot returned to base camp to land on Kahiltna Glacier and wait out the storm. At 5:57 p.m. Cale contacted the ranger station via his park radio, informing them that he and his volunteers would not make it to base camp tonight. They were returning to Talkeetna.

Just before 6:00 p.m. a guide and his clients were fishing along the Yetna River when a wall of cumulus clouds approached from the south. First came the winds, followed by the heaviest rains the Alaskan guide had ever observed. This freak storm moved quickly as it proceeded north, up the Yetna drainage toward the saw-toothed peaks of the Alaska Range.

31

THE RANGER'S BURDEN

In November 1998 Chris Fors left the Grand Canyon to attend the FBI Academy at Quantico, Virginia. He was assigned to an office in Palm Springs, California. Although the bureau dropped plenty of case files on Chris's desk, his workday passed in slow motion compared to the pace he had maintained as a park ranger. Also the NPS set ranger salaries under a unique pay scale. Chris felt a twinge of pity for his ranger friends each time he deposited one of the plump paychecks he received from the Justice Department. The former ranger both missed and didn't miss living and working in a big park. For example, on a weekend trip to nearby Joshua Tree, the scenery recharged Chris's love for the outdoors—until he was chased out of the campground by a deranged man wielding flaming sticks.

Each day, to burn up a few minutes of desk time, Chris sat at his computer and read the "NPS Morning Report." This agency-wide memorandum announced the previous day's incidents and other important events involving parks and park rangers. Some of these reports reminded the FBI agent of his former colleagues and the camaraderie they once shared. Other incidents were so over-the-top, Chris laughed out loud at the absurdity. And there were a tragic few that depressed him, like the one he read on the morning of June 20, 2000.

Denali NP (AK)—Search for Missing Plane, NPS Seasonal/VIPs aboard.

A Hudson Air Service Cessna 185 with an NPS ranger, two NPS volunteers, and the pilot on board was reported overdue yesterday evening and is feared down. Staff at a nearby lodge reported that there were four inches of hail on the ground and heavy thunderstorms with severe downdrafts in the area at the time of the pilot's last radio transmission. The search is continuing, weather permitting. The outlook is for continued poor weather through Thursday. All three NPS employees had portable radios with them. No ELT signal has been reported and no radio contact has been made.

No Emergency Locator Transmitter (ELT) signal had been reported. No radio contact had been made. A park ranger knew too well what that meant, or at least implied. Chris turned to his partner, another FBI agent sitting at a desk nearby, and said, "I think I know the ranger who was on that plane."

* * *

That same morning Brittney Ruland arrived at the Grand Canyon Backcountry Reservation Office and handed out permits to backpackers trekking into the Grand Canyon. That summer she had issued a permit to a guy who ended up dying on the trail. This upset her. Although she didn't do anything wrong, the ranger felt responsible. Maybe, if she could have foreseen the future, if she had refused to give that man a permit, instead of hiking into the canyon when it was 108 degrees, he would have gone to Las Vegas.

At the first lull in her workday, Brittney checked her e-mail. One of the messages in her inbox was the daily "National Park Service Morning Report." The first entry was not a pleasant one: "Great Smoky Mountains NP—Follow-up on Fatal Bear Mauling" was the title.

Brittney shuddered. It reminded her of the time she and Cale had ventured into the Alaska bush in search of a grizzly. She scrolled down to the second entry. Reading the words, she began to hyperventilate. Then she started crying. Her coworkers did their best to comfort her. "They'll find him soon," they said. "He's going to be fine." A few hours later, ranger Bryan Wisher stopped by to see her. Eternally optimistic, Bryan loved life. If there were reason to hope, she would see it in the face of this ranger. Brittney searched Bryan's eyes and immediately knew all those Pollyannas patting her on the back were full of shit. Everything was not going to be okay.

* * *

Sitting in front of a computer in the basement of the Yosemite Jail, Mary Litell Hinson typed her portion of yet another fatality report. "Yesterday afternoon a thirty-four-year-old woman disregarded the warning signs and hiked off-trail until she slid down a granite slab into the Merced River above Vernal Falls. An hour and a half later, park rangers pulled the woman out of the Emerald Pool, initiated CPR, and flew her back down to the valley, where she was pronounced dead at the Yosemite Medical Clinic."

"Hey," another ranger interrupted Mary from her paperwork, "did you read the morning report?"

"No," Mary said. She had been too busy.

"A plane went down in Denali Park. A ranger was on it."

Mary got a real bad feeling that she knew exactly who was on that airplane, and the first person she wanted to call was her old boss. Andy, she hoped, would tell her this was going to have a happy ending.

Around noon, Kent Delbon was on duty when he drove out to my workplace, the Grand Canyon Airport. I assumed that my fiancé was surprising me with a lunch date, until I recognized the stiff jaw and evasive eye contact. At that moment this ranger wasn't the love of my life: He was the man in uniform who had come to deliver bad news.

At 4:15 p.m. that afternoon, a Civil Air Patrol plane spotted the wreckage of the Hudson Air Service Cessna 185 near the confluence of the Yetna and the Lacuna Glaciers. An Alaska State Trooper helicopter crew confirmed that there were no survivors. When the news reached the Talkeetna Ranger Station, ranger Kevin Moore insisted that he be the one to recover the bodies. All of them, but especially Cale. Moore felt it was his responsibility, his duty, to fly out there, pull the body of his friend out of the blueberry bushes, and respectfully secure it in a rubber bag.

District Ranger Darryl Miller disagreed. He had recovered the bodies of friends before—many years ago, when he did two tours as a marine in Vietnam. In theory "bringing in your buddy" sounds like the last, most valiant favor one can do for a friend. In reality the experience had given Miller mental images he could never erase. He'd rather remember how his friends looked when they were alive.

The two rangers went back and forth on the issue of who would recover the bodies before the district ranger pulled rank. It was settled; rescuers from another agency would be the ones to do the recovery. At the time, Miller felt his decision had angered the younger ranger.

Four years later, when ranger Kevin Moore was asked how he now felt about the district ranger's call, he paused long enough that I worried he wasn't going to answer my question, then he said, "It probably was a good decision."

* * *

Denali had delivered her indifference with a cold and monstrous hand, but days after the crash the park was a landscape photographer's mistress. Pink and purple flowers exploded from absurdly green meadows. Snow-dusted ridges pointed to impossibly blue skies. Braids of silver sunlight glittered in milky waters flowing over river-polished stones. Yet these fabulous views provided little comfort to ranger Mark Motsko.

Motsko's task was a solemn one: Drive out to each ranger station, inform the staff, and bring the flags down to half-mast. Miles of rocky, washboarded road stretched between each ranger station, making for a long day. Then, before he could lower the last and most depressing flag—the one flying over the Wonder Lake Ranger Station—a superior gave Motsko another sad assignment.

Rushing to catch his flight, Motsko packed his dress uniform in a suitcase along with a change of clothes. He grabbed his winter hat because the winter hat, which was made of felt, seemed more formal than the summer hat, which was made of straw. At the airport another Park Service employee, an administrator from the regional office, greeted Motsko. She handed him a plastic bag that looked like a hotel laundry bag. Inside the bag was a gray box that looked like a shoebox. The contents of the box were heavier than Motsko expected. He put the box in his backpack and hefted the weight of the pack to his back. *This is weird*, Motsko thought, but then he decided it was exactly what a park ranger would prefer— to be carried home in a backpack.

At the security checkpoint, Motsko placed his green backpack on the conveyer belt. As the pack rolled through the X-ray machine, the security folks became alarmed. "What's this?" they asked.

"It's my friend," Motsko said.

On the flight Motsko had lots of time to think about lots of things. He and his wife were not getting along too well. They had separated a year ago. This summer had been a hard one for Motsko, as the one before had been. Last year, on one of the roughest days, the summer ranger at Wonder Lake had seen the trouble in his supervisor's face. Cale gave Motsko a warm hug. "It's going to be okay, Mark," he said. "You have to trust life."

Summer storms caused several delays. Flights were canceled and rerouted. At one point, afraid he wouldn't catch a connecting flight, Motsko trotted through the crowds, the green pack with the heavy shoebox bouncing on his back. By the time he paid for the rental car, Motsko had driven hundreds of miles, flown on three planes, and had been awake for thirty-five hours.

A three-hour drive from the airport brought him to a well-maintained house. Motsko pulled into the driveway and exhaled in preparation. Carol Shaffer came from the green yard behind the house and walked out to the car. She asked where her child was. Motsko guided her to the trunk, lifted the lid, and pointed to the box inside his backpack. The ranger's mother laid her hand on the cardboard. "Do you mind," she said, "if I have a few moments alone?"

In Pennsylvania, Cale's funeral service was standing room only. Green-and-gray uniforms crowded the small church along with the casual clothes worn by lovers of the outdoors and the stoic black worn by the Shaffers' Amish friends and neighbors. Twenty or so people in ranger uniforms were seated in a position of prominence to the side of the stage. We didn't recognize any of their faces. We didn't know any of their names. We doubted any of them had ever met the ranger inside the engraved wooden box sitting on the pedestal in front of the podium. We were told they were high-level people in the agency and that most of them had come from Washington, D.C.

To us they looked soft, sallow, and doughy as they sat above us, tieless and wearing short sleeves. Their uniforms were a sore spot. It was June—the season for the more casual and cool short-sleeved shirts and straw hats—but we felt the occasion called for the formality expressed by our winter uniforms with the long sleeves, ties, and felt hats. Two days earlier there had been "a discussion" between Washington and the supervisory rangers in the field. We had to appear as a unified agency. As such things are typically handled, a memo from the D.C. office settled the debate. All NPS employees attending the funeral would wear their short-sleeved summer uniforms.

We defied them of course. It seemed important at the time. It was certainly symbolic of the state of things. The side stage filled with upper level managers, their pale arms sticking out of their gray shirts. While our sun-stamped faces, forest-green ties, and long sleeves were scattered among the civilians on the benches below.

Years later I realized our grievances were petty and pointless. And it was painful to learn that some of the people who had known the ranger since childhood resented the way the green and gray swooped in and practically took over the whole affair. The NPS had crowded Cale's memorial with badges, flags, and ranger stories. As if the government owned the ranger. As if the ranger had no life, no experiences, no friends before he joined the National Park Service.

* * *

The day I returned to the Grand Canyon, I received a postcard from the dead. Cale had mailed many cards, gifts, and letters to his friends and family the day before the crash. On the front of the card he chose for me, above a photograph of a sea otter, were the words, "You otter be here!" The postcard brought me to the floor, sobbing. My actions had repercussions far beyond their intent. I had abandoned my friends and colleagues for an easier life, and now one of them was dead. If I had stayed on as a district ranger, I would have hired Cale into that permanent full-time-with-benefits job he wanted at the Grand Canyon. If the Sipapu had not unsettled me, I would have joined him on that fatal flight to Kahiltna Glacier. *You otter be there.*

I may have been a decent park ranger, but I was never a great one like Cale Shaffer. My courage was always a bit shaky. Although my work ethic seemed boundless, my compassion fatigued. I had a smart mouth; but when it came to office politics, I played the fool. I drank too much tequila and picked too many fights. I lost my patience. I lost my temper. I lost my faith. If there are people who can be park rangers in big parks and come out of it unscathed, I'm not one of them.

32

THE LAST CALL

The Shaffer family brought Cale's ashes to the Grand Canyon. Bryan Wisher guided them to the hiker bridge spanning the Colorado River, where they tossed half of the ashes into the jade water. Earlier that morning, Cale's father had thrown a fragile box containing more of Cale's ashes over the rim at Yaki Point. That afternoon a large group of park employees gathered at the same overlook to witness the ranger's "last call."

When we heard the helicopters coming, we turned to face the canyon. The uniformed rangers turned up the volume on their radios, and the patrol cars and fire trucks played the transmission over their loud speakers. "Calling Five-Four-Nine Shaffer" said a steady-voiced dispatcher. Moments later, three rescue helicopters buzzed over our heads and out into the sky in front of us. Immediately, one of them peeled out of the formation and descended straight for the heart of the Grand Canyon as the dispatcher said, "Ranger Five-Four-Nine ... Good luck on your next mission." We watched the rescue helicopter fly deeper and deeper into the canyon until it disappeared.

As the crowd began to disperse, someone pointed out a dark silhouette in the pale blue sky. The large wingspan made the identification impossible to refute. The bird soaring above this ceremony was a California condor.

A few years earlier, biologists had rescued this species from the brink of extinction by breeding more condors out of only twenty-five remaining birds. Eventually there were enough condors to release some of the birds into the wild. The Colorado Plateau, a desert escarpment hundreds of miles from the Grand Canyon, was one location chosen. Wildlife biologists expected the condors to repopulate the wilder, more remote terrain north of the park. Instead an errant few selected a more populated area for their new home—the cliffs around the bustling South Rim of the Grand Canyon. To the chagrin of biologists and the delight of tourists, this camera-friendly flock continues to make frequent public appearances.

Perhaps some saw the condor's presence at Cale's memorial service as an inappropriate or even morbid event. California condors are greasy, homely birds—carrion feeders with supernaturally keen eyesight that scan the landscape for hints of death. Yet this ceremony drew a crowd capable of appreciating the condor's well-timed arrival. We had fallen in love with these awkward creatures that chose our company in the midst of vast wilderness. And they had come bearing gifts, inspiring us by their improbable existence, showing us that a once-doomed species can catch a lift on thermal air currents rising above a ranger's ashes.

EPILOGUE

Death is not a merciful conclusion but a border crossing into a new land that could be more beautiful and majestic than the tallest mansion. Faith, courage, and hope are the characteristics that create happiness. They will stand as remembered monuments for all those left around the bed, and they are the qualities I will strive to obtain.

—From the journal of Cale Shaffer, dated September 7, 1992, written when he was eighteen years old

* * *

The day Cale died, Bryan Wisher's wife, Kim Besom, learned that she was pregnant. The couple named their son for their favorite ranger. I call him "little Cale." The Wisher family moved to Flagstaff, Arizona, after Bryan retired from the NPS.

To honor their son's commitment to helping others enjoy the outdoors, Ron and Carol Shaffer donated funds to create the Cale Shaffer Memorial Scholarship for students studying Outdoor Recreation at Lock Haven University.

Although she had seen mountain tragedies during her time on Denali, the death of Cale and the others on that Cessna changed things for Annie Duquette. After the summer of 2000, she "retired" as the base camp manager on Kahiltna Glacier.

In 2004 the Apache County youth counselor, David Line Denali, obtained his PhD. The title of Denali's thesis dissertation was "The Impact of Medical Training on the Self-Concept of Young Adults."

Brittney Ruland remained single for several years. Eventually she fell in love with another park ranger and later married him. She left her job with the NPS to raise their two young children.

Keith Lober became Yosemite's Emergency Services manager. In 2008 he appeared impressively composed in a Discovery Channel documentary entitled "Dangerous Season: Yosemite Search and Rescue." His colleagues tell me that although Sheriff Lobo has mellowed some over the years, he is still "quite mad."

Former newbie Mike Archer is all grown up now. In 2008 he became the chief ranger of the Grand Canyon. Archer is a highly respected chief ranger—but he takes his orders from Sjors Horstman, the volunteer at Phantom Ranch.

Mary Litell Hinson continues to break glass ceilings. In 2006 she became the first female chief ranger of Lake Mead National Recreation Area, one of the busiest parks in the world. After she was diagnosed with an aggressive form of breast cancer in 2002, Mary continued to work for the NPS during two courses of chemotherapy treatments. (She raised a few eyebrows when she showed up at a rescue scene with a bald head.) So far she remains cancer free. In addition to her duties as a chief ranger, a wife, and a mother of two, Mary raises thousands of dollars every year for breast cancer research and awareness. She rock climbs occasionally, but she will never BASE jump. Instead Mary celebrates her birthdays with a sky dive or a leap from something tall while attached to a bungee cord.

After a short stint with the FBI, Chris Fors returned to the parks to work as a special agent in Yellowstone National Park. Chris's reconciliation with the Park Service was short-lived. He says he left the NPS for good when he accepted a special agent position with the USDA Forest Service (USFS) in Vermont. Chris is content to be back in New England and working for the Department of Agriculture. In 2008 he was anointed "USFS Special Agent of the Year." He now has a wife, a son, and a wonderful home for them to live in—a spacious farmhouse complete with barn, maple trees, apple trees, a trout brook, and a big hayfield. Although Chris no longer has any moody roommates, his farmhouse did come with a few bats in the attic and lots more in the barn, but so far they have been good tenants.

After Cale's funeral, I threw all my ranger uniforms in a dumpster. This shocked my more sentimental ranger friends. I told them the act was incredibly therapeutic. I had to cut the cord. I had to move on.

But I kept the Stetson.

Today my Smokey Bear is taking up space in my garage. The leather band embossed with sequoia cones is faded and frayed. The felt is bruised and moldy. Despite these defects, I could get hundreds for my ranger hat on eBay. Yet I can't bring myself to part with it.

* * *

After my first summer at Cape Hatteras, I thought I'd be a park ranger forever. But life sends you to unexpected places. In 2001 my husband, Kent Delbon, left the NPS for a better-paying job with the U.S. Secret Service. We moved to Los Angeles, a city I once hated, where I became a private duty registered nurse for VIP clients in Beverly Hills.

But old habits are slow to die. One day I was in the middle of a delicate and risky procedure involving a patient's arterial line when an earthquake tried to shake us off the bed. "You're like a Marine," my patient said when the earth finally settled, "but in a good way."

In 2009 Kent accepted a special agent position with the USDA Forest Service, the same agency that has welcomed numerous battle-weary park rangers seeking refuge—including Chris Fors. Kent and I are happy to be living in the Sierra foothills, no more than an hour's drive from where we first met under the ancient cedars that grow wide and tall inside Yosemite Valley.

ACKNOWLEDGMENTS

Among the many heroes in this book are the folks at FalconGuides and Globe Pequot Press, including Scott Adams, Paulette Baker, and John Burbidge. Allen Jones, the manuscript medic, convinced me to excise my tumors, tourniquet my tenses, and suture my structure. Thanks to his advice, this book is a much healthier one.

Audie Alcorn, a former park ranger and a talented editor, read early portions of this manuscript, providing intelligent and practical advice. My work also benefited from the critical reading skills of another former park ranger, Monica McManus Woll.

The research and writings of Michael P. Ghiglieri, Thomas M. Myers, and Charles R. "Butch" Farabee Jr. were most useful to me. Their books *Off the Wall: Death in Yosemite* and *Over the Edge: Death in Grand Canyon* offered another perspective on several incidents I depict here and provided a historical context to the tragedies faced by the rangers who work at Yosemite and the Grand Canyon.

In addition, Cale Shaffer's journals and college reports allowed me to recreate faithfully his experiences at Camp Judy Lane, Lock Haven University, and while rafting the Colorado River. Many of Cale's phrasings are taken verbatim from these texts.

I extend my undying gratitude and admiration to Mary Litell Hinson, Chris Fors, and Brittney Ruland Schramm for having the courage to share some of their most vulnerable moments with us. For certain, I am grateful that Keith Lober's sense of humor is as magnificent as his temper.

The following people were also kind enough to tell me stories that offered additional insights into park ranger culture and/or the events and personalities portrayed in this book. National Park Service employees and volunteers: Mike Archer, Gib Backlund, Werner and Mary Braun, David Line Denali, Paul Downey, K. J. Glover, Scott Hinson, Dan Horner, Sjors Horstman, Jessie Jordan, Ivan Kassovic, Kate McCurdy, Noel McJunkin, Chris Mengel, Darryl Miller, Greg Moore, Kevin Moore, Jim and Lisa Osse, Billie Patrick, Rosie Peragine, Billy Shott, Brian Smith, Patrick Suddath, Jeff Sullivan, Chuck Sypher, Bryan Wisher, and Steve Yu. From Lock Haven University: Judy Elliot, Lenny Long, Jeffrey Walsh, and Tom Wilson. All others: Ryan Booz, Jim Fisher, Kate Henderson, Gren Hinton, Tom and Hazel Martin, Beth Overton, Scott Rossman, and Eric Valentine.

In addition to several names listed above, the following folks went out of their way to help in various ways during the course of my research: Kim Besom, Kris Fister, Todd Gearman, Patricia Lankford, Ray O'Neil, Chris Pergiel, and Deanne Stillman.

Ron, Carol, and Jen Shaffer graciously welcomed me into their home, hearts, and family history. I will forever cherish the week I spent with them, meeting Cale's friends and touring his old stomping grounds. And a special thanks to Cale for visiting Carol and me through our dreams to tell us in no uncertain terms that he approved of my writing about him.

I could not have completed this project and still ended up in one psychological piece if not for my husband, Kent Delbon. Many times he has pulled me back from the edge. This book is dedicated to him.

INDEX

241

ABOUT THE AUTHOR

A former National Park Service ranger, Andrea "Andy" Lankford has trekked the 2,200-mile Appalachian Trail, kayaked from Miami to Key West, cycled to the Arctic Ocean, and was the first to mountain bike eight hundred miles from Utah to Mexico along the Arizona Trail. She is the author of four books, and her stories and photographs have appeared in numerous publications, including *Backpacker, Paddler,* and *Camping Life.* She lives in the Sierra foothills of California.

Kent Delbon